D1258900

WALT DISNEY WORLD
WITH KIDS

WALT DISNEY WORLD WITH KIDS

1998

Kim Wright Wiley

PRIMA PUBLISHING

© 1998 by Kim Wright Wiley

All rights reserved. No part of this book may be reproduced or transmitted in any form or by any means, electronic or mechanical, including photocopying, recording, or by any information storage or retrieval system, without written permission from Prima Publishing, except for the inclusion of quotations in a review.

PRIMA PUBLISHING and colophon are registered trademarks of Prima Communications, Inc.

All products mentioned in this book are trademarks of their respective companies.

Map Designer: Misty Berry
Research Assistant: Melanie Hatfield

ISBN 0-7615-0808-2
ISSN 1083-2424

97 98 99 00 01 HH 10 9 8 7 6 5 4 3 2 1
Printed in the United States of America

How to Order

Single copies may be ordered from Prima Publishing, P.O. Box 1260BK, Rocklin, CA 95677; telephone (916) 632-4400. Quantity discounts are also available. On your letterhead, include information concerning the intended use of the books and the number of books you wish to purchase.

Visit us online at www.primapublishing.com

To my children, Leigh and Jordan,
the best ride-testers in the business.

Contents

SECTION 6: DISNEY–MGM STUDIOS THEME PARK   165

SECTION 7: THE REST OF THE WORLD   189

SECTION 8: DISNEY WORLD
AFTER DARK   235

SECTION 9: AND ANOTHER THING . . .   253

SECTION 10: LIFE BEYOND DISNEY: UNIVERSAL STUDIOS, SEA WORLD, AND OTHER ORLANDO ATTRACTIONS   285

List of Maps

What Makes This Guide Different?

Once upon a time, people with kids didn't travel. Parents lucky enough to have supportive relatives or nannies may have taken off and left the children behind, but more often people with children just stayed home, figuring geographic paralysis was the price of parenthood. Tour buses all over the world are filled with people who deferred their dreams of Maui or Moscow or even Miami until their kids were grown and married.

Things have changed. No one is surprised anymore by the sight of an infant snoozing away in a four-star restaurant, and a recent letter to *Travel and Leisure* magazine inquired about the difficulty of locating Pampers in Nepal. Today people take their kids everywhere, and they especially take them to Orlando, Florida.

Walt Disney World is the most frequently visited manmade tourist attraction on the planet, and at first glance it seems designed to cater specifically to families with young children. But it's not a small world after all, and actually circumnavigating the three major theme parks, five minor parks, 18 on-site hotels, and a shopping plaza requires as much organization and fortitude as a safari.

Guidebooks abound, but they rarely address the questions that the parents of young children ask: Which restaurants are suitable for evening dining with a pooped 5-year-old? Where can we get a sitter? A Band-Aid? Will Epcot bore the kids? Is it worth the extra cost to stay at a hotel on the grounds? Is it OK to take the kids out of school for the trip? Where can I breast-feed? Do the men's restrooms have changing tables? Is the Haunted Mansion really all that scary?

This guidebook takes into account the pace and pocketbook of a couple traveling with young kids and features those attractions, such as the character breakfasts with Mickey and the gang, that first-timers can easily miss but which can make all the difference to a star-struck toddler. Preplanning is essential because, as you well know, a two-hour wait that would be merely annoying to a lone business traveler can be downright disastrous to a single parent with hungry kids in tow. Nonetheless, some families try to wing it. You know the ones—you see them every morning standing flat-footed in the middle of Main Street, kids bouncing in the strollers and parents huddled over their maps, debating how to get to Splash Mountain. This approach is akin to attempting to learn Lamaze after the contractions have begun.

To minimize problems and maximize fun, you must be oriented before you arrive. By following this guide, you'll learn how to get tickets, maps, and reservations in advance and plot your path. Over the past eight years, I have passed out hundreds of questionnaires and interviewed dozens of families; their helpful comments and tips are incorporated throughout this book.

With just a little bit of forethought, you'll be able to go against the crowds—moving clockwise while the thundering hordes are moving counterclockwise, touring Epcot while most people are in the Magic Kingdom, and even the ultimate crowd-busting move: planning your trip during the off-season. If you manage to zig while everyone else zags, you can cut waits to a minimum and see twice as much as you would mindlessly drifting from queue to queue.

The basic rule when traveling with young children is to prepare without overplanning. You want to be familiar enough with the layout of the theme parks that you can find a restroom fast, but not so driven by a timetable that you don't allow plenty of time for resting and savoring spontaneous pleasures. Fun stuff pops up all around the parks, and if you're grimly trying to make it from Fantasyland to Liberty Square on schedule, you'll miss the key pleasures of this amazing attraction.

And pleasures are what this guide is all about. The three bugaboos of the World—the crowds, the heat exhaustion, and the expense—are especially tough on young families, and no amount of preparation will totally eliminate these problems. Walt Disney World, after all, is a 46-square-mile complex in the middle of Florida, visited by as many as 150,000 people a day. It can cost a family of four up to $144 just to get through the front gate. You're going to get hot and tired and you'll spend a lot of money. That's a given.

So why go at all? There's only one reason: It truly is the most fun place on earth.

What Makes Walt Disney World So Special?

The answer to this question is, in a word, *detail*. The entire Disney World fantasy is sustained through painstaking attention to detail.

In an attraction such as Pirates of the Caribbean, the atmospheric mischief begins in the queue, where you wind down into the bowels of a stucco fortress which grows danker and darker with every turn. The ride combines Audio-Animatronics, a catchy theme song, and an attention to detail so relentless that even the hair on the pirates' legs is real. You emerge seven minutes later, blinking into the sunlight, which spills through the market stalls of the Caribbean Plaza, fully understanding why Disney insists that its "rides" be referred to as "attractions." (The illusion holds up just as well at Epcot, where the Disney people have presented themselves a bigger challenge; this time they're out to snooker adults into believing they're actually *in* Norway . . . or the land of the dinosaurs . . . or the human bloodstream.)

The theme parks were designed with the same precision that Disney animators brought to the classic films. Walt Disney was such a perfectionist that he never let four frames per second suffice if eight were possible. Now his successors are successful because of the same sumptuousness. Why not fly in some monkey-puzzle trees for the Japan pavilion? Why not hire George Lucas as creative consultant for the ride based on his *Star Wars* film series? Who says 11,000 dolls are too many for It's a Small World?

The authors of some guidebooks seem immune to the Disney magic, which is why they can describe Dumbo as a "sporadically loading 10-unit cycle ride of the sort common to most midways," and advise you to skip the ride. But it isn't a sporadically loading cycle ride at all—it's Dumbo; and no 4-year-old worth his salt is going to let you pass it up. The special charm of Walt Disney World is that once we pass through those gates, we're all 4-year-olds—impulsive, impatient, curious, easily duped, essentially cheerful, and ready to believe in magic.

Abbreviations and Terms Used in This Book

WDW	Walt Disney World
MK	The Magic Kingdom
Epcot	Epcot Center
MGM	The Disney–MGM Studios Theme Park
The major parks	The Magic Kingdom, Epcot Center, and Disney–MGM Studios
The minor parks	Typhoon Lagoon, River Country, Pleasure Island, Blizzard Beach, and Discovery Island
TTC	Ticket and Transportation Center: the monorail version of a train station, where riders can transfer to monorails bound for Epcot, the MK, or monorail-line hotels. You can also catch buses at the TTC bound for the parks, the on-site hotels, and the Disney Village Marketplace.
On-site	The Disney-owned hotels that are on the WDW property

Off-site	Hotels that are not located on WDW grounds or owned by the Walt Disney Company
On-season	The busiest touring times, including summer and the weeks surrounding major holidays
Off-season	Less busy times of the year, most notably spring and fall
MK resorts	Disney-owned hotels located near the Magic Kingdom (the Grand Floridian, the Polynesian, the Contemporary, and Wilderness Lodge)
Epcot resorts	Disney-owned hotels near Epcot (the Yacht and Beach Clubs, Caribbean Beach Resort, the BoardWalk, Disney Swan, and Disney Dolphin)
Village resorts	Disney-owned hotels near the Disney Village Marketplace (Port Orleans, Dixie Landings, Disney Institute Villas, and Disney's Old Key West)

1

★★★★★★★★★★★★★★★★★★★

Before You Leave Home

WHAT TIME OF YEAR SHOULD WE VISIT?

Fall

September through mid-December is the best time of year to visit for families with young children. Crowds are light—around 30,000 visitors per day compared to 70,000 in the summer months—and many area hotels offer discounted rates. Even the weather cooperates, with highs in the 80s and lows in the 60s.

There are disadvantages to a fall visit. You may not want to take your children out of school, and the theme parks do close earlier at this time of year. The Magic Kingdom and MGM often close as early as 6 P.M., although Epcot generally remains open later. These earlier closings mean that some of the special evening presentations, such as SpectroMagic in the MK, are suspended during the off-season.

Fall is also hurricane season in Florida, so there is some risk that you'll schedule your trip for the exact week Hurricane Laluna pounds the coast. But Orlando is an hour inland, meaning that even the worst coastal storms usually yield only rain. Furthermore, rainy days reach their peak during the summer months, not the fall, so in general the advantages of autumn touring far outweigh the disadvantages.

Spring

If fall isn't possible, spring is nearly as nice. With the exceptions of the holiday weeks around Presidents' Day, Spring Break, and Easter, springtime crowds average around 40,000—not as low as fall but still far better than summer. And the weather is sublime, with highs in the 70s, lows in the 60s, and less rainfall in spring than in any other season of the year.

Disney runs longer park hours in spring than in fall, but schedules vary widely in the weeks between January and May. To check projected hours of operation, call (407) 824-4321 before you leave home.

Summer

The good news is that everything is open and operational and the parks run very long hours. The bad news is that it is hot and crowded, so much so that it is possible to wait 90 minutes per ride. If your children are preschoolers or younger, avoid summer touring at all cost.

If your children's school schedule dictates that you must visit in summer, the first two weeks of June and the last two weeks of August are your best bet. Temperatures and attendance peak in July. Check out "Tips for Extra-Crowded Times" in Section 9, page 282.

Winter

Winter is a mixed bag. The absolute worst times are holidays. Christmas and New Year's can pull in 100,000 visitors per day, which is six times as many people as you'll find on a typical day in October. Extended hours can't compensate for crowds of this size. Although special parades and shows are always planned, you're better off at home watching them on the Disney Channel.

If you avoid the holiday weeks, winter can be an ideal time for touring. January and February are relatively uncrowded and pleasantly cool, although the water parks are sometimes closed during this period, and the parks run the same shortened schedule as in the fall.

The first two weeks of December are another good option. WDW is fetchingly decorated at Christmas, and the decorations go up just after Thanksgiving. So if you make an early-December visit, you'll have all the trees and wreaths and carolers you could wish for—as well as a nearly deserted theme park. Special holiday packages, which include price breaks on lodgings, a party with the characters, and access to the Christmas parades and shows, run from the end of November to mid-December.

HOW LONG SHOULD WE STAY?

It will take at least four days for a family with young kids to tour the MK, Epcot, and MGM. Four- and five-day passes are offered and, since the five-day pass admits holders to Pleasure Island, Typhoon Lagoon, Blizzard Beach, Discovery Island, and River Country as well as the major theme parks, it is the best buy.

Note: Your admission into the minor parks is unlimited and free only within seven days of the first day the pass is used. In other words, buying a five-day pass does not allow you admission entrance to Typhoon Lagoon for life.

If you plan to take in any of the minor theme parks, schedule five days. Five days are also necessary for families who enjoy boating, tennis, swimming, or golf—or those who'd like to tour at a more leisurely pace. Once the Animal Kingdom opens, five days will be necessary if you wish to see what will then be *four* major parks.

If you wish to visit other area attractions such as Sea World or Universal Studios, allow a week.

SHOULD WE TAKE THE KIDS OUT OF SCHOOL?

Even if you're sold on the advantages of fall and spring touring, you may be reluctant to take your children out of school for a week. Here are some ways to temper your guilt.

• Kids remember what they see, so a single day at Epcot can be just as educational as a week of science and geography classes. "That's a Viking ship," my 4-year-old casually observed while we were watching a movie one evening. "You know, like at Epcot." Another mother reports that her son's award-winning science fair project on drip irrigation was inspired by touring Epcot's Land pavilion.

• Since you'll have weeks of advance warning before a trip to Orlando, ask your children's teachers if the kids can do at least some of the lessons they'll miss before you leave. Coming back to piles of makeup work after a vacation can be profoundly depressing.

• Perhaps your children can work out a deal with their teachers whereby they'll do special reports or projects relating to subjects they'll encounter at Epcot or MGM. Here are some suggestions:

■ Into dinosaurs? Check out the Universe of Energy pavilion.

- Students of the natural sciences will find much of interest in the Land pavilion. The greenhouse tour is full of information on space-age farming.

- Marine biology is the theme of the Living Seas pavilion.

- Missing health class? The Wonders of Life pavilion is devoted to that greatest of all machines—the human body.

- Interested in geography? Some students have done reports on the cultures of countries represented in the World Showcase.

- Art students are bound to pick up pointers during the Animation Tour at MGM.

- Drama students or even budding engineers will learn a lot behind the scenes at MGM's Backstage Studio Tour.

- Innoventions at Epcot, although often described as the world's hippest arcade, is also an amazing preview of future technology.

• Along with formal reports on subjects of interest, your child might also want to make a scrapbook or collection display. The mother of one preschooler helped him create an "ABC book" before he left home, and he then spent his WDW week collecting souvenirs for each page—Goofy's autograph on the "G" page, a postcard of a Japanese pagoda on the "P" page, and so on. An older child might gather leaves from the various trees and bushes imported from the countries represented in the World Showcase. Or a young photographer could illustrate his proficiency with various lighting techniques by photographing Cinderella Castle in early morning, at noon, at sunset, and after dark.

CAMP DISNEY AT THE DISNEY INSTITUTE

Disney's half- and full-day seminars for kids are now collectively grouped under the label *Camp Disney* and are run from the Disney Institute. Kids 11 to 15 have their choice of three 6-hour programs and several 3-hour programs, and kids 7 to 10 have eight 3½-hour programs designed especially for them. This is dynamite stuff. My own kids love the Disney Institute, which gives them the chance to go backstage before a live show, and into the zoo nurseries, animation studios, and costuming tunnels. This is what the tourists never see!

As well as being both inspirational and educational, the Camp Disney programs effectively break up the week. Just when you're starting to get on each other's nerves from an overdose of togetherness, you can farm out the kids for a great day at the Institute and take a couple of adult-oriented classes yourself.

Not every program is offered every day, and offerings are constantly being updated and changed. Call the Disney Institute (1-800-496-6337) to order an information packet and (407) WDW-TOUR (939-8687) for more-detailed information. The representatives can describe the programs fully and help you pick those best suited for your children. They can also help with logistics; your 8-year-old will be able to take two short classes, for example, while his 12-year-old sister is off at Show Biz Magic, an all-day class. Teens 16 and up are welcome in the adult programs.

Kids are dropped off and picked up at Youth Central at the Disney Institute. Full-day classes are $79, half-day are $49, and lunch is included in the longer programs. Camp Disney classes are included in some packages such as the Grand Plan, so be sure to check.

The following section gives examples of some of the offerings.

Programs for Kids 11 to 15

• *Art Magic.* Learn the tricks of the trade that Disney artists use to create the magic in the films and theme parks. Kids go backstage at the animation studio, paint a cel, and get tips on drawing from a real Disney animator. Art Magic is the most popular class at Camp Disney, and runs 6 days a week. *6 hours.*

• *Show Biz Magic.* Kids go behind the scenes in the MK to see how a live show is prepared and rehearsed. They get an inside look at the technical side of a production, and go into the famous MK underground tunnel to see the world's largest costume department. Kids meet cast members, who talk about the roles they play in the world of show business, Disney style. *6 hours.*

• *Wildlife Adventure.* With binoculars in hand, kids head for the swamp, where they see alligators, egrets, turtles, and other critters while learning about ecosystems and animal identification. Then it's on to Discovery Island, where they see how the zoo vets care for the animals. This is a physically active tour with lots of animal contact. *6 hours.*

• *Rock Climbing.* Kids learn how to climb the 26-foot Disney Institute rock wall. This is a fun introduction to the sport, with emphasis on rope-handling techniques, safety procedures, and belay systems. *3 hours.*

• *Art Lab.* Kids learn the design basics of form and structure, with plenty of chances to play with the amazing animation gizmos in the Disney Institute art labs. *3 hours.*

- *Deejay for Youth.* The Institute has its own radio station, so kids get to go on the air and see what it's like to create a commercial, concentrating on voice inflection, timing, creative writing, and even sales hooks. *3 hours.*

- *The Funny Papers.* Using storyboarding techniques, kids create their own comic strip, developing both a story line and drawing skills. *3 hours.*

- *Discovery Island Explorers.* A member of the zoological staff leads kids on a tour of Discovery Island, seeing creatures ranging from toucans to tortoises, with a behind-the-scenes look at how the staff cares for the animals. *3 hours.*

Programs for Kids 7 to 10

All of the programs for this age group are 3½ hours long.

- *Broadway Bound.* Kids dance, sing, act, and even learn how to audition in this lively class, in which they don actual Disney costumes and wigs. They'll go underground in the MK to try on parade costumes and see where the parade floats are kept. The program wraps up with a trip to see a full-scale production at MGM.

- *Stealing the Show.* This program focuses on improvisation, mime, and rhythm exercises that professional actors use to sharpen their skills. Then kids move on to Epcot to learn how music, physical movement, and costuming set the tone of a scene.

- *Face Magic!* Kids learn how artists create illusions and special effects through the use of makeup and lighting. At MGM, kids get a chance to apply what they've learned by painting their own face. You'll drop off David and pick up Dracula.

- *ArtSurround.* Epcot is the backdrop for this seminar in how art is inspired by nature, emotions, and music. After seeing how the pros do it, kids get a chance to create art using bubbles, paint, and some rather unusual supplies.

- *Disney's Orient Express.* Kids go to Epcot to visit the Japan and China pavilions. They learn how to eat with chopsticks, create an origami samurai helmet, write in calligraphy, and tell Japanese folk tales that have been passed from generation to generation.

- *Tiles, Temples, and Treasures.* This time it's Mexico and Morocco. Far more than just a tour, kids learn songs, games, and vocabulary native to the countries whose pavilions they visit.

- *Swamp Stomp.* The name is only part of the fun. Kids take a safari through a cypress swamp, scouting for gators and other wild animals. Information on the food chain and the ecosystem are woven into the swamp tour, and the class finishes with the *Circle of Life* show at Epcot.

- *Discovery Island Kidventure.* The lesson here is animal and plant identification. Kids trek through a marsh, go bird-watching by boat, and then move on to Discovery Island for hands-on contact with the zoo animals.

OTHER ORLANDO EDUCATIONAL PROGRAMS

Sea World

Sea World offers daily tours and classes, as well as week-long and overnight programs for kids of all ages. See Section 10, page 314, for details. *(407) 363-2380.*

Orlando Science Center

This impressive facility has oodles of hands-on exhibits, many of them designed to be interesting to kids as young as 4, as well as evening planetarium shows. The highly innovative one-day programs range from "Dirt Safaris" geared toward the kindergarten set to "Gator Watches" for kids 11 and up. The Center even sponsors "Camp-In" sleepovers at the museum, with subjects ranging from Lego Mania to Silly Science—a set of pleasingly messy physics experiments using Silly Putty and slime. Not every class is offered every week, but if you request the brochure, you'll find that something is happening all the time and that the prices are reasonable. All programs must be booked in advance. *(407) 896-7151.*

Spaceport USA

Orlando is only about an hour from Kennedy Space Center, so it's an easy daytrip. Kids will enjoy a ride through the Rocket Garden, which holds eight rockets from the *Mercury* through the *Apollo* programs, as well as the films, projected on the five-story-high screen in the IMAX theater. Call before you leave home and see if a launch is scheduled during the time you'll be in Florida. If so, plan your trip for that day. The crowds will be heavier, but your kids will experience a rare thrill. *(407) 452-2121.*

IS IT WORTH THE EXPENSE TO STAY ON-SITE?

Staying at one of the Disney-owned hotels is very convenient—and with rates as low as $69 a night at the All-Star Resorts, staying on-site is becoming more affordable each year.

Off-site hotels are fighting back with price promotions and perks of their own—such as free child care—arguing that the Disney hotels still cost more and bring you only slightly closer to the action. On-site or off-site? The questions below should help you decide.

- *What time of year are you going and how long are you staying?*

If you're going during the summer or over a major holiday, you'll need every extra minute, so it's worth the cost to stay on-site. (Another reason to book on-site in summer: In the Florida heat, it's nearly a medical necessity to keep young kids out of the sun in mid-afternoon; a nearby hotel room makes that easier.) Likewise, if your visit will be for less than three days, you can't afford to waste much time commuting, so staying on-site is worth considering.

- *What are the ages of your kids?*

If your kids are still young enough to take naps, staying on-site makes it much easier to return to your room after lunch for a snooze. If they're preteens who are up to a full day in the parks, commuting time is less of a factor.

- *Are you flying or driving?*

If you're flying and doing only Disney World, it may make more economic sense to stay on-site. The WDW transportation system is so efficient that you can easily manage without a rental car. But if you're driving to Orlando, consider an off-site location. You'll be able to drive to the parks at the hours that suit you, without being dependent on those sometimes-less-than-prompt off-site buses.

- *How strapped are you for cash?*

If money isn't a major issue, stay on-site. If money is a primary consideration, you'll find the best deals at the budget hotels along I-4. Exits 25 and 27, which flank the Disney exit, are chock-full of chain hotels and restaurants. Exit 27 alone has three Days Inns within two blocks of each other.

- *How much do your kids eat?*

Food is expensive at WDW, both in the parks and at the on-site hotels. If you're staying off-site, you can always eat at the numerous fast-food and family-style restaurants along I-4, Route 192, and International Drive. If you book a suite, fixing simple meals in your room is even cheaper, and kids can really load up at those complimentary buffet breakfasts so frequently offered at the off-site hotels.

- *Do you plan to visit other attractions?*

If you'll be spending half your time at Sea World, Universal Studios, or the other non-WDW attractions, stay off-site, at least during those days. There's no need to pay top dollar for proximity to Disney if you're headed for the Kennedy Space Center.

- *Will your party be splitting up at times?*

Does Dad want to play golf in the afternoon? Do you have teenagers who can head for Blizzard Beach on their own? Will there be times when it would make sense for Dad to take the younger kids back to the hotel while Mom stays in the park with the older ones? Is your 5-year-old raring to go at dawn while your 15-year-old sleeps until noon? If so, stay on-site, where the use of the WDW transportation system makes it easy for you to all go your own way.

- *What's your hassle tolerance level?*

If you simply don't want to be bothered with interstate commutes, parking lots, carrying cash, and maps . . . stay on-site.

THE ADVANTAGES OF STAYING ON-SITE

Surprise Mornings

Under the "Surprise Mornings" program, Disney allows on-site guests each day into one designated theme park an hour earlier than off-site guests. When you check in to your hotel, you are given a brochure which reads something like, "Epcot—Tuesday and Friday, MGM—Sunday and Wednesday, Magic Kingdom—Monday, Thursday, and Saturday."

Note: The surprise-mornings days are sometimes referred to as "early-entry days."

Since visitors are almost always admitted to the theme parks 30 minutes before the stated opening time, this program means that on-site guests may find themselves inside the Magic Kingdom as early as 7:30 on mornings when the official opening time is 9 A.M. Generally, only one part of the park is open during the first hour. For example, in the Magic Kingdom it might be Fantasyland and Tomorrowland, which means you can ride Space Mountain and the other attractions within these sections with minimal waits. Then when the ropes drop at the official opening time, allowing you into the other sections, you're already deep within the park. You can dash straight for Splash Mountain or any other attractions that will be crowded later in the day, beating the surge of people who are still coming down Main Street.

At MGM the shows don't begin until the stated opening time, but the continuous-loading attractions are operative during the surprise-mornings hour—including the Great Movie Ride, the Twilight Zone Tower of Terror, and Star Tours. You can ride them and still be in line for the first showing of Voyage of the Little Mermaid far ahead of the day guests. At Epcot generally Innoventions, Spaceship Earth, and selected Future World pavilions open early.

Note: Because Disney has so many hotels, and thus so many on-site guests, some families responding to our surveys indicated that they use reverse psychology and visit one of the parks *not* featured as that day's surprise-mornings park. "If the sheet says 'MGM,' everyone runs to MGM like lemmings," wrote one father. "Let's face it: If 20,000 people are in on the surprise, it ain't much of a surprise."

There's little doubt that the park featured each day gets more people than it ordinarily would . . . and remains more crowded all day. The answer may be to visit the featured surprise-mornings park as early as possible, stay for a couple of hours, during which time you visit the biggie attractions that opened early, then go to one of the other parks about mid-morning.

Length of Stay Passes

These passes, which can be tailored to fit the length of your stay, offer you unlimited access to the major and minor parks and are slightly cheaper than comparable multiday passes. They also offer park-hopping privileges, even if you're staying only two or three days—a real boon to families with limited time to tour.

Restaurant Reservations

On-site guests can call for reservations at the sit-down restaurants both within the theme parks and at the other on-site hotels in advance. You should make all desired reservations either before you leave home or on the night you check in, thus ensuring that you can eat where you want, when you want, and eliminating standing in line. Since there are so many on-site guests, this perk has the effect of freezing off-site visitors out of the most popular restaurants at the most popular times.

Note: Disney is constantly fiddling with the reservation system and often allows on-site guests to make restaurant and dinner-show reservations a full 60 days in advance. When you book your room, be sure to ask if you can make dining reservations before you leave home.

Transportation

On-site guests have unlimited use of the monorails, buses, and boats of the WDW transportation system, which is your best bet for getting to the major parks. The buses for the on-site hotels, for example, can deliver riders right to the MK gates, eliminating the need to take a ferryboat or monorail from the Ticket and Transportation Center (TTC) and cutting at least 15 minutes off the commute.

If you're headed toward one of the minor parks or another on-site hotel, you'll have to switch buses at the TTC, which takes a little more time. You may save a few minutes by taking your car, but many on-site guests still report that they prefer to leave the driving to Disney.

Use of Other On-site Hotel Facilities

If you want to use the child-care or sporting facilities of other Disney hotels or dine at their restaurants, you'll receive preferential treatment over off-site visitors (although each hotel, reasonably enough, allows its own guests first shot at its services). This means that even if you're staying at the budget Dixie Landings, you can leave your kids at the Neverland Club at the Polynesian or take a tennis lesson at the Grand Floridian.

Access to Parks

The parks never close during operational hours to on-site guests, although when they fill to capacity they may close their gates to day guests. This is a factor only if you're visiting on holidays or during the summer, when the Magic Kingdom and the water parks sometimes reach capacity as early as 10 A.M.

Charging Privileges

If you're staying on-site, everyone in your party will be issued a resort ID the day you arrive. The ID entitles you to full use of the WDW transportation system and allows you to charge to your hotel room food and purchases—either at the hotels or within the parks. This is certainly better than carrying huge amounts of cash, especially at the pools, water parks, and marinas.

It's up to you whether your older kids have charging privileges. It makes it easier to send Johnny to the snack bar for a round of Cokes, but if you opt to give the minors charging privileges, be sure to impress upon them that these IDs work like credit cards; they are *not* an open invitation for the kids to ingratiate themselves with the gang in the arcade by ordering pizza for everyone, purchasing all seven dwarfs from the hotel gift shop, or, heaven forbid, obtaining cash advances. If an ID with charging privileges is lost, it should be reported to the front desk immediately to avoid unauthorized charges.

Family Atmosphere

All the on-site hotels are designed with families in mind, meaning that the ambience is casual, security is very tight, and there are always other kids around to play with. The on-site hotels have fast-food courts; late-night pizza delivery to your room; Laundromats, generally located near the pools and arcades so you can run a load while the youngsters play; and, if there is not a child-care facility at your particular hotel, Guest Services can help you arrange for an in-room sitter. The emphasis at the Disney hotels is on making life more convenient for parents.

Cool Themes

All of the on-site hotels have a theme that is carried out in mega-detail: At the Polynesian, your wake-up call begins "Aloha," jazz music plays all day at Port Orleans, and the bureaus in All-Star Sports look like gym lockers. This makes staying at an on-site hotel almost as exciting for kids as being inside the parks.

In fact, because the on-site hotels are so unspeakably cool, a fun afternoon break from touring can just be visiting the other hotels. Many families mentioned that they ate meals at several different on-site hotels during their visit; the restaurants carry out the themes, too, so if three days at the Polynesian have left you burned out on pineapple juice, try the barbecue at Wilderness Lodge.

THINGS TO ASK WHEN BOOKING AN OFF-SITE HOTEL

If you decide to stay off-site, you should be aware that there is a wide range of amenities and perks among the hundreds of hotels in the Orlando area. To make sure you're getting top value for your dollar, take nothing for granted. Some $250-per-night hotels charge you for shuttle service to the parks; some $75 ones do not. Some hotels count 11-year-olds as adults, and others consider 19-year-olds to be children. Some relatively inexpensive resorts have full-fledged kids' clubs; some larger and far more costly ones are geared to convention and business travel and don't even have an arcade. The moral is: Always ask.

There are three main off-site areas that tourists frequent: exits 25 and 27 off I-4, and International Drive. Both exit 27 and exit 25 are within a 10-minute drive to the theme parks. Exit 27 backs up to the hotels of the Disney Village Hotel Plaza, and any number of upscale eateries and hotels are nearby, mixed in with the Days Inns and fast-food places. (The Hyatt Regency Grand Cypress, Embassy Suites Lake Buena Vista, and Holiday Inn Sunspree are all on exit 27.) Exit 25 is older, seedier, and boasts outlets and gift shops instead of fancy restaurants and resorts, but hotels there run about $30 a night less than at a comparable hotel on exit 27.

International Drive is farther out, about 20 minutes from the theme parks, but it is modern and well kept, the sort of place where you'll find the most beautifully landscaped Pizza Hut in existence. International Drive boasts every chain restaurant you've ever heard of, as well as a funky Ripley's Believe It or Not, which appears to be sinking into the ground. You'll find ice-skating, miniature golf, and a three-story McDonald's. International Drive is the thoroughfare that runs between Sea World, Universal Studios, and Wet 'n Wild and is the most central location if you'll be spending lots of time at these three parks.

An entertainment complex called Pointe Orlando has recently opened on International Drive. It features nightclubs, comedy clubs, and celebrity restaurants developed by Dan Merino and Wynonna Judd, as well as a 20-screen movie theater and upscale shopping. Pointe Orlando, along with the presence of the Peabody and Omni hotels, make International Drive the toniest of the off-site locations.

One note of caution: An extremely cheap hotel rate, say $50 or less, generally means that the hotel is located in a less-desirable part of town, both in regard to proximity to the theme parks and general security. Unless you are personally familiar with the location and quality of the hotel, proceed with caution.

The questions below should help you ferret out the best deal.

• *Does the hotel provide in-room baby-sitters? What are their qualifications? How far in advance should I reserve a sitter? What is the cost? Do you have on-site child care?*

Several of the larger hotels have their own version of a kids' club—a drop-off child-care center with planned activities for the youngsters. See "Great Off-site Resorts for Families" in Section 2, page 67, for details.

- *Do you provide bus service to the Magic Kingdom, Epcot, and MGM? The minor parks? How often? How early—and how late—do the buses run? Is there any charge? Are the buses express or do they stop and pick up riders at other hotels?*

Careful here. Often small off-site hotels share shuttles, which means lots of stops and a long commute time to the parks.

- *Do kids stay free? Up to what age?*

This can be vitally important. On-site Disney hotels allow kids under 18 to lodge free with parents. The policy at off-site hotels varies.

- *Does the hotel provide a free buffet breakfast?*

- *What fast-food or family-style restaurants are nearby?*

- *Do you have any suites with kitchens?*

No one would suggest you should spend a vacation cooking. But many Orlando hotels have villa-style lodgings and, obviously, if you can eat cereal and sandwiches in your room, you'll save significant bucks. Some hotels, such as the Holiday Inn Sunspree, have minikitchens with small refrigerators and a microwave—all you need for simple meals. And the cost is no more than that of a regular room.

- *Does the hotel provide airport pickup?*

This is important if you're not renting a car, because the airport is a half-hour drive from WDW and cab fare is astronomical. There are independent buses that provide hotel service but, again, there's a cost per person.

- *Is there a Laundromat on the premises?*

- *Can I buy tickets to area attractions through the hotel's Guest Services desk? Are the tickets discounted?*

Many Orlando hotels offer discounts to Universal Studios, Sea World, and area dinner shows. Not only do you save dollars, but you save the time you'd otherwise spend waiting in line. Use caution, however, if the off-site hotels try to sell you Disney tickets. They're only slightly cheaper than the nondiscounted ones you'd buy at the theme park gates and they limit your access to the minor parks.

SHOULD WE BUY A PACKAGE?

This is a toughie. There are advantages to package trips, most notable that it is possible to save a good deal of money. It's also helpful to know up front what your vacation will cost. Often packages require hefty prepayments, which are painful at the time but at least you don't return home utterly maxed out on your MasterCard.

Package trips can have drawbacks, however. Like buying a fully loaded car off a dealer's lot, you may find yourself paying for options you don't necessarily want or need. Packages are often padded with perks such as reduced greens fees, which are of interest to only a few families, or rental cars, which you may not need if staying on-site. At the other end of the spectrum are deeply discounted packages which place you in rundown or out-of-the way hotels. Be doubly wary of the very cheap packages offered in Sunday papers. If a deal sounds too good to be true, it probably is.

Common Types of Packages

Disney's Resort Package Vacations
Several families responding to the survey were sold on Disney's own packages, such as the Grand Plan. This

package houses guests in the swank Grand Floridian or the almost-as-swank Yacht and Beach Clubs. It includes all food; all tickets; unlimited golf, boating, and other sporting facilities; as well as such extras as baby-sitting, stroller rental, a personalized itinerary, tuition in one of the Disney Institute programs . . . and a *Fantasia* alarm clock. As a reservation agent laughingly told me, "This one even includes the kitchen sink."

Such luxury, needless to say, doesn't come cheap. A family of four staying five days at the Grand Floridian on the Grand Plan can expect to pay $4,200. Another drawback is that since all meals are included in the plan, you may find yourself gorging as a cruise ship mentality takes over: "We gotta eat it—we paid for it." But families who want to sample a wide variety of Epcot cuisine, who have kids who'd love to rent those $15-per-half-hour water sprites for a whole afternoon, or who want child care every night, may decide that it's worth it.

If all this sounds like a bit too much, Disney also offers a variety of less expensive packages that lodge families at one of the on-site budget hotels such as Dixie Landings, Port Orleans, or the Caribbean Beach Resort. You can opt for meals or not; five days for a family of four without food would be about $1,400. Call (407) W-DISNEY to request a brochure and videotape outlining all the options.

Magic Kingdom Gold Card Packages

Those who hold a Magic Kingdom Club Gold Card have packages developed solely for them, ranging once again from the all-inclusive to the more affordably priced. The difference is that the Magic Kingdom Gold Card packages are 10% to 20% cheaper than comparable Disney packages, so if you're seriously considering booking a package, call 1-800-56-DISNEY. Paying the $65 for the two-year club membership would be smart, especially if you're traveling during the off-season when the biggest discounts are in effect.

Note: Once you purchase a Gold Card, you're in the Magic Kingdom Club automatically. Disney uses the terms *cardholder* and *club member* interchangeably, so it's a bit confusing. See "The Ultimate Cost-Saving Tip: Order a Magic Kingdom Club Gold Card" on page 26.

Airline Packages

If you're flying, check out the Delta Dream Vacations or USAir packages, which include airfare, theme park tickets for both Disney and other Orlando attractions, car rental, and lodging at either on-site or off-site hotels. Again, there's a huge range of amenities—you can have valet parking, character breakfasts, and use of a camcorder if you're willing to pay for them. And, again, the packages can be fine-tuned to meet your needs. If you'll be flying on Delta, call 1-800-872-7786 to request a brochure; the number for USAir is 1-800-455-0123.

Note: The airlines control a limited number of on-site hotel rooms, so call at least six months in advance if you have your heart set on a Disney resort.

Cruise Packages

The Walt Disney Company's long-awaited cruise ship, *Disney Magic,* has its maiden voyage slated for spring 1998, offering families the chance to combine a Bahamas cruise with a Disney World vacation.

Families may opt to spend either three or four nights at sea, the remainder of the week being spent in Orlando. Park admissions are included in the package, as are airfare, a rental car, and all meals while on-board ship. Once on-board you'll find a staggeringly full program for children, including dawn-to-dusk kids' clubs, kids' menus, parties and mixers geared toward teens and preteens, and the Disney characters. Youth counselors squire the kids around, giving worn-out parents the chance to collapse on deck chairs or wander into the casinos and dance clubs if they find the strength.

You can book the cruises through a travel agent or by calling 1-800-334-4017. See "Disney Cruises" in Section 7, page 215, for more information.

Travel Agents

If you'd like to stay on-site and you're not accustomed to using a travel agent, don't worry. Any discounts an agent would be able to get on a Disney resort would be minimal, so you'll come out about as well handling the reservations yourself. Simply call (407) W-DISNEY, and the representative will explain your options.

Travel agents are most helpful to families staying off-site. They are often aware of Orlando hotels that offer packages, and are a good source of comparative rate-shopping. Large travel agencies sometimes put together their own packages that include airfare, lodging at an off-site hotel, and a rental car. If you need all three of these components, you'll probably come out cheaper buying a package through a local agent than trying to book all three separately.

Cheapie Deals

These are frequently seen in the travel sections of major newspapers and offer extremely low rates. Proceed with caution. The hotels are sometimes as far as 50 miles away from the Disney gates. (With a rental car and an alarm clock, even this obstacle can be overcome—but you should know what you're up against.) Other pitfalls include tickets that can be used only at certain times of the year, or extremely inflexible touring arrangements that require you to ride from attraction to attraction in overcrowded, slow-moving buses.

Another consideration is that the hotels featured may not be in a very desirable area of town. Orlando has not suffered the degree of tourist-targeted crime that we've read about in other Florida cities, but unless either you or your travel agent are familiar with the area where the hotel is located, be wary. A family interested in saving money would be far better off driving and camping at Fort Wilderness or trying the All-Star Resorts than signing up for one of these packages.

THE ULTIMATE COST-SAVING TIP: A MAGIC KINGDOM CLUB GOLD CARD

If your family is really dizzy for Disney, it makes economic sense to order a Magic Kingdom Club Gold Card. Because the Disney hotels have no trouble filling up, the offered discounts haven't been quite so great in the past few years, but cardholders still receive a variety of benefits. You can order a Magic Kingdom Club Gold Card by calling 1-800-56-DISNEY. The cost of a two-year membership is $65.

The biggest perk is the discounts on on-site hotels. The 20% discounts coincide with the least crowded times of the year (in the fall), so membership in the club is doubly attractive to families with young kids. There are 10% discounts in spring and early summer. Although the weeks in which the discounts apply vary somewhat from year to year, the following schedule is typical.

From mid-August to mid-December and January to mid-February, expect a 20% discount off the regular rates at the following resorts:

- Disney's Yacht and Beach Clubs
- The Contemporary
- The Disney Institute Villas
- The Grand Floridian
- Fort Wilderness Trailer Homes and Campground
- Disney's Old Key West
- The BoardWalk

From late August to mid-December and from January to mid-February, expect a 20% price break at the following moderately priced resorts:

- Port Orleans
- Dixie Landings
- Caribbean Beach Resort
- Coronado Springs Resort

If your touring plans call for a spring or summer trip, you still get a flat 10% discount on the listed resorts.

Club members get a 10% discount from January to mid-February and mid-August through mid-December at the All-Star Resorts.

Club members get 10% discounts on dining in certain theme park restaurants at certain character breakfasts.

Club members also get a 10% discount on the Disneyland Hotel in California.

Given the high price of WDW lodging and dining, it's easy to see how club membership could pay for itself very quickly. But like the Fairy Godmother told

Cinderella, "There's one catch": If you plan to visit either WDW or Disneyland next year, you should order your card as soon as possible, since you must have it in hand when you make your hotel reservations. Also, only a certain quota of rooms in each hotel is eligible for the discount; call early, at least four months in advance, if you want your choice of dates and resort.

Magic Kingdom Club members receive other benefits, including discounts on National car rentals, theme park tickets, and the Disney cruise line, as well as a subscription to *Disney Magazine*. Also expect 10% discounts on merchandise at Disney stores nationwide (except in Orlando) and on items ordered through the Disney catalog. This perk alone can add up to big savings.

Cardholders have their own travel agency, which offers special packages to WDW, Disneyland, Tokyo Disneyland, and Disneyland Paris. Club members make reservations and get information on packages by calling (407) 824-2600. You'll get a brochure outlining all the perks and packages when you order your card.

Note: If you're really lucky, you can receive many of the goodies listed in this section without having to pay for the card. Many corporations hold Magic Kingdom Club Gold Cards, which qualify their employees for the discounts. Check with the personnel or employee benefits department to see if your company is a member.

WHAT KIND OF TICKET DO WE NEED?

This decision, believe it or not, needs to be made long before you get to the theme park gates. First of all, prepare yourself for the news that, at least in the eyes of the Disney accountants, your 10-year-old is an adult. Then consider how many days you'll need the tickets, whether you'd like to visit the minor parks, and if you plan to visit more than one park in a single day. (Most of the tips and touring plans in this book assume that you will.)

Note: When Disney opens its fourth major park, Disney's Animal Kingdom, in the spring of 1998, there will be a major restructuring of ticket prices. Always call to confirm prices before you leave home.

As this book goes to press, the following ticket options are available. Note that children under 3 are admitted free.

Five-Day World Hopper Pass
Admitting holder to the three major parks and the five minor ones

- Adult: $208
- Child (3–9): $167

Four-Day Park-Hopper Pass
Admitting holder to the three major parks, with the option of visiting more than one park a day

- Adult: $152
- Child (3–9): $122

Four-Day Value Pass
Admitting holder to the three major parks, without the option of moving from park to park in the course of the day

- Adult: $136
- Child (3–9): $109

One-Day Ticket
Admitting holder to one park only

- Adult: $40

- Child (3–9): $32

Holders of the five-day pass have unlimited access to Typhoon Lagoon, Blizzard Beach, Discovery Island, Pleasure Island, and River Country for seven straight days after the first date they use the pass. Considering that a one-day ticket to Typhoon Lagoon is $26 for adults and $20 for kids, the five-day pass is clearly the best value if you're visiting in the summer and want to hit the water parks several times during the week. Not interested in swishing around the water parks or dancing at Pleasure Island? The four-day pass will suffice, but choose the park-hopper option.

It's also worth noting that the four- and five-day passes do not have to be used on consecutive days and, in fact, never expire. Assuming that your kids don't move from the child to the adult category in the meantime, you can return in five years and the unused days on your multiday pass will still be valid, although your access to the minor parks will have expired.

Guests at the on-site hotels should consider the Length of Stay pass, which is good for a stay of any length from one to 10 days. The pass offers unlimited access to the major and minor parks during the time you're staying at a Disney hotel; although the price is obviously tied to how long you stay, the cost is slightly less than that of the Park-Hopper pass.

One final word of caution about buying tickets: The Guest Services desk at off-site hotels may not be run by your hotel at all, but by a separate company that exists solely to sell tickets and bus fares to tourists. These companies offer their own versions of the multiday pass, which they hawk aggressively, usually by telling you that it is much cheaper than the Disney ticket. It isn't. If you are offered a four-day pass with access to River Country, Discovery Island, and Pleasure Island, this is a good buy *only* if you're sure you'll never use that extra day provided on the five-day pass and you don't plan to visit Typhoon Lagoon or Blizzard Beach.

Also, Disney tickets are never discounted, so if you're offered cut-rate tickets you should immediately smell a rat. Sometimes companies offer free or discounted tickets in order to lure you into time-sharing or other vacation club promotions. You'll waste a whole day trying to save 20 bucks.

Be wary of buying bus rides into the parks. For starters, many hotels offer free shuttle service, so if you've chosen your hotel carefully there's no reason you should have to pay for transportation. But even if you need a ride, these independent shuttles may not be your best bet. The agents at the desk may tell you that you'll save the "horrendous" cost of Disney parking by taking their shuttle, but the truth is that it costs $6 to park and the bus tickets run anywhere from $3 to $7 a person. For a family of four, that adds up fast. Also, the shuttles offered by these independent services generally stop at several hotels, making your commute time much longer than if you drove your own car or stayed at a hotel offering a direct shuttle. Don't pay for this abuse.

ADVANCE RESERVATIONS
AND TICKET PURCHASES:
CALL NOW, AVOID LINES LATER

• Get maps of the theme parks and general touring information by calling (407) W-DISNEY. If you're traveling with someone elderly or in a wheelchair, request the *Guidebook for Disabled Visitors.*

• Tickets to the theme parks can be purchased by calling (407) W-DISNEY. MasterCard, Visa, and American Express are all accepted, and the tickets will be mailed to you. If you prefer to pay by check, call first to confirm prices then mail payment to:

WDW Tickets
P.O. Box 10030
Lake Buena Vista, FL 32830-0030

Many area hotels, including all Disney hotels, allow guests to purchase theme park tickets through Guest Services. Inquire when you make reservations.

Theme park ticket prices have spiraled in the past few years, changing about every six months. *Always* call to confirm prices. Once you purchase tickets, however, the price is fixed, so buy in advance when you can. If you live near one of the Disney stores, you can buy theme park tickets there.

• Room reservations for on-site hotels should be made at least four months in advance, especially if you're staying at one of the budget resorts. Call (407) W-DISNEY for information on all Disney-owned hotels. The line is open seven days a week from 8 A.M. to 10 P.M., and you'll have better luck getting through in the evening and on weekends.

Room reservations for off-site hotels can usually be made later, perhaps a month or two before you plan to arrive. Only the wildly optimistic should arrive in Orlando with no reservations at all. Booking mistakes are rare, but it never hurts to call and confirm room reservations before you leave home.

• Disney dinner-show reservations should also be made from home, and reservations are accepted up to 60 days in advance—or upon receipt of confirmed reservations for those staying on-site.

Because on-site guests get first crack at reservations, off-site guests may find themselves shut out of the most popular shows. If you're staying off-site, visiting during a busy time of the year, and want to see a popular dinner show like the Hoop-Dee-Doo Musical Revue, be sure to call (407) W-DISNEY at least 60 days in advance.

• In general, the character breakfasts are buffet-style and require no advance reservations, but this policy is subject to constant revision. Call (407) 939-3463 to inquire which character breakfasts are running during the time you plan to visit and whether you can make advance reservations.

• You'd like to make dining reservations in advance? This is where it gets complicated, so hold on.

If you're staying at one of the Disney hotels, dinner reservations for restaurants within the theme parks can generally be made up to 60 days in advance by calling (407) W-DISNEY. If you can't make reservations in advance or would like to wait until you're actually there and can see which restaurant looks the coolest, make reservations after you arrive by calling 55 from your hotel.

If you're not staying on-site, you'll need to make reservations in person on the day you plan to visit—by dropping by the actual restaurant in the MK, at the reservations booth at MGM, or at the WorldKey Information System inside the Earth Station under Spaceship Earth at Epcot.

• Members of the Entertainment Club may be surprised to learn that some spiffy area hotels, such as the Hotel Royal Plaza, Marriott Orlando, and Delta Orlando, offer 50% discounts to cardholders, making an upscale resort as inexpensive as an interstate cheapie. But because only a certain number of rooms are set aside for club members, reservations must be made well in advance to get the discounts. (Becoming a member of the Entertainment Club is as simple as buying one of the discount coupon books in your hometown. The books generally cost between $35 and $50 and are best known for their restaurant coupons. Few people seem to realize that a nationwide directory of hotels offering 50% discounts can be found in the back of the books.)

• Another great source of discounts is to call the Orlando Visitor's Bureau at 1-800-255-5786 and request their Vacation Planner and Magic Card. It takes about three to four weeks to get the package, but inside is lots of discount coupons for hotels, off-site dinner shows, and area attractions.

• Decide in advance if you need a rental car. If you're staying off-site or if you plan to visit non-Disney attractions, the answer may well be yes. Some rental car companies—Avis, Budget, Dollar, and National—have desks in the Orlando airport, with the cars in an adjacent lot. Others, such as Hertz or the huge and popular Alamo, are located away from the airport and require a separate shuttle ride. The shuttle adds 20 minutes to your commute, both going to and arriving from the airport, but Alamo offers slightly lower rental fees to compensate.

To reserve a car, call:

Hertz	1-800-654-3131
Avis	1-800-331-1212
National	1-800-227-7368
Alamo	1-800-327-9633

If you're staying on-site and doing only Disney, you may not need a rental car. Call Guest Services at the hotel where you'll be staying and ask the best way to get from the airport to the hotel. Some hotels run their own shuttles, and others use independent services such as Mears.

• It's always a good idea to read up on Disney as much as possible before you go. Although the company's own material is helpful, it does have an everything-is-wonderful tone, which is not much help to a family with limited vacation time, who must make some hard choices about what to see and do. Your travel plans should definitely include boning up on some "unofficial" sources, like this book.

Another good source of timely tips is the *Mousetales* newsletter. *Mousetales* contains lots of advice from parents as well as honest critiques of new shows and attractions. To subscribe, send $12.95 to:

Mousetales
P.O. Box 383
Columbus, OH 43216

THINGS TO DISCUSS WITH YOUR
KIDS BEFORE YOU LEAVE HOME

• *The Trip Itself.* There are two schools of thought on just how far in advance you should let the kids in on the plan. Because many families make reservations six or more months in advance, it's easy to fall into a "waiting for Christmas" syndrome, with the kids nearly in a lather of anticipation weeks before you leave. In order to avoid the agony of a long countdown, one couple packed in secret, then woke the children at 5 a.m. and announced, "Get in the car—we're going to Disney World!" Probably the best method is somewhere in between the two extremes. Tell the kids at the time you make your reservations, but don't begin poring over the brochures in earnest until about two weeks before the trip.

• *Height Requirements.* Get out your yardstick, because if your kids fall under the required height for riding Space Mountain and Splash Mountain (44 inches), or the Twilight Zone Tower of Terror and Big Thunder Mountain Railroad (40 inches), you should break it to them now. Disney vigilantly enforces these requirements, and there is nothing worse than waiting in line for an hour only to have little Nathan ejected unceremoniously just as you approach the ride.

• *The Layout of the Parks.* Kids 7 or over should have some idea of the layout of the parks; and if you're letting preteens and teens roam about on their own, they definitely should be briefed on the location of major attractions and where and when to meet up with the family again.

Among the more than 200 families surveyed or interviewed for this book, there was a direct correlation between the amount of advance research they had done and how much they enjoyed the trip. Visitors who show up at WDW without any preparation can still have fun, but their comment sheets were sprinkled with "Next time I'll know . . ." and "If only we had . . ." The pleasures of being prepared extend even to preschoolers. If you purchase a few WDW coloring books to enjoy on the trip down to Orlando, or watch one of the Disney Channel specials featuring the parks, even the youngest child will arrive able to identify the Swiss Family Robinson Treehouse and the Living Seas pavilion. A little knowledge prior to entering the gates helps you decide how to best spend your time and eliminates those "Whadda-we-do-now" debates.

• *The Classic Stories of Disney.* If your children are under 7, another good pre-trip purchase is a set of Disney paperbacks with audiotapes. Even though parental eyes may glaze over when *Dumbo* rewinds for its thirty-fourth straight hearing, these tapes and books help to pass the trip and familiarize kids with the characters and rides they'll be seeing once they arrive. (If you find kiddie tapes too annoying, you can always bring along Walkmans for the children to use.)

Some families rent Disney movies just before the trip: The videotape *Disneyland Fun* is especially good for getting the whole family revved up and in the mood. The park featured is Disneyland in California and not the Magic Kingdom in Florida, but the attractions are similar enough to make the tape an exciting preview. Renting *Honey, I Shrunk the Kids* before you leave will vastly improve your kids' appreciation of

Epcot's *Honey, I Shrunk the Audience* show, as well as the Honey, I Shrunk the Kids Adventure Zone at MGM.

The Disneyland Game, which is available through major toy store chains such as Toys R Us, is also a fun way to orient kids ages 2 to 8 to the general attractions of the theme parks. Players are required to move about the board, gathering cards from different attractions; the goal of the game—to visit as many rides as possible before the park closes—is considerably like that of the real-life game you'll play when you hit Orlando.

• *Special Academic Projects.* See "Should We Take the Kids Out of School?" on page 5 for ideas on special projects and seminars.

• *Souvenirs and Money.* Will you save all souvenir purchases for the last day? Buy one small souvenir every day? Are the children expected to spend their own money, or will Mom and Dad spring for the T-shirts? Whatever you decide will depend on your pocketbooks and your particular interpretation of fiscal responsibility, but do set your rules before you're in the park. Otherwise, the selection of goodies will lure you into spending far more than you anticipated.

One excellent technique for limiting impulse buys is to request Disney Dollars at the time you order your theme park tickets. Disney Dollars come in denominations of $1 (Mickey), $5 (Goofy), and $10 (Minnie) and are accepted throughout the theme parks, shops, restaurants, and resorts of WDW. Some wily parents have managed to convince their tots that these bills are the only currency the parks accept, and have given them a certain number of Disney Dollars before leaving home, explaining that this money and this money alone is for souvenirs.

You can purchase Disney Dollars at the Disney stores or by writing to:

Walt Disney World Ticket Mail Order
P.O. Box 10030
Lake Buena Vista, Florida 32830-0030

DON'T LEAVE HOME WITHOUT . . .

* *Comfortable Shoes.* This is no time to be breaking in new Reeboks.

* *Minimal Clothing.* Many hotels have Laundromats, and you can always use Woolite to wash out underwear in the sink. Most families make the mistake of overpacking, not figuring in all the souvenirs they'll be bringing back. (Guest Services at area hotels report that many families buy so much stuff that they end up shipping their dirty clothes home via UPS.) Disney T-shirts are not only great for touring, but can serve as swimsuit cover-ups and pajamas. And unless you're planning a romantic evening out at Victoria and Albert's, casual clothing is accepted everywhere.

* *Lightweight Jackets.* It rains in Orlando off and on all year around, so jackets should be preferably water-resistant.

* *Basic Necessities.* Disposable diapers, film, blank camcorder tapes, and baby formula are all available within WDW, but at premium prices.

* *Sunscreen.* Keep a tube with you and reapply it often. Sunburn is the number one complaint at the first-aid clinic in the MK. *Note:* You need sunburn protection all through the year in Orlando, not just during the summer.

- *Juiceboxes.* Not only are these handy in the car for the trip down, but you might want to keep a couple in your bag while touring. There are few places in the parks where you can grab a healthy drink fast, and kids can become dehydrated rapidly.

- *A Waist Pouch or Fanny-pack.* This is a good alternative to dragging along a purse while touring and frees up your hands for boarding rides, pushing strollers, and holding on to your kids.

- *Sunglasses.* The Florida sun is so blindingly bright that more than once I've reached into my purse for my sunglasses only to realize that I already had them on. Kids too young for sunglasses need wide-billed caps to cut down on the glare.

- *Strollers.* Earlier versions of this guide suggested renting strollers at the theme parks, because they're rather a hassle on the monorails and boats. But since Disney has raised its stroller rental fee to an unconscionable $6 per day, you're better off bringing a stroller from home. If you're staying at one of the more sprawling resorts, such as the Caribbean Beach Resort, the All-Star Resorts, Dixie Landings, or the Fort Wilderness Campground, you'll need your own stroller just to get around your hotel.

- *A Credit Card.* It's no joke. The Sun Bank, with locations throughout WDW, gives cash advances on most major cards, which can be a lifesaver.

HELPFUL PHONE NUMBERS

All Orlando numbers have a 407 area code. *Note:* Make all reservations through the (407) W-DISNEY number and use the resort's direct line only to call Guest Services or reach a registered guest.

General information on accommodations	W-DISNEY
General information on WDW	824-4321
All-Star Music Resort	939-6000
All-Star Sports Resort	939-5000
Beach Club	934-8000
BoardWalk	939-5100
Caribbean Beach Resort	934-3400
Contemporary Resort	824-1000
Dinner-show and character breakfast reservations	W-DISNEY or 939-3463
Discovery Island	824-3784
Disney Institute	1-800-496-6337
Disney Institute Villas	827-1100
Disney's Old Key West	827-7700
Disney Village Marketplace	828-3800
Dixie Landings	934-6000
Dolphin	934-4000
Fort Wilderness Campground	434-7639
Grand Floridian Resort	824-3000
Pleasure Island	934-6374
Polynesian Resort	824-2000
Port Orleans	934-5000
River Country	824-2760
Swan	934-3000
Typhoon Lagoon	560-4141
Wilderness Lodge	824-3200
Yacht Club	934-7000

2

★★★★★★★★★★★★★★★★★

Choosing a Hotel

RATING THE ON-SITE DISNEY HOTELS

Not content with merely dominating the entertainment market, the Walt Disney Company has also turned its attention to lodging the 10 million visitors who stream into Orlando each year. Orlando has over 100,000 hotel rooms, more than any other U.S. city, and an increasing percentage of these rooms are Disney-owned, that is, on-site.

The majority of the new hotels added by Disney fall into the budget and midpriced category. With the exception of the BoardWalk, the new resorts are bigger and less expensive than those built 10 years ago. Port Orleans and Dixie Landings have joined the Caribbean Beach Resort to bring the total of rooms in the $115 to $145 price category to well over 5,000. The opening of the new Coronado Springs Resort adds 1,900 more rooms and even convention space to the midpriced market.

In an effort to go after even the most budget-minded families, the mammoth All-Star Sports and All-Star Music Resorts have 4,000 rooms in the $69 to $89 category. Until now, cost has been the primary reason for visitors to opt to stay off-site; but with the explosion in on-site budget and midpriced resorts, Disney is working to eliminate even that objection. Each time Disney opens a new resort, your options increase.

And so do your decisions. All this expansion means that even if a family has decided to stay on-site, they still face a bewildering number of choices. Does the convenience of being on the monorail line justify the increase in price? Do you want to stay amid turn-of-the-century Victorian splendor or is a fort more your style? Is it important to be near the swimming, golf courses, stables, and other sporting activities, or do you plan to spend most of your time in the parks? As in all of WDW, making the best choice hinges upon your awareness of your family's particular needs.

Magic Kingdom Hotels

The Grand Floridian

Modeled after the famed Florida beach resorts of the 1800s and possibly the prettiest of all Disney hotels, the Grand Floridian has 900 rooms encased among its gabled roofs, soaring ceilings, and broad white verandas.

Proximity to the MK: Excellent, via direct monorail or launch.

Proximity to Epcot: Good, via monorail with a change at the TTC.

Proximity to MGM: Fair, via bus.

Pluses

- Convenient location on the monorail line.
- A private beach on the Seven Seas Lagoon and numerous water sports.
- Excellent dining choices, including 1900 Park Fare, which serves a buffet with the characters.
- On-site child care.
- On-site health club.
- Exceptionally lovely rooms. The Grand Floridian is a favorite with honeymooners and others seeking a romantic ambience. (It's within sight of Disney's wedding chapel.)

Minuses

- Extremely pricey, with rooms about $300 to $530 a night.

- The elegance puts off some families who feel funny trooping past a grand piano in dripping bathing suits.

Overall grade: B. Expensive but luxurious.

The Contemporary Resort

You'll either love or hate the Contemporary, which has 1,050 rooms surrounding a mammoth high-tech lobby full of shops and restaurants. This place is always hopping.

Proximity to the MK: Excellent, via direct monorail.

Proximity to Epcot: Good, via monorail with a change at the TTC.

Proximity to MGM: Fair, via bus.

Pluses

- Located on the monorail line.

- Fairly easy to book, and discounts are available.

- Disney movies are shown nightly, and the Contemporary is also home to the Fiesta Fun Center, a giant arcade.

- The standard water sports are available, along with tennis and a spa.

- Chef Mickey is one of the best restaurants in all of WDW for families, offering a chance to visit with the characters while enjoying an all-you-can-eat buffet.

Minuses

- It's loud, with a big-city feel, which is exactly what many families come to Florida to escape. "Like sleeping in the middle of Space Mountain," wrote one mother. *Note:* The Garden Wings are both quieter and cheaper than the main building.

- Like the other hotels on the monorail line, the Contemporary is expensive. Expect around $230 to $315 per night, unless discounts apply.
- This is the original WDW resort and, although constantly refurbished, it looks a bit tired in comparison with the others.

Overall grade: C. Convenient and lively—perhaps a little too lively.

The Polynesian Resort

Designed to emulate an island village, the Polynesian is relaxed and casual. The main desk as well as most of the restaurants and shops are in the Great Ceremonial House, along with orchids, parrots, and fountains. Guests stay in one of the 863 rooms in the sprawling "long houses." The Polynesian enjoys a loyal repeat business, with many of the families surveyed raving about the laid-back ambience and pretty lagoon views.

Proximity to the MK: Excellent, via direct monorail, launch, or ferryboat.

Proximity to Epcot: Good, via monorail with one change at the TTC.

Proximity to MGM: Fair, via bus.

Pluses

- The Polynesian offers the most options for transport to the MK. You're on the monorail line but are also within walking distance of the ferryboats. Launches leave from the docks regularly, as do buses from the Great Ceremonial House. Your best route to the MK depends on the location of your room. Near the lagoon? Take the launch. Near the Great Ceremonial House? The monorail is faster. On the beach? Walk to the ferryboat.

- Private beach with an attractive pool and numerous water sports available. Like the beach at the Grand Floridian, the Polynesian has canvas shells that provide shade for napping babies and toddlers digging in the sand.
- On-site child care.

Minuses
- Without a discount, expect to pay $250 to $400 a night.
- Like the Contemporary, it's an older resort, which is sometimes reflected in the color schemes.

Overall grade: A–. An outstanding resort, and your best choice if you're willing to pay the bucks required to be on the monorail line.

The Wilderness Lodge

Disney opened the Wilderness Lodge near the campgrounds of Fort Wilderness in 1994. At about $200 a night, the rustic-looking, western-spirited resort is aimed at filling the gap between the midpriced and luxury hotels.

As is typical with the newer resorts, the theme of Wilderness Lodge is extended to every aspect of the hotel's design—the pool begins indoors as a hot spring, then flows into a meandering creek, culminating in a waterfall into the rocky caverns of the outdoor pool. The awe-inspiring lobby, which looks like a Lincoln log project run amok, centers around an 82-foot fireplace which blazes year-round. The quilted bedspreads and Native American–motif wallpaper of the guest rooms, the staff dressed like park rangers, and even the stick ponies children ride to their tables in the Whispering Canyon Cafe—all combine to evoke the feel of a National Park Service lodge built a hundred years ago.

When you check in, you're given a brochure on Wilderness Lodge lore, which will help you find the 100 animals hidden in the lobby, many of them carved into totems or branded into chandeliers. And you'll learn that "it took over 2 billion years to build the fireplace," as the rock represents strata from all the layers of the Grand Canyon. They even play audiotaped animal sounds in the parking lot, so don't panic if you hear a moose call while you're getting into your Mazda.

For those who just like to *appear* to be roughing it, Wilderness Lodge is perfect—you can jump into the Jacuzzi right after your trail ride.

Proximity to the MK: Good, via launch.

Proximity to Epcot: Fair, via bus.

Proximity to MGM: Fair, via bus.

Pluses

- The lodge is relatively new—and looks it. The pool area is especially dramatic.

- You have close access to River Country and all the down-home fun of Fort Wilderness without having to camp.

- On-site child care.

- Wilderness Lodge is small for a Disney resort— 760 rooms in contrast to the budget hotels that have as many as 2,000—which gives it a more intimate feel and makes it easier to get around.

Minuses

- At $185 to $235 a night, it's still not cheap.

- This is the only Magic Kingdom resort without monorail access to the MK. The boat takes slightly longer.

- The rooms sleep four people, whereas the other full-priced resorts sleep five.

- The Wilderness Lodge has received many complaints about its bus service. Part of the problem is due to its out-of-the-way location—you have to ride through the woods to get anywhere—so expect a slightly longer commute time.

Overall grade: B+

On-site Midpriced Hotels

Midpriced is somewhat of a misnomer, because both the price and the quality are higher than a typical chain hotel in Orlando. For paying about $30 more a night than a comparable off-site hotel, you get an ambience that's pure Disney. As you sip a drink and watch your kids zoom down the tongue of the beloved sea serpent slide at the Port Orleans pool, you certainly won't feel like you're slumming. The hotels are well maintained and landscaped, with gobs of atmosphere thrown in to carry their motifs to the *n*th degree.

Port Orleans and Dixie Landings

Both of these hotels are based on an Old South theme and offer unbeatable amenities and ambience for the price. Port Orleans transports guests to the heart of the French Quarter with manicured gardens, wrought-iron railings, and street names such as Rue d'Baga. The Mardi Gras mood extends to the pool area, dubbed the Doubloon Lagoon, where alligators play jazz while King Triton sits atop the water slide, regally surveying his domain.

Dixie Landings is a bit more down-home, with a steamboat-shaped lobby, general stores run by gingham-clad gals in braids, and Ol' Man Island—a swimming area based on the Disney film *Song of the South*. A bit schizophrenic in architecture, with white-column buildings encircling fishin' holes and cotton mills,

Dixie Landings manages to mix in a variety of southern clichés without losing its ditsy charm. If Huck
Finn ever married Scarlett O'Hara, this is where
they'd come on their honeymoon.

Comparatively speaking, Port Orleans is only half the
size of Dixie Landings, the major reason why it gets our
nod as the best. At Port Orleans the odds are you'll be
close to the pool, lobby, food court, and shuttle-bus
station; at Dixie Landings getting around is a bit more
of a headache. Both resorts have a fast-food court, a sit-
down restaurant, and a bar that features live entertainment.
The food court at Dixie Landings is more complete, but
the sit-down restaurant at Port Orleans is quieter and
more relaxing. If you're in a rush, the Creole munchies
in the Port Orleans bar and the Cajun ones at the Dixie
Landings bar make an adequate meal.

Proximity to the MK, Epcot, and MGM: Fair, via bus.

Pluses

- Great water areas, which can easily keep the kids
  entertained for a full afternoon.

- So cleverly designed and beautifully maintained
  that you won't believe you're staying on-site for
  half the price of the other resorts. (Rooms are
  $115 to $145 a night.)

- Both hotels have marinas with the standard selection of watercraft.

- The *Sassagoula* steamboat offers both resorts
  easy water access to the Disney Village Marketplace and Pleasure Island.

Minuses

- Unless you drive your own car, you are dependent
  upon buses for transport to the major and minor
  parks, which means a slightly longer commute

time. The fact that the two resorts share buses slows you down a bit.

- No on-site child care.

Overall rating: A. You get a good deal here in more ways than one.

Caribbean Beach Resort

This family-priced 2,112-room resort is located on 200 acres with a private lake and white-sand beaches. Each section of this mammoth hotel is painted a different tropical color and named after a Caribbean island. Each "island" has its own shuttle-bus stop, private beach, and pool. The rooms, although small, are attractively decorated.

Proximity to the MK, Epcot, and MGM: Fair, via bus.

Pluses

- The price is right, at $115 to $145 per night.
- Parrot Cay, a manmade island with a playground, climbing fort, and small aviary, is fun for young kids.
- Water sports abound; Toobies—small, motorized bumper boats that can be rented at the marina for $10 per half-hour—are especially popular.
- This is one of the best places in all of WDW to explore by bike. Bikes can be rented at the marina for $3 an hour or $7 a day, with specialty bikes like tandems costing a bit more. (If you're driving to Orlando and plan to bike a lot, it's definitely cost-effective to bring your own wheels.)
- Inexpensive food can be found in the Old Port Royale fast-food plaza. A full-service restaurant has also been added.

Minuses
- Although the buses are regular, they're not as swift as the water-taxis or monorails. Expect a longer commute time.
- The place is huge. It may be a major hike from your hotel room to the food plaza or marina. If you have young kids, bring your own stroller.
- No on-site child care.

Overall grade: B. Solid value for the money.

Coronado Springs Resort

As this book goes to press, Disney's first moderately priced convention hotel is set to open in fall of 1997 (and will continue to open in stages through 1998). The theme is Mexican, with Spanish tiled roofs, adobe walls, and a pool area dominated by an imposing Mayan temple. The playground doubles as an archeological dig site, and the rooms are scattered around a 15-acre lake and a series of rocky streams. Most of the action will center around the 95,000-square-foot convention space, but the resort will be open to regular vacationers as well. Coronado Springs should be in the same $115 to $135 price range as the other midpriced hotels.

The resort will feature the main pool with its water slide, as well as hot tubs and three smaller "quiet pools." Expect a volleyball court, swimming beach beside the lake, and a marina with the standard boat rentals. There will also be a health club—a rarity in the midpriced range—and a food court and sit-down Mexican restaurant. Coronado Springs will be reviewed more extensively in next year's guide.

On-site Budget Hotels

After opening only three years ago, the All-Star Resorts have rapidly built such a loyal following that they are now among the first to fill up. There are three reasons for the resorts' success—price, price, and price. The All-Star Resorts make staying on-site possible for families who previously could only dream of such a splurge.

It's worth noting that the budget and midpriced hotels don't run with quite the legendary efficiency of the more expensive resorts. I recently endured a 40-minute check-in procedure at All-Star Sports, something that would be unheard of at the Grand Floridian. A woman behind me was grousing that there was no freebie Mickey Mouse lotion in her room like they had at the Yacht Club. But these minor inconveniences pale when you consider that most of the on-site benefits—easy transportation to the parks, help with tickets and reservations, and the surprise-mornings perk—are just as available to those paying $69 a night at the All-Star Resorts as to those paying $369 at the BoardWalk. And, hey, the maids still leave your kids' stuffed animals in the window to greet them in the evening, so who can complain?

All-Star Sports and All-Star Music Resorts

This nearly 4,000 room complex opened in stages throughout 1994 and 1995. All-Star Sports contains five sections—tennis, football, surfing, basketball, and baseball—with the decor themed appropriately. At the All-Star Music Resort, you can choose between jazz, rock 'n roll, country, calypso, and Broadway tunes.

The pow graphics of the brightly colored buildings and the general zaniness appeal to kids. There are giant tennis ball cans and cowboy boots, a walk-through jukebox, and footballs the size of houses. At the calypso pool in All-Star Music, the buildings are lime green and punctuated with maracas; pitcher Goofy throws water in the baseball diamond–shaped pool at All-Star Sports. Palm trees are set to tip off before a gargantuan backboard in the basketball section, and show tunes play all day under the marquee on the streets of the Broadway section. It's budget, but it ain't boring.

Proximity to the MK, Epcot, and MGM: Fair, via bus.

Pluses

- In a word, *cost*. Rooms start at $69.

- The All-Star Resorts offer an affordable option for families with a handicapped member. For $79 a night, you can have a slightly larger ground-floor suite with roll-in showers.

- The shuttle buses are a good transportation option considering the price. When you get into this price range at the off-site hotels, you often have to pay for a shuttle. These run every 15 minutes and service is prompt.

- Proximity to Blizzard Beach.

- There's a food court which, although crowded, provides a fair selection.

Minuses

- Food options are limited. Fast-food courts only, with no restaurants or indoor bar.

- Sporting options are limited; swimming is about it.

- The rooms are very small. They sleep four, but you'll be bunched.

- By breaking each resort into five separate sections, Disney is striving to eliminate that sleeping-in-the-middle-of-Penn-Station feel. But there's no way around the fact that it takes more effort to get around a huge hotel than a small one.

- Longer check-in than is typical for Disney resorts.

Overall grade: A–. Lots of bang for the buck here.

Epcot Center Resorts

The Disney Swan and Disney Dolphin

This convention/resort complex is connected to Epcot and MGM by water-taxi and bridges. The Swan and Dolphin are "twin" hotels (like the nearby Yacht and Beach Clubs), meaning that although they have separate check-ins (and are in fact owned by separate companies), the resorts are alike in architecture and mood. Both the Swan and the Dolphin have an emphatically sophisticated feel, but since their openings both have made great strides to become more family-oriented and offer amenities directed toward the parents of young children.

Proximity to the MK: Fair, via bus.

Proximity to Epcot: Excellent, via tram or a moderate walk.

Proximity to MGM: Excellent, via water-taxi.

Pluses

- Disney is aggressively going after the convention trade with the Swan and Dolphin. If a working parent is lucky, she can score a free family vacation here.

- Transportation to MGM by water-taxi and Epcot by shuttle tram takes less than 10 minutes from lobby to theme park gate, with a slightly longer shuttle ride to the MK. These hotels offer extremely easy access to Epcot, with a private entrance into the back of the World Showcase, allowing Dolphin and Swan guests to completely avoid arriving and departing crowds. You even have your own stroller-rental booth at the World Traveler Shop, and breakfast at the Boulangerie Patisserie in the nearby France pavilion is sublime. (During the off-season, when the World Showcase section of Epcot often doesn't open until 11 A.M., guests are transported directly to Future World in double-decker buses.) If you like MGM and Epcot, it's hard to beat the location of these two.

- Camp Swan and Camp Dolphin offer excellent on-site child care. Planned activities range from tennis programs to craft classes; they are geared toward kids as young as 3 and are reasonably priced.

- The new, expanded beach area offers a playground, kiddie pools, water slides, and a small marina with paddleboats.

- Bike rentals, tennis courts, and health clubs are also available.

Minuses
- Expensive, at $220 to $400 per night.

- Because of the proximity to Epcot and MGM and the fact they're gunning for the convention trade, these are adult-oriented resorts, with a citified atmosphere.

Overall grade: B. A great place to go if the company is picking up the tab. Otherwise, try the Yacht and Beach Clubs first.

The Disney Yacht and Beach Clubs

Designed to resemble a turn-of-the-century Nantucket seaside resort, the Yacht and Beach Clubs are situated on a 25-acre freshwater lake. The Yacht Club, with 635 rooms, is the more elegant of the two, but the sunny gingham-and-wicker-filled Beach Club, with 580 rooms, is equally charming. The Yacht and Beach Clubs hit the perfect balance for families with young kids in tow—homey, lovely, and not one bit fancy.

Proximity to the MK: Fair, via bus.

Proximity to Epcot: Excellent, via a short stroll over a bridge.

Proximity to MGM: Excellent, via water-taxi.

Pluses

- Stormalong Bay, the water recreation area that separates the two resorts, is almost like being next door to a private water park. The sand-bottomed "bay" contains pools of varying depths, water slides, and a wrecked ship for atmosphere. It's especially fun to climb the shipwreck nearly to the top of its rigging, then zoom through a long tube into the middle of the pool. In fact, the water areas at the Yacht and Beach Clubs are so nice you'll have no trouble convincing the kids to return "home" for a dip in lieu of a more time-consuming trek to Typhoon Lagoon or Blizzard Beach.

- Like the Dolphin and Swan, the Yacht and Beach Clubs are on the doorstep of the Epcot World Showcase and are just an easy boat commute away from MGM as well.

- The Sandcastle Club offers on-site child care for children 3 to 12.

- Disney characters are on hand for breakfast at the Cape May Cafe in the Beach Club.

- The two resorts share an on-site health club.

- The Bayside Marina offers paddleboats, pontoons, and Toobies.

Minuses
- Rates run about $235 to $425 per night, but discounts do apply in the off-season.

Overall grade: A. These hotels enjoy a large repeat business from satisfied families. If your kids like water sports, and you all like Epcot, try the Yacht or Beach Resort on your next trip down.

The BoardWalk

The BoardWalk and the BoardWalk Villas (see page 60) form the hub of a large complex with convention space, four restaurants, the ESPN sports club, dance clubs, comedy shows, and a cool arcade with state-of-the-art virtual-reality games. The mood? Turn-of-the-century Atlantic City. Cheery, attractive rooms are clustered above an old-fashioned boardwalk, and the action on the waterfront continues late into the night.

In fact, some readers have written in to claim that the BoardWalk is a far more affordable version of Pleasure Island. The two nightclubs, Atlantic Dance and Jellyrolls, charge a small cover during the on-season, but even with this you'll be paying far less than the $19 Pleasure Island admission fee. The midway-style games, carnival barkers, and arcades can keep older kids busy. A fun extra is renting a surrey bike ($10.75 per half-hour) and taking the whole gang for a loop around the lagoon (you'll be gasping for air by the time you pass the Yacht Club). The BoardWalk area is stunningly beautiful at night.

Proximity to the MK: Fair, via bus.
Proximity to Epcot: Excellent, via a short stroll.
Proximity to MGM: Excellent, via water-taxi.

Pluses
- Great location for both Epcot and MGM.
- A far wider selection of restaurants and entertainment than most of the other resorts.
- The resort is brand-new—and looks it. The rooms are spacious, modern, and attractive.
- On-site health club.
- An excellent selection of water activities.
- Proximity to the ESPN sports club.
- You'll have no trouble keeping older kids entertained here—although you may go broke in the process.
- On-site kids' club.

Minuses
- Expensive, at $220 to $340 a night.
- May be too lively and hopping for families with very young kids.

Overall grade: A–. You'll feel like you're right in the middle of the action—because you are.

Villa-Style Accommodations

BoardWalk Villas

The villa side of the BoardWalk complex offers the same lively activities and great restaurant selection— as well as more room upstairs. Many of the suites have whirlpool tubs, and the minikitchens are well stocked. Villa units are a bit more expensive than the regular rooms, ranging from $260 to $510 per night.

Pluses and Minuses: See "The BoardWalk" on page 59.

Overall grade: A–. New, fresh, and fun—and a great option if you have a large family and need the space of a villa.

Disney's Old Key West

Designed to be sold as time-shares, the villas of Disney's Old Key West (formerly known as the Vacation Club) are available for nightly rentals. You get all the standard amenities of a Disney resort—plus a lot more room.

Proximity to MK, Epcot, and MGM: Fair, via bus.

Pluses

- If you have more than two children and need to spread out, or if you'd like a kitchen where you can prepare your own meals, Disney's Old Key West is a good on-site option. The villas are larger than those at the BoardWalk.

- Tennis, pools, a cute sand play area with a permanent castle, and a marina are on-site. There's an arcade and fitness room, and free Disney movies are shown nightly.

- Prices run from $260 for a studio with a kitchenette to $725 for a three-bedroom Grand Villa, which could easily accommodate 12 people. A roomy two-bedroom villa with full kitchen is about $450, which compares with a room at the Grand Floridian or Yacht Club. If you're willing to swap proximity to the parks for more space and the chance to cook your own meals, Disney's Old Key West may be just what you need.

Minuses

- Still much pricier than off-site villas such as Embassy Suites.

- Quieter, with less going on than the resorts.
- No child-care options.

Overall grade: B

Disney Institute Villas

Designed for families—large families—these villas are far from the maddening crowd, tucked behind the Disney Village Marketplace. Formerly known as the Disney Village Resort Villas, the Disney Institute Villas offer one, two, or three rooms. Many of the guests are taking classes at the Disney Institute or are golfers looking for action on the nearby courses.

Proximity to the MK, Epcot, and MGM: Fair, via bus.

Pluses

- Close to Disney Village Marketplace and Pleasure Island.
- Proximity to golf.
- Best choice for those traveling with a huge brood, such as a family reunion; several villas easily sleep up to 12 people. Some of the villas are designed like treehouses; others have lofts and skylights.
- As well as great access to golf, you'll find tennis, boating, biking, and six small swimming pools.
- Proximity to all the activities of the Disney Institute, including the huge health club—by far the best in all of WDW, if not Florida.

Minuses

- You're a fairly long way from the theme parks, even by bus.
- There's only one restaurant, although if you're cooking in your villa a lot, this may not be a problem. You also have access to the many eateries at

nearby Disney Village Marketplace and Pleasure Island.

- The villas, although recently refurbished, are much older than those at Disney's Old Key West or the BoardWalk. The architecture is very low-key, and the resort is not as thematic as the other on-site hotels.

- It's quite expensive, with villas ranging from $195 to $775 per night. Average villas run about $340, and far cheaper suites can be found off-site.

- Guests of the Disney Institute get first crack at the villas. If the Institute isn't full, other people are welcome to rent the villas—but you may feel like a stranger at someone else's party.

Overall grade: B–. Lots of space, but you have to rely on buses or your own car to get to where the action is.

On-site Camping

Fort Wilderness Trailer Homes and Campground

A resort into itself, Fort Wilderness offers campsites for tents and RVs as well as air-conditioned trailers for rent. The wide-open spaces, perfect for volleyball, biking, and hiking, are a relief for families with kids old enough to explore on their own.

Proximity to the MK: Good, via bus or launch.

Proximity to Epcot: Fair, via bus, or bus to the TTC, where you can change to the monorail.

Proximity to MGM: Fair, via bus.

Pluses

- Fort Wilderness offers a huge variety of activities for kids, such as hay rides, horseback and pony riding, and a petting farm with pigs, goats, and geese.

- Proximity to River Country, Discovery Island, and the Hoop-Dee-Doo Musical Revue
- This is your least expensive on-site option, with hookups and tent sites as low as $43 a night. The trailers rent for about $185 a night, sleep six people, and offer full kitchens.
- Groceries are available at the on-site trading post.
- Daily maid service is free in the rental trailers.

Minuses
- Camping may not seem like a vacation to you.
- A large number of people are sharing relatively few facilities, and the pools and beach can get very crowded.
- The place is so spread out that it requires its own in-resort bus system to get guests from one area to another. You can rent golf carts or bikes, but make no mistake: Fort Wilderness is large and hard to navigate.

Overall grade: B. If you like to camp and are willing to put up with a little inconvenience for great savings, this is a good option.

Disney Village Hotels

The Disney Village Hotels include the Buena Vista Palace, the Grosvenor Resort, the Guest Quarters Suite Resort, the Hilton, the Royal Plaza, the Courtyard by Marriott, the Howard Johnson Resort Hotel, and the Travelodge Hotel.

Because they're neither owned by Disney nor built on Disney property, the Disney Village Hotels are somewhat of a hybrid between the on-site and off-site lodgings. Located just across the road from the Disney Village Marketplace and Pleasure Island, these hotels are also considered to be "official" WDW hotels, meaning that they run very frequent shuttles to all Disney theme parks and offer access to the restaurant reservation system and price breaks on admission tickets.

Proximity to the MK, Epcot, and MGM: Fair, via bus.

BEST ON-SITE CHOICES AT A GLANCE

Best Magic Kingdom Resort: The Polynesian

People who come here always seem to come back, and that says something.

Best Epcot Resort: The Beach Club

You like Epcot? It's just a stroll away.

Best Midpriced Resort: Port Orleans

The best of both worlds—all the charm and intimacy of a full-priced hotel at a reduced cost.

Best Budget Resorts: All-Star Sports and All-Star Music Resorts

The All-Star Resorts have the distinction of being both the winner and the only entry in the category . . . but they're still worth mentioning because of strong reader support.

Best Villa: BoardWalk Villas

The resort has been open only a year as this book goes to press, but the people who write to us seem to love it. The only drawback is the noise. If you prefer a more quiet, out-of-the-way hotel, try Disney's Old Key West.

GENERAL INFORMATION ABOUT
THE ON-SITE DISNEY HOTELS

- A deposit equal to the price of one night's lodging is required within 21 days of making your reservation. You may pay by check or with MasterCard, Visa, or American Express. If you cancel at least 48 hours in advance, your deposit will be fully refunded.

- All Disney hotels operate under the family plan, meaning kids 18 and under stay free with parents. The rooms at the midpriced and budget hotels, as well as Wilderness Lodge and the Swan and Dolphin, are designed for four people; the other on-site hotels can easily sleep five in a room. If your family is larger, consider either a villa or a trailer home.

- Check-in time is 3 P.M. at most Disney resorts, but 4 P.M. at the villas. You can drop off your bags and pick up your tickets and resort IDs in the morning and tour until midafternoon. Then return to your hotel to check in.

- Check-out time is 11 A.M. but, again, you needn't let this interfere with your touring. Check out early in the morning and store your bags with the concierge or valet parking. Then enjoy your last day in the parks. If you pay with a credit card, you can arrange for automatic check-out: an itemized charge statement is slipped under your door early on the morning you'll be leaving—a definite timesaver.

- The resort ID that you are issued when you check in allows you to charge meals, drinks, tickets, and souvenirs to your room, and also gives you access to all WDW transportation.

- Room service, with the exception of pizza delivery, can be painfully slow, with 45-minute waits not uncommon. Breakfast can be ordered the evening before and is more prompt, but even then it is far quicker to get your own food. Each hotel has a fast-food restaurant or snack bar on-site that is open very early; the larger hotels send around pastry and beverage carts. If you're in a rush to get to the parks, one parent can go out for muffins and cereal and take the food back to the room so you can eat while you dress.

GREAT OFF-SITE RESORTS
FOR FAMILIES

In this edition of the book, you won't find several of the hotels that were previously listed in this category. As Disney has opened more resorts and increased the perks offered to on-site guests, it's become difficult to advise any family to pay $200 a night for an off-site hotel. At that price, you could be staying at one of the best Disney resorts and enjoying all the on-site benefits.

In response to Disney's attack on their turf, several of Orlando's luxury hotels, such as the Peabody and the Renaissance Resort, have begun gearing themselves even more toward convention traffic. As the off-site hotels have dropped family-oriented programs, I have in turn dropped them from my recommended lists. They're still great hotels—just a little too adult and swank for the typical family traveling with young kids. The hotels listed here have maintained their youth-oriented programs and remain good choices for families.

Hilton at Disney Village Hotel Plaza

Conveniently located with shuttle service to nearly all area attractions, the Hilton has the additional boon of a kids' club, called Vacation Station, for kids 4 to 12. It's open from 5 P.M. until midnight and charges $4 an hour, with a $1 add-on for siblings. Kids can eat dinner at the Soda Shoppe next door while their parents are out on the town. (The Hilton is a mere stroll away from Pleasure Island.) There's a playroom, big-screen TV with Disney movies, Nintendo games, and even a six-bed dormitory complete with teddy bears, so sleepy preschoolers can be bedded down.

The Hilton concierge has a lending library of games, and kids get a Family Fun Kit with freebies and discount coupons when they check in. Rates are $150 to $250 per night. Call 1-800-782-4414 or (407) 827-4000.

The Hyatt Regency Grand Cypress Resort

The Grand Cypress isn't a hotel—it's an event. With 750 rooms, golf courses, lakes, riding trails, and an enormous pool and grotto area with waterfalls and caves, you could spend a vacation here without ever leaving the hotel. (But should you decide to venture out, WDW is only three miles away.) The Grand Cypress is home to Camp Hyatt, a child-care center that plans daily activities for children 5 to 15, at a cost of $5 an hour or $25 a day. Rock Hyatt, a weekend evening program that gives teenagers the chance to hang out with other kids their age, provides specially trained counselors to oversee volleyball and Ping Pong, video tournaments, and dances. The Grand Cypress also boasts five restaurants—including Hemingway's, a Key West–style getaway perched dramatically atop the resort waterfall—and a stellar Sunday brunch that's widely conceded to be the best in town, even by the staffs at other hotels.

Rates are $200 to $260. Call 1-800-233-1234 for reservations and (407) 239-1234 for information about Camp Hyatt and Rock Hyatt.

Delta Orlando Resort

Located just across from Universal Studios and convenient to both Wet 'n Wild and the Mystery Fun House, the Delta Orlando offers resort-style amenities at budget prices. Wally's Kids Club, named after resort mascot Wally Gator, provides free daily activities for children 4 to 12 from 11 A.M. to 5 P.M. As well as scavenger hunts, pool games, and crafts, special activities are highlighted on a regular basis: There may be a cooking lesson with the resort chef (the kids return wearing chef hats and clutching sacks of chocolate cookies that they made themselves), a scuba demonstration in the pool, a tennis clinic, or a magic class taught by a professional magician. There's a small fee (usually around $6) for these special activities. Each evening from 6 to 10 P.M., there's a themed Kid's Night Out featuring dinner, games, and movies at $10 per child, $20 if a special activity is planned as well as dinner.

Action centers around The Oasis, a recreation area in the center of the resort, with an enormous pool, three hot tubs and saunas, two kiddie pools, a small putt-putt course, volleyball, and two playgrounds. Parents can relax and let the kids explore. Fishing, tennis, and golf lie farther out.

The Delta's commitment to pleasing families shows through in small ways, such as the fact that kids under 6 eat free in the Bistro Boulevard food court, where they have a separate dining section with chalkboard drawings on the wall and cartoons on TV. The weekly resort newsletter keeps you up-to-date on scheduled sandcastle-building contests, Frisbee golf, and water volleyball. Wally Gator is frequently on hand for the activities and will come to your room at night for tuck-in service. All in all, the Delta is a clear winner in its price range.

Rates are $99 to $149. Call 1-800-776-3358 or (407) 351-3340.

The Holiday Inn Sunspree

Located less than two miles from the Disney gates, the Holiday Inn Sunspree provides a minikitchen with refrigerator, microwave, and coffee maker in every room. It's a nice option for families who don't need a full suite (and who don't want to pay suite prices) but who'd like save a few bucks by eating cereal and sandwiches in their room. The Sunspree offers a food court, where kids eat free. Children also have their own special check-in, where they receive a bag full of small gifts and surprises, which is a fun way to start the vacation and makes the kids feel terribly special.

As you walk through the Sunspree, it's immediately evident that children aren't just tolerated here—they're welcomed guests. Camp Holiday posts daily activities, such as kids' karaoke and the kids' kazoo band, and the works of winners of coloring and essay contests are prominently displayed in the hall. Many of the rooms have VCRs, and a wide selection of movies are available for rent; there's also a small theater, where kiddie movies play all day long. Max's Cyber Arcade is so swell that there's a section where kids can surf the Internet. You'll find few convention-eers or business travelers at the Holiday Inn Sunspree—the clientele is overwhelmingly families.

Each evening from 5 to 10 P.M., Camp Holiday activities are provided for kids 2 to 12 at Max's Magic Castle
for a nominal charge. Hotel mascot Max the Raccoon
and his friends supervise Bingo games, magic shows,
and movies. (Note that the Holiday Inn is licensed to
take kids in the 2-to-4 age range—a rarity.) Beepers
are available for rent, which adds to parental peace of
mind, and daytime child care is available on-site. Max
will even come to your room to tuck in tired toddlers
after a tough day in the parks.

The Holiday Inn Sunspree offers kids' suites—a special block of themed rooms, each done up like a child's
fantasy-come-to-life. You can sleep, for example, in the
Western Jailhouse, Noah's Ark, or in a Polar Bear
Igloo. Or perhaps it would be more accurate to say you
can *try* to sleep; these rooms are so cool they can whip
kids into a total frenzy.

Rates for the Sunspree are $104 to $149 per night.
Call 1-800-HOLIDAY or (407) 239-4500.

Embassy Suites Resort Lake Buena Vista

This resort, with a beautiful coral stucco exterior and
dramatic open-air atrium decorated in Caribbean
shades of teal and purple, offers very good deals for
families. The 280 suites have pleasant sitting areas,
can sleep as many as six people easily, and feature
kitchens with microwaves, refrigerators, and coffee
makers. A full range of sporting activities—an in-
door/outdoor pool, tennis, basketball, volleyball, shuf-
fleboard, and a jogging trail with exercise stations—is
close at hand, and the resort offers several significant
freebies to guests: shuttle service to the Disney parks,
drinks at the manager's daily cocktail party from 5:30
to 7:30 P.M., and a bountiful breakfast buffet. (What

many hotels advertise as a free breakfast often turns out to be a paper cup of orange juice and a wrapped roll, but this spread features a fruit bar, sausage, bacon, eggs, pancakes, French toast, and made-to-order omelets.)

The Crazy Cat Kids' Club cranks up from 4 to 10 P.M. for kids 3 to 12; cost is $8 for dinner, $6 to make a craft. Beeper service is provided for parents, and the kids' club has plenty of Nintendo games, a video wall with five separate TV sets, a crawl castle, and a small ball pit. You can order the Crazy Cat Tuck-In Service for $1, which includes a snapshot. (You'll need the picture, because otherwise it would be impossible to prove that you can get anything in Orlando for a dollar.)

Poolside games—such as egg tosses, relay races, and the popular "Daddy Splash" wherein the dad with the most impressive belly flop wins a prize for his kid—keep things hopping all day. The guests at this resort are almost exclusively families, so it is easy for a child in any age group to meet new friends.

At $169 to $249 for a suite, and so many perks included in the price, the Embassy Suites offers a decent value and a great location just off exit 27 on I-4, a mere 10-minute ride from the Disney parks. Call 1-800-EMBASSY or (407) 239-1144.

HOW TO FIND A CHEAP OFF-SITE HOTEL

At least two months before you leave home, call 1-900-89-MAGIC. There will be a $4 charge for the call, but in return you'll get a visitor's guide and accommodation information from the Orlando Chamber of Commerce and Visitors' Bureau. The guide will give you info on all

Orlando hotels, from the interstate truck stops to the full-service resorts, and there will be numerous discount coupons for hotels, restaurants, and attractions included in the package.

Unless you are familiar with the specific hotel, your best bet is to choose a reliable chain like Days Inn or Quality Inn, and then look for a location off I-4, preferably at either exit 25 or exit 27, the two exits that flank Disney. Exit 27 is the newer and more upscale of the two; the rate at an exit 27 Days Inn or Holiday Inn, for example, will run about $30 more than a hotel of the same chain on exit 25. Beware of an extremely low rate (below $50), which generally indicates that you're both far from the theme parks and probably in a rundown side of town.

3

★★★★★★★★★★★★★★★★★

Touring Plans

GENERAL WALT DISNEY WORLD TOURING TIPS

The size of Walt Disney World is often a shock to first-time visitors, many of whom arrive with vague notions that they can walk from Epcot to the Magic Kingdom or even that they are separate sections of the same theme park. There is also some confusion over the names; some people use *Walt Disney World* and *Magic Kingdom* synonymously, when in reality the Magic Kingdom is a relatively small part of the much larger Walt Disney World complex. There's more to this place than Cinderella Castle and Space Mountain.

Hence, an understanding of the WDW transportation system is vital, since you'll be covering many miles in the course of your touring. Despite the distances involved, the tips below encourage you to visit more than one park a day, using the ever-present WDW transportation system to allow you to follow a morning of bodysurfing at Typhoon Lagoon with an afternoon show at MGM. The best way to avoid over-stimulation and burnout is to work a variety of experiences—some active, some passive, some educational, some silly—into each day.

Most of the tips in this section assume that you'll be visiting WDW for more than one day. If you aren't staying longer, see "A One-Day Touring Plan" on page 93.

• *Come Early!* This is the single most important piece of advice in this entire book. By beating the crowds, you can not only visit attractions in quick succession, but you also avoid the parking and transport nightmares that occur when the parks fill to peak capacity around 11 A.M.

For families with kids, it is especially important to avoid the exhaustion that comes with just trying to get there. If you're staying off-site, it can take a full two hours from the point you leave your hotel to the point where you board your first ride, which is enough to shatter the equanimity of even the best-behaved kid. They've been waiting for this vacation a long time, and flying and riding a long time: You owe it to them to get into the parks quickly.

• On the evening you arrive, call 824-4321 or check with your hotel to confirm the opening time of the theme park you plan to visit the next morning. If you learn, for example, that the Magic Kingdom is scheduled to open at 9 A.M., be at the gate by 8:30. Frequently—for no apparent reason—the gates open a half-hour early. This is a gift from the gods, and you should be prepared to capitalize on it. On the mornings the park is opened ahead of the stated time, you can ride a dozen attractions while the other 50,000 poor saps are still out on I-4.

• Even if the park doesn't open ahead of schedule, guests are frequently ushered in to one section early. This means you can get maps and entertainment schedules before you enter the body of the park, and have breakfast if you order something simple and eat fast.

In the MK, visitors are usually allowed to travel the length of Main Street before the park actually opens. You can window-shop, grab a muffin at the Main Street Bakery, and still be at the ropes blocking the end of Main Street by 9 A.M. Similarly, at MGM visitors are often allowed onto Hollywood Boulevard to browse the shops and nibble a bite at Starring Rolls before the main park opens. If you have young kids

and a special morning showing of Voyage of the Little
Mermaid is scheduled, you should go there first. Older
kids? Try the Twilight Zone Tower of Terror first, then
head for Voyage of the Little Mermaid.

At Epcot the advantages of an early arrival are even
greater. Spaceship Earth (aka "the Big Ball") stands
silent and empty at the day's beginning. A family can
get strollers, ride Spaceship Earth, make dinner
reservations at the WorldKey Information System
(inside the Earth Station under Spaceship Earth), and
have a quick breakfast at the Electric Umbrella—all
before the park officially opens.

• Plan to see the most popular attractions either
early in the day, late at night, or during a time where a
big event siphons off other potential riders (such as the
3 P.M. parade in the MK).

• Eat at "off" times. Some families eat lightly at
breakfast, have an early lunch around 11 A.M., and
dinner at 5 P.M. Others eat a huge breakfast, have a
late lunch around 3 P.M., then a final meal after the
parks close. If you tour late and you're really bushed,
all on-site hotels and many off-site hotels have in-room
pizza delivery service.

• Be aware that that kids usually want to revisit
their favorite attractions. (My daughter insisted on
riding Dumbo every single day the first time we visited
WDW, something I hadn't foreseen and which radically
restructured our touring plans.) Parents who over-
schedule to the point that there is no time to revisit
favorites risk a mutiny.

One way to handle this is to leave the entire last day
of your trip free as a "greatest hits" day so that you can
go back to all your favorites one more time. If you feel

like lugging the camcorder around only once, make this the day.

• Use the touring plan to cut down on arguments and debates. It's a hapless parent indeed who sits down at breakfast and asks, "What do you want to do today?" Three kids will have three different answers, and the indecision and bickering waste valuable time.

• When making plans, keep the size of the parks in mind. MGM is small and can be easily crisscrossed to take in various shows. The MK is larger and though some cutting back and forth is possible, you'll probably want to tour one "land" thoroughly before heading to another. Epcot is so enormous you're almost forced to visit attractions in geographic sequence or you'll spend all your time and energy in transit.

• If you're going to be in the MK for two days or longer, plan to visit the most popular attractions on different days. Many families arrive in the MK determined to take in Space Mountain, Splash Mountain, Big Thunder Mountain Railroad, Alien Encounter, and Pirates of the Caribbean their first day . . . then wind up spending hours in line. Better to try to see a couple of the biggies during the first hour after the park opens. After that, move on to less popular attractions, saving the other biggies for subsequent mornings.

• If you leave a park and plan to return to either that park or another, save your stroller receipt and have your hand stamped. You won't have to pay a new stroller deposit at the new park if you can show a receipt and you can reenter the new park swiftly by showing your hand stamp and ticket. (Don't worry if you're leaving to swim—the hand stamps are waterproof, although sunscreen can smear them.)

Likewise, if you're staying off-site and using your own car to visit more than one park in a day, save your parking receipt so you won't have to pay the fee more than once.

- Park-hop. Many families with a five-day pass figure: We'll spend Monday in the MK, Tuesday at MGM, Wednesday at Blizzard Beach, Thursday at Epcot, and Friday back in the MK. . . . Sounds logical, but a day in the MK is too much riding, 12 hours at Epcot is too much walking, a whole day at MGM is too much sitting, and anyone who stays at Blizzard Beach from dusk to dawn will wind up waterlogged. It's especially essential to take Epcot in small doses; if you do all the Future World attractions at once, the Audio-Animatronics will run together in the kids' heads, they'll likely get antsy from too much sitting, and any educational potential will be lost.

- If you're trying to predict how crowded a ride or show will be, four factors come into effect:

  - *The Newness of the Attraction.* In general, the newer it is the hotter it is, particularly if it's a thrill ride like Test Track.

  - *The Quality of the Attraction.* Space Mountain, the Beauty and the Beast Stage Show, Illumi-Nations, and other Disney "classics" will be mobbed five years from now.

  - *Speed of Loading.* Continuous-loading attractions such as Pirates of the Caribbean, It's a Small World, Spaceship Earth, and the Great Movie Ride can move thousands of riders through in an hour. The lines at the start-and-stop rides such as Dumbo, Astro Orbiter, and the Mad Tea Party move much more slowly.

- *Capacity.* Movies like *O Canada!* at Epcot, shows like *MuppetVision 3-D* at MGM, and the Country Bear Vacation Hoedown in the MK can seat large crowds at once. Lines form then disappear rapidly as hundreds of people enter the theater. For this reason, theater-style attractions are good choices for the afternoon when the park is crowded.

• At some rides you might opt to do a "baby swap" (which does not mean you can trade your shrieking 2-year-old for that angelically napping infant behind you!). It enables the family that has some coaster-warriors and some uneasy-riders to enter the line together, rather than split up or go through the lines twice.

As you approach the ride, inform the attendant that you'll need to swap off the baby or younger kid. One parent rides, then the waiting parent passes the baby through and rides himself. (Older kids are often allowed to ride back-to-back with Mom and Dad if the lines aren't too bad.)

If you're unsure if a ride is too intense for your kids, you can use the baby swap as a test: Let one parent ride, then return with the verdict. If the first parent thinks it's OK, the second parent can then immediately board the ride with the child.

• When planning your touring days, take time to familiarize yourself with the Ticket and Transportation Center (TTC). Located near the MK, the TTC is the main station for the monorails and buses and where you'll make all your transfers.

If you're staying on-site, you'll be able to take a direct bus, boat, or monorail to any of the three major theme parks; but if you're trying to get to a minor park, you'll have to go through the TTC.

Off-site visitors can drive directly to Epcot, MGM, or any of the minor parks, all of which have their own parking lots and shuttle trams. But the parking lot for the MK is so far from the actual park that off-site visitors will have to park, catch the shuttle tram, and then go through the TTC in order to catch a monorail or ferryboat to get to the Magic Kingdom. (This is why we recommend that off-site visitors allow 45 minutes to get to the MK, even if their hotel is close to the park.) Likewise, if you're park hopping, you'll need to go through the TTC to get, say, from Epcot to the MK, or from the MK to Typhoon Lagoon.

It may sound like a big bowl of alphabet soup, but everything is very well marked, and there are always plenty of Disney employees on hand to answer your questions. Once you get the hang of the system, you'll find using the WDW transportation services easier than trying to get around on your own.

• If you'll be at WDW for more than four days, consider planning a "day off" in the middle of your vacation. Families sometimes feel so compelled to do it all that they come back from their trip exhausted and irritable. But a day in the middle of the trip devoted to sleeping in, hanging around the hotel pool, taking in a character breakfast, visiting the other hotels, or shopping can make all the difference. You'll start the next day refreshed and energized.

• Tickets are expensive, so use them wisely. Each time you enter the gates of a major park, you get a day marked off your multiday pass—even if you visit for just a couple of hours. So on the days when you'll be in a major park, make sure that the hours spent warrant losing a day of your multiday pass.

One way to stretch your ticket is to spend one day solely in the minor parks. If you visit Blizzard Beach in the morning and Pleasure Island at night, for example, you won't have a day marked off your World-Hopper pass.

TOURING TIPS FOR STAYING ON-SITE

• By far the greatest advantage of staying at one of the hotels within WDW is the easy commute to the theme parks. Visitors with small kids can return to the their hotel in midafternoon, then reenter the parks about 5 or 6 P.M. Remember the mantra: Come early, stay late, and take a break in the middle of the day.

If you arrive early, you'll have been touring for five or six hours by 1 P.M. and will be more than ready for a rest. Have a late lunch either at one of the Main Street restaurants, which are reasonably empty at midday, or back at your hotel. Once "home," nap or take a dip in the pool.

At least one day you'll want to remain in the Magic Kingdom until 3 P.M. for the Main Street parade. Be sure to watch near the Railroad Station, at the Main Street hub, so you'll be close to the main gates and can make a clean getaway once the parade has passed.

• In the off-season the MK and MGM sometimes close at 6 P.M., but Epcot stays open later, even during the least crowded weeks of the year. The solution? Spend mornings in the MK or MGM, return to your hotel for a break, and then spend late afternoons and evenings at Epcot. Not only does this buy you more hours per day in the theme parks, but the best places for dinner are all at Epcot anyway.

• It's hard to overemphasize the importance of the "Surprise Mornings" program. If Epcot is the featured park on Tuesday, go to Epcot on Tuesday. By getting in the park an hour and a half ahead of the stated opening time, you can easily ride the most popular attractions before the crowds arrive; during Christmas week my family was able to ride nine rides in the Fantasyland and Tomorrowland sections of the MK during our first hour. Later in the day, we noticed that some of those same rides were posting 90-minute waits.

Since the program has been in effect, however, many families have pointed out that the designated park for that day draws a disproportionate number of visitors, who come early and stay all day. The solution is to park-hop: If the park of the day is the MK, and it's mobbed by 10 A.M., take the monorail over to Epcot.

TOURING TIPS FOR STAYING OFF-SITE

• Time your commute. If you can make it from your hotel to the theme park gates within 30 minutes, it may still be worth your while to return to the hotel for a midday break. This is a distinct possibility for guests of the hotels at the Disney Village Hotel Plaza and some I-4 establishments. If your hotel is farther out, it's doubtful you'll want to make the drive four times a day.

• If it isn't feasible to return to your hotel, find afternoon resting places within the parks. (See the "Afternoon Resting Places" sections in the discussions of each theme park.) Sometimes kids aren't so much tired as full of pent-up energy. If you suspect that that's the case, take preschoolers to Ariel's Grotto or the Toontown playground in the MK; let older kids run free among the forts and backwoods paths of Tom Sawyer Island. The Honey, I Shrunk the Kids Adventure Zone at MGM is also perfect for burning off excess energy.

• If you're willing to leave the parks in the middle of the afternoon, you have even more options. Cool off at a water park or in the 24-screen movie theater beside Pleasure Island. *Note:* River Country is an easy commute from the MK, since it runs its own launch. If you stash your bathing suits in one of the lockers under the Railroad Station in the MK, you can retrieve them around lunchtime and go straight to River Country without having to return to your car.

The hotel restaurants in the MK resorts are never crowded at lunch, and the dining is much more leisurely than in the parks. An early dinner around 5 P.M. can also effectively break up a summer day, when you may be staying at the park until midnight. The buffets at 1900 Park Fare in the Grand Floridian and Chef Mickey in the Contemporary are especially good bets. *Note:* If you take the monorail, be sure to line up for the train marked *Monorail to the MK Resorts.* Most of the monorails are expresses back to the TTC.

• If you'll be touring all day, get strollers for all preschool-age kids. Few 5-year-olds can walk through a 14-hour day.

• Visit one of the parks *not* featured as the "Surprise Mornings" park for the on-site guests. (You can find out which is the featured park by calling 824-4321.)

• Staying for a late-evening show such as Illumi-Nations at Epcot or SpectroMagic in the MK? Either choose a location near the main exit, so you can get a jump on the rest of the departing crowd, or stop for shopping and a snack after the show and exit the park about 20 minutes behind the main surge of people. Not staying for the late show? Leave the park while it's in progress and you'll miss the departing crowds altogether.

HOW TO CUSTOMIZE A TOURING PLAN

There's no substitute for a good touring plan, especially if it's geared toward the ages, interests, and risk tolerance of your family.

In creating a personalized touring plan, your first step is to request maps when you make your hotel reservations. Familiarize yourself with the overall map of WDW and those of the three major theme parks so you can arrive in Orlando with some sense of proximity and the location of major attractions. Getting to Big Thunder Mountain Railroad early is considerably easier if you know where Big Thunder Mountain Railroad is. Next, poll your family on which attractions they most want to see and build these priorities into the plan.

Third, divide each day of your visit into three components: morning, afternoon, and evening. It isn't necessary that you specify where you'll be every hour—that's too confining—but you need some sense of how you'll break up each day. Check out the plan below, which is an adaptation of the perfect four-day touring plan described on page 89. This plan is custom-designed for a family with a 4-year-old girl and 7-year-old boy who will be at WDW for five days in October, staying at the on-site Caribbean Beach Resort. The younger child is sold on the characters and most yearns to meet Minnie Mouse up close and personal. She still naps in the afternoon. The older child likes action rides, is pretty fearless when it comes to special effects, and especially wants to see the Indiana Jones Epic Stunt Spectacular show at MGM. The dad asks only that one afternoon be left open for golf. Mom would like some time in the parks without the kids to get an early jump on Christmas shopping and wants to get a sitter one evening for a parents' night out.

A touring plan for this family might look something like this:

Wednesday morning:	The Magic Kingdom—tour Fantasyland, Toontown, and Tomorrowland.
Wednesday afternoon:	Return to the hotel for lunch and naps around 2 P.M.
Wednesday night:	Epcot—tour a couple of Future World pavilions.
Thursday morning:	MGM Studios Theme Park.
Thursday afternoon:	Return to the hotel after the parade. Mom supervises swimming and naps while Dad golfs.
Thursday night:	Hoop-Dee-Doo Musical Revue at Fort Wilderness; afterward watch Electrical Water Pageant.
Friday morning:	The Magic Kingdom—Ride Big Thunder Mountain Railroad and Splash Mountain first, then tour Adventureland, Liberty Square, and Frontierland.
Friday afternoon:	While Dad takes the kids to River Country via the launch,

	Mom stays behind to shop. Lunch late at King Stefan's in Cinderella Castle, then take in the 3 P.M. parade.
Friday night:	Sitter comes to hotel room for kids while Mom and Dad visit Pleasure Island.
Saturday morning:	Return to the Magic Kingdom and reride all the favorites.
Saturday afternoon:	Lunch at the Mexico pavilion at Epcot. Tour the World Showcase, encouraging kids to rest and/or nap during films, since this is the only day they won't be returning to the the room for an afternoon nap.
Saturday night:	Dinner at Coral Reef restaurant. Then tour the rest of Future World and see IllumiNations.
Sunday morning:	Take in a character breakfast. Return to room to check out, then leave bags with the concierge or go ahead and load the car. Return to MGM to see anything missed on the first morning.

This touring plan has much to recommend it:

- You can get an early start every day.
- A nap, or at least downtime, is built into the afternoon.
- You see the characters every day.
- Minimal time is spent waiting in line, because major attractions are visited first thing in the morning.

If your kids are older, the plan can be easily adapted. Substitute the wilder rides for the tamer, Typhoon Lagoon or Blizzard Beach for River Country, cut out the naps and character breakfasts, and you still have the prototype of a workable plan.

THE PERFECT TOURING PLAN FOR FOUR- OR FIVE-DAY VISITS

This touring plan assumes that you have a multiday pass and are visiting at a time when all three parks are open past 8 P.M.

Day 1

Be at the end of Main Street in the MK 30 minutes before the stated opening time. When the ropes drop (assuming your kids are 7 or older and up to it) head directly for Space Mountain.

After you ride Space Mountain, go to Fantasyland. (If your children are younger or frightened by roller coasters, go to Fantasyland first.) If you want to eat lunch inside Cinderella Castle, make your reservation at King Stefan's Banquet Hall. Visit these Fantasyland rides in rapid succession:

- Dumbo
- Cinderella's Golden Carousel
- Snow White's Scary Adventures
- Peter Pan's Flight
- It's a Small World
- Legend of the Lion King
- Mr. Toad's Wild Ride
- The Mad Tea Party

After you exit the Mad Tea Party, teeter on to Toontown. Ride Goofy's Barnstormer first, then the kids can enjoy the character houses and play areas.

After you've met Mickey and the other characters, stop for a snack before you head toward Adventureland. It's a fairly long walk.

In Adventureland, visit Pirates of the Caribbean, the Jungle Cruise, and the Swiss Family Robinson Treehouse. By now it should be late in the morning and some of the lines may be prohibitive. If you face a wait of more than 20 minutes at an attraction, skip it. You'll need to be back out on Main Street by 2 P.M., and you'll be returning to the MK on other days.

As you exit Adventureland and head toward Main Street, stop at either the Crystal Palace, the Plaza Restaurant, or Tony's Town Square Cafe to eat lunch. (If you've made lunch reservations for King Stefan's in Cinderella Castle, go there now.)

Watch the 3 P.M. parade from the Main Street hub.

After the parade, exit the theme park. It is now time for your well-deserved midday break. Be sure to have your hand stamped as you exit the park.

About 6 P.M. go to MGM. Pick up an entertainment schedule at Guest Services as you enter. You should easily be able to catch the Indiana Jones Epic Stunt Spectacular, SuperStar Television, one of the stage shows, and *MuppetVision 3-D*.

Eat last of all; the restaurants stay open after the attractions close down. Enjoy the fireworks presentation. (Times for this finale vary, so consult the entertainment schedule.)

Day 2

Spend most of the day at either Typhoon Lagoon or Blizzard Beach. Exit the water park in the afternoon, take a break in your hotel room if needed, then head for Epcot.

Enter Epcot in early evening. If you haven't made advance reservations and you want a sit-down meal, stop by the WorldKey Information System (inside the Earth Station under Spaceship Earth) and see which restaurants still have seating times left. Avoid booking a time just before IllumiNations—you don't want to miss the show.

Tour the Living Seas and the Land pavilions and Journey Into Imagination. See *Honey, I Shrunk the Audience.*

Eat dinner, then watch the closing presentation of IllumiNations.

Day 3

Be through the MK gates early. This time when the ropes drop, hoof it to Big Thunder Mountain Railroad and Splash Mountain.

Tour the Haunted Mansion in Liberty Square.

See the Country Bear Vacation Hoedown.

If you missed any Adventureland or Fantasyland attractions on the previous day, tour them now. If the kids are restless, you might opt to visit Tom Sawyer Island and have a snack at Aunt Polly's Landing while they explore. If they're tired, take in the Hall of Presidents.

Visit the Tomorrowland Grand Prix Raceway, Alien Encounter (for older kids), and any other Tomorrowland attractions that appeal to your family. Eat a fast-food lunch.

Exit the park and take an early midday break.

Either take in a family-style dinner show such as the Hoop-Dee-Doo Musical Revue, go shopping at the Disney Village Marketplace, or try out the water sprites or some other sort of boating fun. If your kids are older, consider visiting the other major water park. The crowds taper off in the evenings.

Day 4

Start your day at MGM. If you dare, ride the Twilight Zone Tower of Terror immediately upon entering. If an early showing of Voyage of the Little Mermaid is scheduled, go there next.

Make lunch reservations for either the 50's Prime Time Cafe or the SciFi Drive-In at the reservations booth on Hollywood Boulevard.

See Star Tours and the Great Movie Ride.

Visit the Honey, I Shrunk the Kids Adventure Zone.

See the earliest Beauty and the Beast Stage Show.

Take the Animation Tour.

See the parade.

Have lunch, then take the Backstage Studio Tour.

Visit the Monster Sound Show and the Hunchback of Notre Dame Stage Show.

Exit the park around 4 P.M. for swimming and resting.

This is parents' night out. If your hotel does not have a kids' club or if you plan to be out past 10 or 11 P.M., you should have arranged a sitter in advance. Orlando has many elegant restaurants (some of them inside Epcot), or you may prefer a rowdier evening at Pleasure Island.

Day 5

Start your day early at Epcot. With any luck, you should be able to make lunch reservations and tour Spaceship Earth before the ropes drop.

Head straight for Test Track. Ride Body Wars in the Wonders of Life pavilion next, then proceed to Cranium Command and Horizons.

Head toward the World Showcase Lagoon.

Ride El Rio del Tiempo in Mexico and Maelstrom in Norway, then have lunch in either pavilion.

Continue circling the World Showcase Lagoon. The presentations at the China, America, France, and Canada pavilions are all compelling and extremely well done, as are the comedy street shows in Italy and the United Kingdom. Take in as many of these as time and your children's stamina permit. Finish with the Universe of Energy pavilion on your way out of the park.

Exit Epcot and enjoy an afternoon rest.

Enter the MK in early evening. Revisit a couple of favorite rides—Splash Mountain and Big Thunder Mountain Railroad are especially neat at night. See SpectroMagic, Tinkerbell's Flight, and the fireworks at closing.

A ONE-DAY TOURING PLAN

If you're going to be in WDW only one day, your task is challenging indeed. A one-day ticket entitles you to the use of a single Disney park, so select carefully. Time will be at a premium, so you'll probably want to forgo your midday break, opting instead for finding afternoon resting places inside the theme park.

1. If you have only one day, it is imperative that you be at the park and through the gates a half-hour before the stated opening time. (In the MK, with its convoluted transportation system, this will mean leaving your hotel 60 to 75 minutes before the stated park opening time.)

2. Turn to the section of this book that refers to your theme park of choice and read the section on your first hour in the park.

3. See as many attractions as possible in the morning, moving swiftly from one to the next. If any attraction requires more than a 30-minute wait, skip it for now. You can try it again just before park closing when lines are usually shorter.

4. Have lunch, then move on to theater-style attractions that allow you to sit, or consult the "Afternoon Resting Places" list for your theme park.

5. The parades and character shows are quite worthwhile, even on a packed schedule. They're what make Disney, Disney.

6. Around 6 P.M. crowds thin out a bit. Eat a snack supper then return to any sections of the park you missed or which had long lines earlier. Save the most popular attraction for last.

7. At park closing, one parent should stake out a spot as near as possible to the main exit, where you can watch the closing festivities while the other parent takes the kids to pick out a souvenir. Turn in your strollers and make a final potty run. It may also be a good time to grab a dessert or ice cream while waiting for the parade/fireworks/laser show to begin.

8. As soon as the finale concludes, head directly out of the park. Don't look back—the crowds behind you will be the scariest thing you've seen all day.

A ONE-DAY TOURING PLAN FOR THE HIGHLY ENERGETIC

The following is an eclectic but efficient touring plan for families with a Park-Hopper pass who are driving their own car.

This plan works well as a wrap-up on your final day, because it allows you to visit two major parks, revisit favorite attractions, eat in an Epcot restaurant, and see as many as three major presentations. Admittedly, this plan requires a lot of energy and probably shouldn't be attempted with preschoolers. But for families determined to see as much as possible in the smallest amount of time, it can't be beat!

1. Epcot is much easier to access by car than the Magic Kingdom is. Early-arriving visitors can park very close to the main entrance and simply walk in, often circumventing even the need for a tram.

2. Drive to Epcot at least 30 minutes before the stated opening time; get strollers and maps, and make your evening dinner reservations at the WorldKey Information System inside the Earth Station under Spaceship Earth.

3. Have breakfast if you haven't eaten, and ride Spaceship Earth.

4. Tour Future World until about 11 A.M., then exit Epcot, turning in your stroller and keeping the receipt. Take the monorail to the TTC and transfer to the MK monorail. You'll be running just behind the surge of visitors who usually glut the MK main gates between 10 and 11 A.M. Use your receipt to get a new stroller in the MK and have lunch on Main Street.

5. Tour the MK until 2:45 P.M. Return to the Main Street hub and watch the 3 P.M. parade.

6. Exit the MK immediately after the parade. Again, monorail traffic should be light, as most MK visitors are still watching the parade snake its way through the rest of the route. Go back to

the TTC and take the monorail to Epcot. Eat at the Epcot restaurant for which you made your reservations that morning, and tour the World Showcase until the closing presentation of Illumi-Nations.

7. After IllumiNations, you'll feel mighty smug as you bypass the horrendous crowds in line for the monorails and parking trams. Walk to your car and exit the park.

Note: An alternative to this plan is to exit Epcot around lunchtime via the "backdoor" located between the France and United Kingdom pavilions in the World Showcase. Walk to the Yacht and Beach Clubs' marina and catch the water-taxi to MGM. Tour MGM until 5 P.M., then return to Epcot via the same water-taxi for your evening activities.

4

★★★★★★★★★★★★★★★★★★

*The Magic
Kingdom*

THE MAGIC KINGDOM

FANTASYLAND

Dumbo

FRONTIERLAND

TOONTOWN

Big Thunder
Mountain
Railroad

Legend of the
Lion King

LIBERTY
SQUARE

CINDERELLA
CASTLE

Splash Mountain

Pirates of the
Caribbean

Space
Mountain

Jungle
Cruise

TOMORROWLAND

Baby
Services
Center

ADVENTURELAND

MAIN STREET
USA

City Hall

WDW Railroad
Station

Stroller
Shop

MONORAIL

LAUNCH

FERRYBOAT

GETTING TO THE MAGIC KINGDOM

• If you're staying off-site, prepare for a complicated journey. Either drive or take a shuttle to the Ticket and Transportation Center (TTC). From the TTC, you can cross the Seven Seas Lagoon by ferryboat or monorail.

Note: Make it a habit each time you board the monorail to ask if the driver's cab is vacant; people who'd like to ride up front wait in a special holding area. Since monorails run every three minutes during peak times, you shouldn't have to wait long and the view is spectacular.

As you enter the front gates, the turnstiles to the right are usually less crowded than those to the left.

• If you're staying at the Contemporary, you can bypass the TTC and take the monorail directly to the MK.

• Likewise, if you're staying at the Grand Floridian, the monorail will have you in the MK within minutes. Or you can take the launch from the marina dock.

• Guests at the Polynesian have the most choices of all: the launch, the monorail, or the ferryboat. If your room is on the lagoon, walk to the ferryboat. If you're in one of the buildings near the Great Ceremonial House, the monorail is a better bet. If your room is close to the pool, take the launch.

• From Fort Wilderness Campground or Wilderness Lodge, take the launch.

• Guests at Disney hotels that are not on the monorail line can take shuttles directly to the MK, bypassing the TTC. This saves you at least 10 minutes of commuting time, more during the morning rush hour.

LEAVING THE MAGIC KINGDOM

• When leaving at the end of the day, visitors staying off-site should pause for a second as they exit the gates. If a ferryboat is in the dock to your far left, that's the fastest route back to the TTC. If there's no boat in sight, you're probably better off queuing up for the monorail that runs directly back to the TTC.

• Guests at the Contemporary should always exit via the monorail, making sure that they take the one designated for the resorts.

• Those staying at the Polynesian or the Grand Floridian should glance down at the launch dock, which is straight ahead as you exit the MK gates. If a launch is in the dock, take it back to your hotel; otherwise, head for the resort monorail.

• Guests staying at the other Disney hotels should return to the shuttle-bus station.

Note: The launches, which are not to be confused with the gargantuan ferryboats, are a pleasant alternative to the monorails, especially in the afternoon. As well as transporting guests directly to the Grand Floridian, the Polynesian, Fort Wilderness, and Wilderness Lodge, launches also run to Discovery Island and River Country.

GETTING AROUND THE MAGIC KINGDOM

Walking is by far the fastest means of transport in the MK. The trolleys, vintage cars, and horse-drawn carriages are fun, but think of them as pleasant rides that offer charming views, not as a serious means of getting around the park.

The WDW Railroad, which leaves from the main gate with stops near Splash Mountain in Frontierland and Toontown, can save you a bit of time and effort if you happen to hit it right. Don't think, however, that catching the train to Splash Mountain in the morning is your fastest way there. The Railroad Station is busy in midmorning, and you may have to wait for a second or third train; by that time, you could have walked. If you're entering in the afternoon or some other time when the station is less crowded, the odds are you can catch the next train. This may save you a few steps, especially if you're headed toward Toontown.

Be prepared to make frequent rest stops while touring the MK. You won't walk as much as you do at Epcot, but you're likely to spend more time waiting in line. Standing still is ultimately harder on the feet—and the nerves—than walking.

YOUR FIRST HOUR IN THE MAGIC KINGDOM

• Be through the gates 20 minutes earlier than the stated opening time, 40 minutes if you plan to have breakfast on Main Street. Get strollers and pick up a map and entertainment schedule at City Hall.

• Be at the end of Main Street by the stated opening time. When the ropes drop, if your kids are 6 or older, head for Splash Mountain, then Big Thunder Mountain Railroad, then across to Space Mountain.

• If your kids are under 6, head straight through Cinderella Castle to Fantasyland. When most people reach the end of Main Street, they tend to veer either left toward Adventureland or right toward Tomorrowland, and thus begin touring in a clockwise or counterclockwise fashion.

If you go straight to Fantasyland, you'll not only be able to tour five or six attractions before 10 A.M., you'll also spend the rest of your day moving against the crowds.

• If there's a gap in the ages of your children and the 9-year-old is ready for the roller coasters but the 4-year-old isn't, split up. Mom can take one child, Dad the other, and you can meet up again in an hour.

MAIN STREET TOURING TIPS

• Although you might want to spend a few minutes mingling with the characters who greet you as you enter, don't stop to check out the shops or minor attractions of Main Street in the morning; you need to hurry on to the big rides.

• Return to Main Street to shop in midafternoon. Especially worthwhile are Disney Clothiers, Uptown Jewelers, and the Emporium. Main Street is also a good place for lunch.

• If you're looking for souvenirs, be aware that there's no point in comparison shopping within the confines of WDW. A $22.50 stuffed Simba at the Emporium will also be $22.50 at a gift shop in the Polynesian Resort or the Disney Village Marketplace.

• After shopping, stow your purchases in the lockers beneath the Railroad Station. If you're not planning to see the parade, be sure to be off Main Street by 2:30 P.M. After that, it's a mob scene.

• A fun diversion for kids is having their bangs trimmed amid the old-fashioned splendor of the Harmony Barber Shop beside the flower market on Main Street. The barbers are jovial, even by Disney employee standards, and happy to explain the history of the mustache cups, shaving mugs, and other tonsorial paraphernalia. Many families wait to have their baby's first trim on Main Street; Dean, one of the longtime barbers, has a scrapbook of first-haircut photos.

• If you're touring the MK late and your party splits up, make sure you choose a spot on Main Street as your meeting place. Disney employees clear people out of the other sections of the park promptly at closing time, remaining firm even if you explain that you were supposed to meet Lauren by Dumbo at 10 P.M. But Main Street stays open up to an hour after the rides shut down, and is the best place to reassemble the family before heading for the parking lot.

• A blackboard posted at the end of Main Street provides up-to-date information about the approximate waiting times for MK rides, as well as all showtimes and where to meet the characters. Consult it whenever you're unsure about what to do next.

FANTASYLAND

The aptly named Fantasyland, located directly behind Cinderella Castle, is a cross between a Bavarian village and a medieval fair. Most of the kiddie rides are here, and it is the most congested section of the Magic Kingdom.

Fantasyland Attractions
It's a Small World
During this 11-minute boat ride, dolls representing children of all nations greet you with a song so

infectious you'll be humming it at bedtime. The ride loads steadily, so the lines move fast, making this a good choice for afternoon. And it's one of the best of all attractions to film with a camcorder.

Note: Although beloved by preschoolers, this ride can be torturous for older siblings. One family's 10-year-old wrote that Disney should offer an "I survived It's a Small World" T-shirt similar to those they sell outside of Alien Encounter or the Twilight Zone Tower of Terror.

Peter Pan's Flight

Tinkerbell flutters overhead as you board miniature pirate ships and sail above Nana's doghouse, the sparkling night streets of London, the Indian camp, and Captain Hook's cove. Of all the MK attractions, this one is most true to the movie that inspired it.

Legend of the Lion King

This show is a huge hit with kids, combining complex human-controlled puppets, live action, special effects, and music to retell Simba's familiar story. Like Voyage of the Little Mermaid at MGM, the show is sophisticated enough to charm even the most cynical parents.

The show runs every 30 minutes, and 480 people are seated at once, meaning that even if the line looks discouraging, you should still queue up. Afternoons are mobbed, sometimes requiring that you wait through two shows before being seated, so visit midmorning after you've ridden several rides and the kids could use a rest.

Mr. Toad's Wild Ride

Cars careen through a funhouse, narrowly missing a chicken coop, an oncoming train, and being crushed by a teetering grandfather clock. Although the special effects are nowhere near up to the standard of Peter Pan's Flight, younger kids enjoy "driving" the cars.

Cinderella's Golden Carousel

Seventy-two white horses prance while a pipe organ toots out "Chim-Chim-Cheree" and other Disney classics. The carousel is gorgeous at night, and benches nearby let Mom and Dad take a breather.

Snow White's Scary Adventures

This ride was updated three years ago, devoting more time to Snow White herself and cutting down a bit on the scary elements. You still ride mining cars through the dark, however, and the Wicked Queen appears several times quite suddenly, giving a few toddlers the willies. The acid test: How well did your kids handle the scene in the movie when Snow White flees through the forest? My 4-year-old liked the ride while she was on it but, perhaps significantly, didn't want to try it again the next day.

Skyway to Tomorrowland

This overhead cable car offers great views, especially at night.

Dumbo

This happy little elephant has become the center of some controversy: Is he worth the wait or not? Although the lines do indeed move slowly, making a one-hour wait possible for a 90-second ride, there's something special about this attraction. It's frequently featured in the ads, so it has become an integral part of our collective Disney consciousness.

Recognizing that Dumbo lines can bottleneck, Disney recently added more elephants to the fleet and created a second holding area, which does cut down somewhat on the wait. Obviously, if you visit this ride first thing in the morning, you can minimize the wait even more, perhaps to only a few minutes. The height of your Dumbo flight can be controlled by a joystick, making the ride appropriate for any age.

The Mad Tea Party

Spinning pastel cups, propelled by their riders, swirl around the Soused Mouse, who periodically pops out of the teapot. Because you largely control how fast your teacup spins, this ride can be enjoyed by people of all ages.

Note: Rider volume ebbs and flows at this attraction. If the line looks too daunting, grab a drink or make a bathroom stop. By the time you emerge, the crowd may have dispersed.

Ariel's Grotto

This small play area with squirt fountains is a good place for toddlers and preschoolers to cool off on a hot afternoon. Go inside the cave to meet Ariel and get her autograph.

Note: 20,000 Leagues Under the Sea, beside Ariel's Grotto, has been permanently scrapped in order to clear the lagoon for a new interactive ride based on *The Little Mermaid,* set to open sometime in 1998. When it does open, expect it to be crowded, as all new attractions are, and visit it first thing in the morning.

FANTASYLAND TOURING TIPS

• Visit Fantasyland either before 11 A.M., after 5 P.M., or during the 3 P.M. parade.

• Don't eat or shop in Fantasyland. Similar food and toys can be found elsewhere in far less crowded areas of the MK.

• Park your strollers in one spot and walk from ride to ride. Fantasyland is geographically small, so this is easier than constantly loading and reloading the kids only to push them a few steps.

• Stay alert. Because the kiddie rides tempt them to wander off, this is the most likely spot in all of WDW to become separated from your child.

MICKEY'S TOONTOWN FAIR

Revamped from Mickey's Starland in late 1996, Mickey's Toontown Fair (most often referred to as just "Toontown") is like being immersed in a giant cartoon. There is a lively, campy, county fair theme and many attractions designed to appeal exclusively to the 2-to-8-year-old set.

The centerpiece is a zippy little roller coaster called Goofy's Barnstormer, which takes you on a wild trip through Wise Acre Farm with you-know-who as the pilot. The ride lasts only 50 seconds, so the line moves fast, and this is the sort of ride many kids insist on doing again and again. Goofy's Barnstormer is a good choice for kids not quite up to Splash Mountain or Space Mountain; the thrills are there, but the ride is so short that you barely get out one good scream before it's over.

Toontown is full of great photo opportunities, such as the bright blue car outside of Pete's Garage, or

Minnie's House where the oven bakes a cake before your eyes and kids can make popcorn pop by pushing a microwave button. Donald's boat, the *Miss Daisy,* is a great play area with squirting fountains, making Toontown a good choice after you've finished Fantasyland and the kids just want to run and play for a while.

Toontown is the best place in the park to meet the characters. After you tour Mickey's House, enter the main tent and you'll see lines marked *Mickey's Pals, Villains,* and *Princesses.* Follow the signs to Mickey's Pals and you'll meet Goofy, Pluto, Chip 'n Dale, and Donald Duck. The Princesses tent will have some combination of Belle, Jasmine, Mary Poppins, Cinderella, and Snow White; and the Villains assemblage comprises (in some combination) Captain Hook, Cruella De Vil, Jafar, the Sheriff of Nottingham, and the Wicked Queen from *Snow White.* There is plenty of time for photos and autographs; and because guests are admitted only 10 at a time, young children can visit the characters without being trampled or mobbed. After you've visited one group, you can always rejoin the line and visit another.

TOMORROWLAND

After years of trying to constantly update Tomorrowland and keep it fresh, the Disney imagineers have decided to go with a '50s sci-fi look that reflects "the future that never was." In this new, completely redesigned Tomorrowland, the mood is decidedly camp—as evidenced by the robot paperboy hawking tomorrow's news and the street sweepers on rollerblades.

Tomorrowland Attractions

Space Mountain

This three-minute roller-coaster ride through inky darkness is one of the few scream-rippers in the MK. The cars move at 28 mph, a fairly tame pace compared with that of the monster roller coasters at some theme parks, but the entire ride takes place inside Space Mountain, and it's impossible to anticipate the turns and dips in the blackness, which adds considerably to the thrill. Space Mountain is the most popular MK attraction with visitors between 11 and 21 years of age.

Children under 7 must be 44 inches tall and have an adult present to ride. Children under 3 and pregnant women are prohibited. Some kids 3 to 7 loved the ride, but many surveyed found it too scary. Only you know whether your children are up to this.

Tomorrowland Raceway

These tiny sports cars circle a nifty-looking racetrack, and although the ride isn't anything unusual, kids under 11 rated it very highly, perhaps due to the fact that even young drivers can steer the cars themselves. (If Jennifer's legs are too short to reach the gas pedal, Mom or Dad can handle the floor pedals while she steers.) Kids 52 inches and taller can drive solo.

Note: Try to convince your child not to rush through the ride; loading and unloading the race cars takes time, and you may as well drive slowly, savoring the loops of the track, rather than sit for five minutes in the pit, waiting to be unloaded.

Galaxy Palace

This large outdoor theater hosts a variety of shows, including a character show in midafternoon. Check your entertainment schedule or the blackboard at the end of Main Street for details.

The shows are fun and fast-paced and, since the theater is so huge, you can almost always be seated by showing up 10 to 15 minutes before showtime.

Skyway to Fantasyland

This has pretty views, especially at night, but by the time you wait in line to board, you could have walked.

Take Flight

This happy, upbeat ride traces the history of flight. It's very tame, and nothing terribly special, at least not compared with similar Epcot attractions, but it loads quickly and preschoolers like it.

Astro Orbiter

The Tomorrowland makeover has turned this ride into one of the jazziest-looking ones in the park.

A circular thrill ride—sort of a Dumbo on steroids—Astro Orbiter is a bit too much for preschoolers and a bit too little for teens. It's a good alternative for those kids 5 to 9 who would be overwhelmed by Space Mountain. Like Dumbo, it loads slowly; if you wait to ride at night, the crowds are lighter and the astro-ambience is even more convincing.

Timekeeper

In this CircleVision 360 film, Jules Verne and H. G. Wells take the audience from nineteenth-century Paris into the future. The voices of Robin Williams and Rhea Perlman, your time-travel pilot and navigator, add to the fun.

The show is well done, but guests stand throughout the presentation, and strollers are not allowed inside the theater, which means babies and toddlers have to be held during the show, a condition that eliminates it for many families.

Note: Lines disappear every 20 minutes, making *Timekeeper* a good choice for the most crowded times of the afternoon.

Tomorrowland Transit Authority

This little tram circles Tomorrowland and provides fun views, including a glimpse inside Space Mountain.

Carousel of Progress

This is another fairly long show (22 minutes), another high-capacity attraction, and thus another good choice for crowded afternoons. Kids under 10, however, may be bored by this salute to the uses of electricity, especially once they've seen the more high-tech presentations at Epcot.

ExtraTerrorestrial Alien Encounter

Alien Encounter opened two years ago amid considerable controversy. After the original version was dubbed too tame, the second manifestation was too terrifying; people were literally screaming so loudly they couldn't hear the story.

The present version of Alien Encounter is about a time-travel experiment that runs amok, "releasing" an alien into the theater. Although you never totally see the beast, you see flashes of parts of his body and hear him rattling around above your head and behind you. Like *Honey, I Shrunk the Audience,* some of the special effects are tactile; the shoulder harness gives the sensation that the monster is just behind you, slipping around your shoulders and down your back. The danger is mostly implied, since the imagineers working on the attraction theorized that the mind can conjure up far worse things than they can create. At one point in the presentation, when the tactile and aural effects are at their peak, you sit in total darkness for more than a minute.

Teens and preteens love Alien Encounter, but most parents conclude it is too much for younger kids. One mother pointed out that the shoulder harness not only gave her 8-year-old the sense he was strapped down, but also prevented her from putting her arm around him or comforting him when he panicked. I've received a lot of mail on this one, with most letters describing how thoroughly terrorized young kids were. "There is fun scary and scary scary," one 7-year-old wrote. "Alien Encounter is scary scary."

Kids must be 44 inches tall to enter, and kids 44 to 48 inches must see the preshow as a preview before they enter. I'd send a parent through first to preview the experience before going in with kids under 10.

Note: ExtraTerrorestrial Alien Encounter has a surprisingly small sign, and is not that easy to find. It's directly across from *Timekeeper* as you enter Tomorrowland via the Main Street bridge.

TOONTOWN AND TOMORROWLAND TOURING TIPS

• If you plan to ride Space Mountain, make a beeline for it immediately upon entering the park gates. After 9:30 A.M. there are substantial lines. By midmorning, Alien Encounter also has lines.

• When you enter Toontown, ride Goofy's Barnstormer first, then move on to Minnie's house. Both of these attractions can draw long lines by midmorning.

• If you don't plan to ride Space Mountain or see Alien Encounter, save Tomorrowland for afternoons, when the park is at its most crowded. Several Tomorrowland attractions such as *Timekeeper* and Carousel of Progress are high capacity and relatively easy to get in to even in the most packed part of the day. Others such as the Tomorrowland Transit Authority and Take Flight board quickly and offer the added bonus of letting you rest for a while.

• Looking for fast food during peak dining hours? Tomorrowland food stands are rarely as busy as those in other areas of the MK. The large Starlight Cafe can move you in and out fast.

• Tomorrowland has its own tip board across from Alien Encounter, listing approximate wait times for rides. Check the tip board if you're headed for Space Mountain; if the wait is longer than 40 minutes, come back another time.

• The arcade across from Space Mountain is a good place for the less adventurous members of your party to wait while the coaster warriors tackle Space Mountain. Be aware, however, that it's tough to drop in to this enormous arcade for "just a minute."

• Like Fantasyland, Toontown can become unbearably crowded in midafternoon. By early evening, however, the crowds thin. If you missed Goofy's Barnstormer in the morning, check back in the evening, when waits are minimal.

ADVENTURELAND

Thematically the most bizarre of all the lands, sort of a Bourbon Street meets Trinidad by way of the Congo, Adventureland still manages to convey an exotic mood.

Adventureland Attractions

Jungle Cruise

You'll meet up with headhunters, hyenas, water-spewing elephants, and other varieties of frankly fake wildlife on this 10-minute boat ride. What distinguishes this attraction is the amusing patter of the tour guides—these young adventurers in pith helmets are the unsung heroes of Disney casting genius.

The Jungle Cruise is not at all scary and is fine for any age, but the lines move with agonizing slowness. It's skippable, but if you decide to take the cruise, go in the morning or during the 3 P.M. parade.

Swiss Family Robinson Treehouse

There's a real split of opinion here—some visitors love this replica of the ultimate treehouse, others rate it as dull. One word of warning: This is a tough attraction to tour with toddlers. The steps are numerous, and at times the climbing is a bit too precarious for unsteady little legs. Lugging a 2-year-old through the exhibit is tiring, but the real problem is that the bamboo and rigging look so enticing that kids want to climb on their own—and at their own pace. This may not sit well with the 800 people in line behind you.

The Enchanted Tiki Birds,
aka Tropical Serenade

Interestingly, these singing/talking birds, and the singing/talking flowers and statues around them, represent Disney's first attempt at the Audio-Animatronics that are now such an integral part of Epcot magic. This attraction is dated and boring in comparison with the newer robotics, however, and is quite skippable unless you're just looking for a cool, quiet place to sit down in midafternoon.

Pirates of the Caribbean

The Pirates inspire great loyalty, and a significant number of guests of all ages name this ride as their favorite in all of the MK. Your boat goes over a small waterfall and there is a bit of menace on the faces of some buccaneers, but very few kids leave the Pirates frightened. Most would agree with the 5-year-old who voted the ride "best reason to leave Fantasyland."

FRONTIERLAND

Kids of all ages love the rough-and-tumble, Wild West feel of Frontierland, which is home to several of the MK's most popular attractions.

Frontierland Attractions

Big Thunder Mountain Railroad

A roller coaster disguised as a runaway mine train, Big Thunder is considerably less scary than Space Mountain but almost as popular. The glory of the ride is in the setting. You zoom through a deserted mining town populated with bats, rainmakers, and saloon denizens—crafted Disney-style.

If you're wondering if the roller coaster may be too much for your kids, be advised that Big Thunder Mountain Railroad is more in the rattle-back-and-forth school than the lose-your-lunch-as-you-plunge genre. Almost any child over 7 should be able to handle the dips and twists, and many preschoolers adore the ride as well.

Note: Children under 7 must ride with an adult, and no one under 40 inches tall is allowed to board.

Splash Mountain

Based on *Song of the South* and inhabited by Brer Rabbit, Brer Bear, Brer Fox, and the other characters from that film, Splash Mountain takes riders on a watery, winding journey through swamps and bayous, culminating in a 40-mph drop over a five-story waterfall. "Zip-A-Dee-Doo-Dah," perhaps the most hummable of all Disney theme songs, fills the air, making the ride both charming and exhilarating—truly the best of both worlds.

Note: Splash Mountain can get very crowded; ride early in the morning or in the last hour before closing. The intensity of that last drop, along with the 44-inch height requirement, will eliminate some preschoolers as riders. If your kids aren't sure if they're up to it, watch a few cars make the final drop before you decide.

Also, you can get really soaked on this ride, which is great fun at noon in June, but less of a thrill at midnight in January. During the chilly season, some people bring big black Hefty bags to use as ponchos, then discard them after the ride.

The Diamond Horseshoe Jamboree

Snacks and drinks are served during this 30-minute saloon show full of hokey humor and lively dance. Some of the puns will go over the heads of younger children, but the material is delivered in such a broad style that kids find themselves laughing even when they're not quite sure why. Audience "volunteers" are often dragged into the action.

The Jamboree is a great place to get off your feet for a midday break—almost like a free dinner show. In fact, the Jamboree is a good alternative to the Hoop-Dee-Doo Musical Revue at Fort Wilderness for families on a budget.

Frontierland Shootin' Arcade

Bring your quarters. This is a pretty standard shooting gallery, but a good place for the kids to kill a few minutes while adults wait in line at the Country Bear Vacation Hoedown.

Country Bear Vacation Hoedown

Younger kids fall for the funny, furry Audio-Animatronic critters featured in this 15-minute show. From the coy Teddi Barra to the incomparable Big Al, from Bubbles, Bunny, and Beulah (a sort of Andrews Sisters meets the Beach Boys) to Melvin the Moosehead, each face is distinctive and lovable.

The Hoedown is popular, but you can slip in easily in the evening or during the 3 P.M. parade. (But don't, for heaven's sake, try to get in just after the parade, when thousands of tourists suddenly find themselves on the streets of Frontierland with nothing to do.) Kids 9 and up rate the bears as hokey; if there's a split in your children's ages, one parent can take the little kids to the Hoedown while the other rides nearby Splash Mountain with the older ones.

Note: A different but equally charming show runs at Christmas.

Tom Sawyer Island

A getaway playground full of caves, bridges, forts, and windmills, Tom Sawyer Island is a good destination when the kids become too rambunctious to handle. Adults can sip a lemonade at Aunt Polly's Landing, the island fast-food restaurant, while the kids run free.

The big drawback is that the island is accessible only by raft, which means you often have to wait to get there and wait to get back. If your kids are under 5, don't bother making the trip. The terrain is too widespread for preschoolers to play without supervision, and young kids can better blow off steam in Toontown. Likewise, there is little on the island for adults and teenagers to do. But if your kids are 5 to 9 and getting squirrelly, stop off at Tom Sawyer Island, where such behavior is not only acceptable, it's de rigeur.

LIBERTY SQUARE

Walk on a few feet from Frontierland and you'll find yourself transported back another hundred years, to Colonial America, strolling the cobblestone streets of Liberty Square.

Liberty Square Attractions

Liberty Square Riverboat

The second tier of this paddle-wheel riverboat offers outstanding views of Liberty Square and Frontierland but, as with the other Rivers of America craft, board only if you have time to kill and the boat is in the dock. *Note:* There are some seats but most riders stand.

The Hall of Presidents

This attraction may remind you that one of the villains in the movie *The Stepford Wives* was a Disney engineer. The Hall of Presidents indeed puts a Stepford spin on the presidency, with eerily lifelike and quietly dignified chief executives, each responding to his name in the roll call with a nod or tilt of the head. In the background other presidents fidget and whisper. Bill Clinton made his debut in 1994, and Maya Angelou narrates the show.

The presidential roll call and the film that precedes it will probably bore most kids under 10. Older children will find the 20-minute presentation educational.

Babies and toddlers consider the Hall of Presidents a fine place to nap. A good choice for afternoon.

Note: The theater holds up to 700 people, which means that lines disappear every 25 minutes. Ask one of the attendants at the lobby doors how long before the next show, and amble in about 10 minutes before showtime.

Mike Fink Keelboats

These small boats follow the same route as the riverboat. The riverboat holds more people at a time, however, so if you're in a rush, take the riverboat.

The Haunted Mansion

More apt to elicit a giggle than a scream, the Haunted Mansion is full of clever special effects—at one point a ghost "hitchhikes" a ride in your own "doom buggy"! The cast members, who dress as morticians and never smile, add to the fun with such instructions as, "Drag your wretched bodies to the dead center of the room." A significant number of kids 7 to 11 listed the Haunted Mansion as one of their favorite attractions, but the mothers of several children under 7 reported that their kids were frightened. The spooks are played for laughs, but the entire ride does take place in darkness. The Mansion is best viewed before noon or, if you have the courage, in the last two hours before closing.

ADVENTURELAND, FRONTIERLAND, AND LIBERTY SQUARE TOURING TIPS

• If you have two days to spend touring the MK, begin your second in Frontierland at Splash Mountain. Move on to Big Thunder Mountain Railroad, then the Haunted Mansion in Liberty Square. All three attractions are relatively easy to board before 10 A.M., and you can return to ride less-crowded Liberty Square and Frontierland attractions later in the day.

• Because most visitors tour the lands in a clockwise or counterclockwise fashion, these three lands reach peak capacity around noon and stay crowded until around 4:30 P.M., when the people lined up to watch the 3 P.M. parade finally disperse. So if you miss Splash Mountain, the Jungle Cruise, the Haunted Mansion, or Big Thunder Mountain Railroad in the morning, wait until evening to revisit them.

• Should you, despite your best intentions, wind up in one of these three sections in midafternoon, you'll find a bit of breathing space on Tom Sawyer Island, with the Enchanted Tiki Birds, in the Hall of Presidents, or among the shops in the shady Adventureland Pavilion. Surprisingly, Pirates of the Caribbean isn't that difficult to board in midafternoon. The lines look terrible, but at least you wait inside, and this is one of the fastest-loading attractions in WDW.

• Splash Mountain stays mobbed almost all day long, so anytime you find a wait of less than 20 minutes, you should queue up immediately and thank your lucky stars.

Everyone dashes to Splash Mountain the minute the ropes drop in the morning; on very busy days, this means the line may be massive within minutes after the park opens. If you hustle straight to Frontierland and arrive only to find yourself facing a wait longer than 30 minutes, move on to Big Thunder Mountain Railroad; check Splash Mountain again immediately afterward, and you may find that the initial surge of people has moved through and the line is a bit shorter.

The lines also shorten in the last hour before closing, especially on the nights when a parade is scheduled. Even if you've already ridden once, you'll find that Splash Mountain is a whole new experience after dark.

FULL-SERVICE RESTAURANTS IN THE MAGIC KINGDOM

Tony's Town Square Cafe
Located in the Main Street Hub

This thoroughly enjoyable restaurant is dedicated to *Lady and the Tramp,* with scenes from the popular film dotting the walls, and a statue of the canine romantics in the center. The cuisine, like that of the cafe where Tramp wooed Lady, is classic Italian, and the portions are generous.

Tony's is a good choice for breakfast because, along with the other Main Street eateries, it begins serving before the park officially opens.

The kiddie menus, which feature pictures of Lady and the Tramp to color, are handed out with crayons, and the wait is rarely long, making Tony's a good choice for families with toddlers. Tony's is moderately priced (although still expensive for Italian food), and open for breakfast, lunch, and dinner.

The Plaza Restaurant
Located on Main Street

The sandwiches, burgers, and salads served at the Plaza are very filling. Try the milkshakes or the staggeringly large sundaes, which are trotted over from the Sealtest Ice Cream Parlor next door. The Plaza is moderately priced and open for lunch and dinner.

Crystal Palace

Located between Main Street and Adventureland

The MK's only cafeteria offers something for everyone and allows picky eaters a chance to pick. You can find salads and sandwiches at lunch, and nearly anything you please at dinner—even that most elusive of all MK foods: vegetables. And the setting is absolutely lovely.

One warning: Because of its central location and distinctive architecture, few visitors pass by the Crystal Palace without checking it out. The cafeteria is especially crowded from noon to 2 P.M., so you should aim to go around 11 A.M. or in midafternoon. Presently it is used for character breakfasts and is not a cafeteria in the morning. The Crystal Palace is moderately priced and open for breakfast, lunch, and dinner.

Liberty Tree Tavern

Located in Liberty Square

Crammed with antiques and decorated in a style reminiscent of Colonial Williamsburg, the tavern serves salads, sandwiches, and clam chowder at lunch. The evening menu offers classic American cuisine—a sort of "dinner at Grandma's" with turkey and dressing, or pot roast and mashed potatoes. A local food critic voted Liberty Tree Tavern as having the best food in the MK—which, admittedly, is an honor a bit like being the tallest building in North Dakota. A character dinner, featuring the characters in Revolutionary War–era garb, has recently been added.

The buffet is $20 for adults, $11 for kids 3 to 10.

King Stefan's Banquet Hall

Located in Cinderella Castle, Fantasyland

Nestled high amid the spires of the castle, this restaurant—named, mysteriously enough, for Sleeping Beauty's father—is the most glamorous in the MK. Make reservations at the restaurant door first thing in the morning; but even with reservations, you can expect to wait for both your table and your food. Because the service is slow and the menu pricey, King Stefan's is not a place to drop into casually.

Cinderella appears downstairs throughout the day to greet diners and pose for pictures. (Ask what times she is scheduled before you make your reservation.) Kids love the distinctive pumpkin-shaped kiddie menus, and often bring them back downstairs for Cinderella to autograph. The setting of the massive banquet hall with its high ceiling is spectacular, and the leaded-glass windows overlook the rides of Fantasyland, offering a stunning view, especially at night. King Stefan's offers a relatively ambitious menu, including a gorgeous fruit plate, but in general the food is only so-so.

Note: At certain times of the year, the "Once Upon a Time" character breakfast is offered, featuring the Cinderella gang.

DECENT FAST-FOOD PLACES IN THE MAGIC KINGDOM

• The **Mile Long Bar** in Frontierland is a good place for tame Tex-Mex, and lines move more swiftly than those at the **Pecos Bill Cafe** next door.

• The **Starlight Cafe** in Tomorrowland is by far the fastest of the sandwich-and-fries places.

• **Sleepy Hollow** in Liberty Square offers the best sandwiches and cookies in the MK. The shady park across the street is a great place to relax while you eat.

- Try a citrus swirl at the **Sunshine Tree Terrace** in Adventureland. Like Sleepy Hollow, this snack shop is tucked out of the way with its own quiet courtyard.

- Families who demand healthy snacks should stop by the **Liberty Square Market**, where fresh fruit and juices are available.

- **Lumiere's Kitchen** in Fantasyland provides the Disney version of a Happy Meal, featuring a cartoon-covered box with a burger, fries, and a souvenir pin inside. If you buy one of these meals, carry the food to a less crowded part of the park and look for a bench.

In general, the overcrowded fast-food places in Fantasyland should be avoided completely; likewise the Adventureland Veranda, where you wait far too long for mediocre Chinese food.

AFTERNOON RESTING PLACES

- The WDW Railroad (you can rest while you ride)
- The small park across from Sleepy Hollow in Liberty Square
- The Diamond Horseshoe Jamboree
- The Hall of Presidents
- Legend of the Lion King
- Galaxy Palace
- Tom Sawyer Island
- Guests with a five-day pass can take the launch marked *Campground and Discovery Island* to either River Country or Discovery Island. If it's hot, bring your suits along or wear them under your clothes—an hour or two at River Country can cool you off and revive your spirits.

- And if you want a quiet, leisurely lunch, take the resort monorail to one of the MK hotels. The coffee shops and restaurants are rarely crowded in the middle of the day.

BEST VANTAGE POINTS FOR WATCHING THE PARADES

- The absolute best location is at the very beginning of Main Street, along the hub in front of the Railroad Station. (The parade begins here, emerging from behind City Hall.) You do lose the vantage point of the floats coming down Main Street, but it's worth it to not have to fight the crowds.

The crowds grow less manageable as you proceed down Main Street and are at their worst in front of Cinderella Castle. In fact, if you find yourself four-people-deep on Main Street, send one of your party toward the main entrance to check out the situation at the hub; you may find there's still curb space there when the rest of the route is mobbed.

- If you find yourself deep in the theme park at parade time, don't try to fight your way up Main Street to the hub—you'll never make it. Instead, go to the end of the route, in front of Pecos Bill Cafe in Frontierland. The crowds there are thinner than in front of Cinderella Castle or in Liberty Square.

- On very busy days, the parade may run more than once—going from Main Street to Frontierland and then back from Frontierland to Main Street. Ask the nearest Disney attendant from which direction the parade will be coming and try to get as close as possible to the beginning of the route. Being near the beginning saves the kids a 20-minute wait to see the show and also ensures that you won't be caught among the exiting crowd.

BEST RESTROOM LOCATIONS IN THE MAGIC KINGDOM

By *best* I mean least crowded. You can get in and out of these rather quickly:

- Behind the Enchanted Grove snack bar near the Mad Tea Party.
- In the passageway between Adventureland and Frontierland. This one draws traffic, but is so huge that you never have to wait long.
- Near the Skyway to Fantasyland in Tomorrowland.
- If you're in the Baby Services center for other reasons, make a pit stop.
- The sit-down restaurants have their own restrooms, which are rarely crowded.
- And as you leave Pirates of the Caribbean, make a stop at the restroom behind the market stalls. This one is so secluded that I found it myself only on my seventeenth fact-finding trip to WDW.

THE MAGIC KINGDOM DON'T-MISS LIST

If your kids are 7 or older:

- Space Mountain
- Splash Mountain
- Pirates of the Caribbean

- Big Thunder Mountain Railroad
- The Haunted Mansion
- Legend of the Lion King
- Alien Encounter—if they're 10 or older
- The parades
- Any Fantasyland rides that catch their fancy

If your kids are under 7:

- Dumbo, the Flying Elephant
- Tomorrowland Raceway
- Mad Tea Party
- It's a Small World
- Peter Pan's Flight
- Toontown—especially Goofy's Barnstormer
- Pirates of the Caribbean
- Country Bear Vacation Hoedown
- Legend of the Lion King
- The parades
- Splash Mountain—if they pass the
  height requirement
- Big Thunder Mountain Railroad—if they pass the
  height requirement

YOUR LAST HOUR IN
THE MAGIC KINGDOM

- Some rides—most notably Big Thunder Mountain Railroad, Cinderella's Golden Carousel, Dumbo, Splash Mountain, and the Skyway between Tomorrowland and Fantasyland—are particularly beautiful at night.

• If you missed any of the biggie rides earlier in the day, return in the last hour; lines are shorter just before closing, especially in Fantasyland.

• If you're visiting on an evening when a parade is scheduled, move as far as possible up Main Street and stake out your curb space near the hub. Turn in your strollers and make a final potty run before the parade starts so you'll be ready to make a fast exit once the final float rolls by.

THE SCARE FACTOR IN THE MAGIC KINGDOM

I get more mail on this subject than any other. Many families arrive eager to sample every ride, especially the big-deal attractions that get so much hype. But a whole day can be ruined if a child becomes sick or frightened.

Few attractions at WDW are truly terrifying in the physical sense. In fact, young visitors raised on a steady diet of roller coasters called "Corkscrew" and "Python" are apt to find Disney offerings pretty tame. With the exception of Space Mountain, nothing in the MK will knock off your glasses or shake out your fillings.

But Disney plays on your emotions in more subtle ways. Children who would seem to be anesthetized by the violence of movies like *Halloween VIII* have been known to sob inconsolably over the demise of Old Yeller. Walt, you'll remember, is the guy who bumped off Bambi's mother, and some preschoolers leave the rides psychologically shaken. In addition, the attention to detail which is so much a Disney trademark is especially evident in attractions like the Alien Encounter—he's believable.

This makes the scare factor tough to gauge. I'd ask myself: Is my child more afraid of physical sensations, such as dipping or twirling or falling, or is he more likely to be scared by eerie music, darkness, and bad guys? Then read the ride descriptions and make up your mind which rides, in the words of my 7-year-old adviser, are "fun scary" and which are "scary scary." Remember: When in doubt, do the baby swap first—let a parent preview the ride and return with the verdict.

Snow White's Scary Adventures

Don't expect to leave this attraction humming "Whistle While You Work." Riders take the role of Snow White as she flees through the woods, and the Wicked Queen does leap out at you several times. But the ride is a short one, and the special effects are fairly simple.

Final verdict: Not too scary; fine for most kids over 4.

Mr. Toad's Wild Ride

Your car careens through a funhouse. At one point you make a wrong turn onto a railroad track with a train approaching. Mr. Toad also—briefly—goes to hell.

Final verdict: Not too scary; fine for most kids over 4.

Big Thunder Mountain Railroad

This exciting three-minute ride is one of the best-loved in the Magic Kingdom. At no time does the train go very high, although it does travel fairly fast. Riders exit giggly but not shaken.

Final verdict: Fine for the 7-and-above crowd. Children must be 40 inches tall to ride, and some kids under 7 who rode with their parents loved Big Thunder. If you're debating which of the three "mountains" (i.e., Splash Mountain, Big Thunder Mountain Railroad, and Space Mountain) is most suitable for a preschooler, Big Thunder is your best bet.

Goofy's Barnstormer

A good first roller coaster for preschoolers, mostly because the ride is less than a minute long. You can see the whole path of the ride from the ground, so watch it make a couple of trips and then make your call.

The Haunted Mansion

This is more funny than scary. The cast members who load you into your black "doom buggy" are dressed like morticians and never smile or make eye contact; the ceiling in the portrait hall moves up; and the mansion is home to ravens, floating objects, swirling ghosts, glowing crystal balls, and doors that rap when there's no one there.

Final verdict: Fine for any child over 7—and most younger kids. A few parents reported that their preschoolers got nervous.

Alien Encounter

This is risky business. A shoulder harness secures you in your seat but also holds you hostage to a variety of creepy sensations. The theater is totally darkened for long stretches of time, and the visual and sound effects were overwhelming to some kids.

Final verdict: An intense show, best suited for kids over 10. There's a 44-inch height requirement, and kids 44 to 48 inches must watch the preshow before they're allowed to enter.

Pirates of the Caribbean

My 4-year-old daughter grew a bit apprehensive as we wove our way through the drafty, dungeonlike queue area, but she loved the ride that followed. Although there are gunshots, skeletons, cannons, mangy-looking buccaneers, and even a brief drop over a "waterfall" in the dark, the mood is generally up-tempo.

Final verdict: Fine for anyone.

Splash Mountain

The atmosphere inside the mountain is so happy and kid-oriented that it's a shame the final plunge over the waterfall is so steep. This last drop gives you the feeling that you're coming out of your seat and momentarily takes your breath away. The same 44-inch height requirement applies as at Space Mountain, meaning that many children under 7 technically qualify to ride; the final verdict rests with the parents.

Final verdict: The general consensus among the families we surveyed is that the ride is OK for any child 5 and over.

Note: Don't let the fact that Splash Mountain has the same height requirement as Space Mountain fool you—it's nowhere near as wild. The height requirement is partially due to the construction of the log boats, which are built with high walls to limit how much riders are soaked during the final drop. But an unhappy side effect of the log construction is that a child shorter than 44 inches wouldn't be able to see much—and might be tempted to stand.

Astro Orbiter

You can control how high your spaceship flies in this cyclic ride. A good choice for those not quite up to Space Mountain, unless you're prone to motion sickness or vertigo.

Final verdict: Fun for kids 7 to 11.

Space Mountain

It's not just the fact that this is a roller coaster—it's the fact that you plunge through darkness, which makes Space Mountain unique. There are lots of sharp dips with very little warning. Kids under 7 must pass the 44-inch height requirement and be accompanied by an adult. Children under 3 cannot ride.

Final verdict: Forget it for preschoolers. Kids in the 7-to-11 age range in general like Space Mountain. Teens adore it.

5

★★★★★★★★★★★★★★★★★★

Epcot Center

EPCOT CENTER

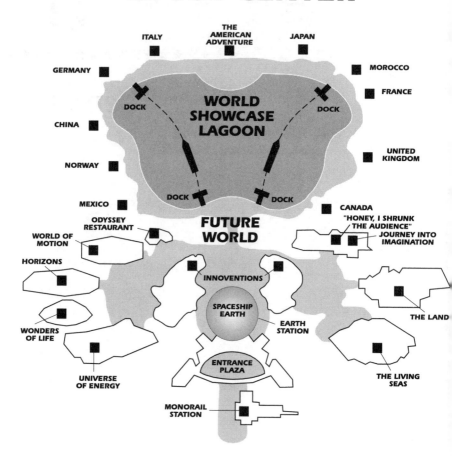

GETTING TO EPCOT CENTER

• Epcot is easy to reach by car. If you arrive early in the morning, you can park very close to the main entrance and forgo the tram ride. If you arrive a bit later, the trams do run quickly and efficiently. Just be sure to write down the number of the row where you parked your car.

• Many off-site hotels offer shuttle buses to Epcot. Fort Wilderness, Port Orleans, Dixie Landings, the Disney Institute Villas, Coronado Springs, Wilderness Lodge, the All-Star Resorts, Disney's Old Key West, and the Caribbean Beach Resort all run shuttles as well.

• If you're staying at the Polynesian, Grand Floridian, or Contemporary, it's fastest to take the monorail to the TTC and then transfer to the Epcot monorail.

• The Swan, the Dolphin, the BoardWalk, and the Yacht and Beach Clubs are connected by bridge to a "backdoor" entrance to the World Showcase. Either take the shuttle, or, if you're staying at the Yacht or Beach Club, simply walk over the bridge.

GETTING AROUND EPCOT CENTER

As any Disneyophile can tell you, *Epcot* is an acronym for the Experimental Prototype City of Tomorrow. But as one of the players at the Comedy Warehouse on Pleasure Island suggests, maybe Epcot really stands for Every Person Comes Out Tired.

Epcot is indeed sprawling—more than twice the size of the MK—but the FriendShips that crisscross the World Showcase Lagoon and the double-decker buses that encircle it should be viewed as fun rides, not transportation. The fastest means of getting around is walking.

YOUR FIRST HOUR AT EPCOT

• As soon as you enter the main gate, veer left to rent strollers. Then, assuming it's operative, ride Spaceship Earth.

• One parent should take the kids and the camera and order breakfast at the Electric Umbrella or Pasta Piazza (both near Innoventions). The characters, dressed in nifty spacesuit garb, sometimes show up around 8:30 A.M. The entertainment schedule notes which restaurant is hosting the characters, and there's usually a sign outside the door as well.

The other parent should stop by the WorldKey Information System inside the Earth Station under Spaceship Earth and make dinner reservations, then enter Guest Services and pick up an entertainment schedule.

• If you have time before the rest of the park opens, browse through Innoventions. It's probably a mistake to let the kids at the games—once they start, it'll be hard to get them out—but scope out the exhibits you'd like to return to later.

• After the ropes drop and you're allowed to enter the body of the park, veer sharply left and ride Test Track first, then Body Wars in the Wonders of Life pavilion.

• After Body Wars, leave the Wonders of Life pavilion—knowing you can always return for the films and interactive exhibits later—and head for the first showing of *Honey, I Shrunk the Audience.* If Test Track and Body Wars are too wild for you, go to *Honey, I Shrunk the Audience* first.

EPCOT TOURING TIPS

• Take Epcot in small doses if your kids are young; three to four hours at a time are enough.

• Visit newer attractions such as *Honey, I Shrunk the Audience* and Test Track first thing in the morning.

• In the off-season, Epcot hours are often staggered. Future World is generally open from 9 A.M. to 7 P.M., and the World Showcase from 11 A.M. to 9 P.M.

• Avoid the high-capacity shows such as Universe of Energy or *O Canada!* in the morning. Your time is better spent moving among the continuous-loading attractions such as Body Wars, Test Track, Horizons, the Land pavilion, World of Motion, the Living Seas pavilion, and Journey Into Imagination. With the exception of *Honey, I Shrunk the Audience,* save the theater-style attractions until afternoon.

• Touring Epcot is easier if you zig when everyone else zags. During the summer and other busy times, Future World stays crowded from midmorning until late afternoon, then empties as people head toward their dinner reservations in the World Showcase.

You can avoid crowds by touring Future World until midmorning, then drifting toward the World Showcase in the afternoon, where you can escape to the films and indoor exhibits during the hottest and busiest times.

Then, after an early dinner, head back into Future World. Attractions such as Journey Into Imagination,

Innoventions, and the Living Seas pavilion are rarely packed in the evening.

• If you are touring off-season and plan to spend mornings in the MK or at MGM and your evenings at Epcot, make Epcot dinner reservations for as early as possible, leaving yourself several hours to tour after you eat.

Another alternative: If your children have had a good afternoon nap and can keep going until 10 P.M., make your dinner reservations for very late. The restaurants accept their final seating just before the park shuts down, and all the transportation stays operative for at least 90 minutes after the park officially closes. Eating late buys you maximum hours in the park, assuming your kids can handle the schedule.

• Upon entering a World Showcase pavilion that has a show or film—France, Canada, America, or China— ask the attendant how long until the show begins. If the wait is 10 minutes or less, queue up. If the wait is longer, browse the shops of the pavilion until about 10 minutes before showtime. The World Showcase theaters are large, and everyone who shows up within 10 minutes of showtime will be seated.

• Most people circle the World Showcase Lagoon in a clockwise fashion, beginning with the Mexico pavilion. You'll make better time if you move counterclockwise, beginning with Canada.

• Innoventions and the interactive exhibits in the Wonders of Life, Journey Into Imagination, and Spaceship Earth pavilions are very worthwhile—and a nice break from the enforced passivity of all the rides. But do the rides first and save the interactive games for midafternoon or early evening.

- If you're not staying for IllumiNations, begin moving toward the exit gates while the show is in progress.

If you miss the chance to exit before the Illumi-Nations crowd, or you've opted to stay for the show, don't join in the throngs that mob the exit turnstiles and shuttles just after the show has ended. Pick up dessert before the show and then, after IllumiNations, find a table, sit down, relax, and let the crowds pass you by. The trams and monorails will still be running long after your finish your snack, and the lines waiting for them will be far shorter.

FUTURE WORLD

Future World comprises nine large pavilions, each containing at least one major attraction, and is very much like a permanent World's Fair, mixing educational opportunities with pure entertainment. Most visitors are drawn first to the rides with their spectacular special effects, but don't miss Innoventions and the chance to play with the smaller interactive exhibits. Many of these encourage young visitors to learn while doing, and stopping to try them out helps kids avoid what one mother termed "Audio-Animatronics overload."

Sensitive to complaints that Epcot "was boring" and "never changed," Disney has endeavored to make Future World more appealing to kids. Three pavilions—Horizons, World of Motion, and Universe of Energy—have undergone substantial alterations to make the preshows and technical presentations shorter and the special effects zippier. And Innoventions is constantly changing, with new exhibits moving in and out on a regular basis.

Future World Attractions

Spaceship Earth

Few travelers, whatever their age, can remain blasé at the sight of Spaceship Earth, the most photographed and readily recognizable symbol of Epcot.

The ride inside, which coils toward the top of the 17-story geosphere, traces developments in communication, from cave drawings to computers. The voice of Jeremy Irons croons in your ear as you climb past scenes of Egyptian temples, the Gutenberg press, and a performance of *Oedipus Rex*. Even preschoolers rated Spaceship Earth highly, probably due to the excitement of actually entering "the Big Ball" and the impressive finale, which flashes a planetarium sky above you as you swirl backward down through the darkness.

Note: If you can't ride Spaceship Earth early in the morning, save it for evening.

The Living Seas

The Living Seas features a saltwater aquarium so enormous that Spaceship Earth could float inside it. You begin with a short film that discusses the critical role of the ocean as a source of energy, then swiftly move on to board a gondola that takes you through an underwater viewing tunnel. More than 200 varieties of marine life, including stingrays, dolphins, barracuda, sharks, and an occasional scuba-clad Mickey, swim above you. Unfortunately, the gondola ride is so short that there's not much time to look.

The most enjoyable part of the attraction comes after you disembark at Seabase Alpha. You can remain here as long as you choose, wandering through two levels of observation tanks that allow you to view the fish and human divers at startlingly close range. (A new program allows visitors—for $125—to suit up and enter the tank with a guide.)

Note: It's easy to spend an entire afternoon at the Living Seas. But if you plan to devote a day to Sea World while in Orlando, you'll find much of the same stuff there, so hold your time at the Living Seas to a minimum.

The Land

This cheerful pavilion, sponsored by Nestle and devoted to the subject of food and how we get it, is home to three separate attractions as well as a rotating restaurant and fast-food court. Because it is the hub of so much activity, the Land pavilion is crowded from midmorning on.

• *Living with the Land.* Visitors travel by boat past scenes of various farming environments, ending with a peek at fish farming, drip irrigation, and other innovative agricultural technologies. Perhaps because there are few special effects and no cute tour guide like Figment, who lives in the Journey Into Imagination pavilion next door, this attraction is less interesting to preschoolers. But, as is the case in all of Future World, the presentation moves swiftly. In short, this won't be your children's favorite attraction, but they won't complain either. (Hour-long guided tours of the greenhouse are also available: $6 for adults, $4 for kids. Ask a host for details.)

• *Circle of Life.* This film, presented in the Harvest Theatre, graphically illustrates how we interact—both positively and negatively—with our environment. It has been revamped to make it more appealing to kids, with Pumbaa and Timon from *The Lion King* as the hosts.

- *Food Rocks.* This funny 15-minute show features famous rock 'n roll stars masquerading as food. The Peach Boys sing about "Good Nutrition," an eggplant is dubbed "Neil Moussaka," and the Refrigerator Police oversee "Every Bite You Take."

Note: Both *Circle of Life* and *Food Rocks* are good choices for the most crowded times of the afternoon.

Journey Into Imagination and Honey, I Shrunk the Audience

One of the best pavilions in Future World for young kids, the ride inside features Dreamfinder and the charming purple Figment of his imagination. Together they take you through a variety of scenes celebrating art, literature, music, and other products of human creativity. Be forewarned: There's a sudden flash of light near the end of the ride. This pavilion is sponsored by Kodak, and a wide-screen photograph of you in all your glory is waiting around the next corner.

Beside Journey Into Imagination is Epcot's new sleeper hit, the 3-D film *Honey, I Shrunk the Audience.* This show is so fun that several families reported that their kids insisted on seeing it more than once. Based on the popular movie series, the presentation begins as Dr. Wayne Szalinski is about to pick up the award for Inventor of the Year. The scene quickly dissolves into mayhem as the audience is accidentally "shrunk," one son's pet snake gets loose, and the other's pet mouse is reproduced 999 times. Although the 3-D images are dazzling, the effects go far beyond the visual—you actually feel the "mice" running up your legs. The kid-pleasing, dog-sneezing finale is not to be missed.

After you disembark from Journey Into Imagination, it's fun to explore the Image Works, a series of hands-on exhibits such as the Magic Palette, with an electronic paintbrush, or Stepping Tones, where kids can create music by jumping into different-colored puddles of light. Volunteers may get the chance to act as characters in a video short story told by the Dreamfinder himself: Five or six children selected from the crowd are "inserted" into the background of a space adventure and, by following such simple commands as "jump" or "run in place," they appear to be interacting with the figures onscreen. Image Works is especially fun from 6 P.M. on, when the crowds disperse and kids don't have to wait in line to try everything out.

As you leave the Journey Into Imagination pavilion, take time to check out Splashtacular, a fountain show full of special effects.

Note: If your kids are freaked out by the special effects in *Honey, I Shrunk the Audience,* tell them to lift their legs off the floor and take off the 3-D glasses. The effects are brief, and they can put the glasses back on and resume sitting normally within a minute or two.

Test Track

Test Track, which debuted in the spring of 1997, is the longest, fastest ride in all of WDW, and the only Epcot attraction that can honestly be called a thrill ride.

The premise is that guests are testing automobiles before they are brought to market. You begin the ride inside, checking out how your vehicle responds to conditions of cold, heat, and stress—but it's the stress level of the passengers that soars when you "accidentally" break through a barrier and burst outside of the building. Once outside, the cars reach speeds of up to 65 mph, with hills, hairpin turns, and what is euphemistically called "changes in road surfaces." The track in total is almost a mile long, and it all adds up to a powerfully exciting ride.

Note: New rides get lots of press and draw big crowds. Go early or during IllumiNations.

Horizons

How will the average family live in the future? Horizons takes riders into the next century, where robots clean house, families visit via holographic telephone, and cities flourish on the ocean floor. Needless to say, Disney's predictions for the year 2020 are all sunny.

Note: Horizons loads fast and is rarely too crowded. It's a good choice when Test Track and the Wonders of Life pavilion next door are swamped.

Wonders of Life

Devoted to celebrating the human body, the Wonders of Life pavilion resembles a brightly colored street fair full of hands-on exhibits. You can check out your health profile via computer, get advice on your tennis or golf swing, and test your endurance on a motorized bike. Kids enjoy the film *Goofy About Health* as well as the Sensory Funhouse. (Despite the provocative name, this exhibit is devoted to only the most wholesome of tactile sensations.) Like the Land pavilion, the Wonders of Life pavilion houses three major attractions and is crowded by 11 A.M.

• *Body Wars.* Incorporating the same flight-simulation technology found at MGM's Star Tours, Body Wars takes riders on a turbulent high-speed chase through the human body. After being miniaturized to the size of a pinhead and injected into a patient, the crew is briefed to expect a routine medical mission for the purpose of removing a splinter from the "safe zone just under the skin." But when shapely Dr. Lair is sucked into a capillary, your crew is off on a rescue chase through the heart, lungs, and brain.

No expectant mothers or kids under 3 are allowed to board, and Body Wars does indeed have its queasy moments, due more to the accuracy of flight-simulation technology—and perhaps the subject matter—than the bouncing of the ship. Those prone to motion sickness should skip the trip.

• *The Making of Me.* This 15-minute film provides a fetus-eye view of conception, gestation, and birth. Martin Short travels back in time to show us his own parents as babies, then chronicles how they met and ultimately produced him. (One glaring anachronism: Martin must have been the only kid born in America in the fifties who was delivered through Lamaze.) Although the film is direct and unflinching, it's appropriate for any age.

The line for the film can be long, so let one parent queue up while the other takes the kids around to some of the interactive exhibits. Coach's Corner, which gives visitors a chance to have their golf, tennis, or baseball swing videotaped, replayed in slo-mo, and then analyzed by Nancy Lopez, Chris Evert, or Gary Carter, is especially fun.

• *Cranium Command.* One of the funniest presentations in Epcot, Cranium Command mixes Audio-Animatronics with film. General Knowledge taps an unfortunate recruit, Fuzzy, to pilot "the most unstable craft in the fleet"—the brain of a 12-year-old boy. If he fails in his mission, Fuzzy will be demoted to flying the brain of a chicken or, worse, a talk-show host. Fuzzy tries to guide his boy through a typical day of junior high school without overloading his system—which isn't easy, especially when the body parts are played by this cast: Charles Grodin as the right brain, Jon Lovitz as the left brain, Hans and Franz from "Saturday Night Live" pumping it up in the role of the heart, Norm from

"Cheers" as the stomach, and, in a particularly convincing performance, Bobcat Goldthwait as adrenaline.

Universe of Energy

This technologically complex presentation can be enjoyed by any age on any level. Kids are dazzled by the dinosaurs, and parents leave the pavilion muttering, "How did they do that?" A digital clock at the entryway keeps you posted on when the next show begins; don't file in until the wait is 10 minutes or less. This is an almost 30-minute presentation, and there's no point in wearing out the kids before you begin.

Last year Disney made the preshow and postshow a lot snappier by bringing in Ellen DeGeneres, Alex Trebek, and Jamie Lee Curtis. The premise is that Ellen dreams she goes on "Jeopardy!" She is thoroughly skunked in the science category by smarty-pants Jamie; Bill Nye the Science Guy convinces her that we all need to know more about energy.

The Disney twist comes when the 97-seat theater begins to break apart in sections, which align themselves in sequence and move toward a curtain. Your theater has become your train, and the curtain slowly lifts to reveal an Audio-Animatronic version of the age when coal deposits first began being formed. The air reeks of sulfur, as it presumably did during prehistoric times, the light is an eerie blue, and all around you are those darn dinosaurs—the largest Disney robots ever created, and quite authentic. After your train has once again metamorphosed into a theater, there's a final film segment in which a newly educated Ellen gets her "Jeopardy!" revenge.

Note: Despite its proximity to the front gate, this is not a good choice for the morning; save it for afternoon or early evening when you'll welcome the chance to sit for a half-hour. Also, the Universe of Energy seats a large number people, meaning that lines form and dissipate quickly. If the line looks prohibitive, check out nearby pavilions and return in 20 minutes. You may be able to walk right in.

Innoventions

Innoventions is the arcade of the future, where you can try out new Sega Genesis games before they hit the market, fly on a virtual-reality magic carpet, and play with beyond-state-of-the-art technology such as video controller chairs and computers that translate voice dictation directly into the printed word.

Innoventions is a showcase for such corporations as Apple, IBM, Motorola, Sega, and AT&T. The products displayed have either just come on the market or are straight from the inventor and not yet available. Choices range from toilets that clean themselves to a stationary bike with a Nintendo attached—the idea being that you'll become so absorbed in the game that you won't notice how hard you're pedaling.

The most popular by far are the virtual-reality games; people line up for five minutes on a machine, and many become so hooked that they reenter the line over and over for the chance to be a cue ball in a pool game, a driver in the Indy 500, or to visit the great museums of the world. (Observers can see what the player sees, via an overhead screen.) Cast members are quick to point out that these much-maligned games are what pushed the envelope in computer technology, especially in the area of graphics. Preteens and teens will obviously be dazzled, but there are Pico computer games for preschoolers as well.

If you plan to spend much time in Innoventions, pick up a map as you enter. Well-informed cast members are always on hand to answer questions or help you get the hang of the games and experiments. Exhibits change frequently, keeping things fresh.

If the blinking and beeping become too overwhelming, parents can take a break outside at the nearby Expresso and Pastry Cafe. The Fountain of Nations between Innoventions East and West—so named because it contains water from all the countries of the World Showcase—puts on a lovely evening show.

Note: Innoventions becomes unbearably crowded in midmorning, as people enter the Epcot gates and make a dash for the first thing they see. Visit in late afternoon or during IllumiNations.

WORLD SHOWCASE

Pretty by day and gorgeous by night, the World Showcase comprises the pavilions of eleven nations—Mexico, Norway, China, Germany, Italy, America, Japan, Morocco, France, the United Kingdom, and Canada—stretching around a large lagoon. Some of the pavilions have full-scale attractions, listed as follows; others have only shops and restaurants. Demonstrations, music, and shows are scheduled throughout the day, and the characters, dressed in culturally correct costumes, frequently appear in the afternoon.

Most important from an educational and cultural perspective, each pavilion is staffed by citizens of the country it represents. Disney goes to great pains to recruit, relocate, and, if necessary, teach English to the shopkeepers and waiters you see in these pavilions, bringing them to Orlando for a year and housing them with the representatives from the other World Showcase nations. It's a cultural exchange program on the highest level. (One Norwegian guide told me that her roommates were from China, Mexico, and Canada.) These young men and women save the World Showcase from being merely touristy, add an air of authenticity to every aspect of the experience, and provide your kids with the chance to rub elbows, however briefly, with other cultures. So even if pavilions such as Morocco or Japan don't have a ride or film, don't rush past them: Stop for a honeyed pastry or an origami demonstration and chat with the person behind the counter.

Note: The World Showcase can be a big yawn for kids under 8. But if you buy them a World Showcase Passport at Port of Entry, they can collect stamps and a handwritten message from each World Showcase nation they visit. Given kids' passion for collecting, a desire to fill their passport will motivate them to move from country to country. It's the Epcot equivalent of collecting character autographs and makes a great souvenir.

World Showcase Attractions

O Canada!
This 20-minute CircleVision 360 film is gorgeous, stirring—and impossible to view with kids under 6. In order to enjoy the effect of the circular screen, guests are required to stand during the presentation, and strollers are not allowed into the theater. This means babies and toddlers must be held, and preschoolers, who can't see anything in a room of standing adults, often clamor to be lifted up as well. So we regretfully suggest that families with young kids pass up this presentation, as well as the equally lovely *Wonders of China: Land of Beauty, Land of Time.* If this is the

case, and you're dining at Epcot on your parents' night out, that would be a good time to take in those World Showcase attractions that just aren't oriented toward kids.

Impressions de France

What a difference a seat makes! Like all the Epcot films, *Impressions de France* is exceedingly well done, with lush music and a 200-degree wide-screen feel. It's fairly easy to get in, even in the afternoon, and no one minds if babies take a little nap.

The American Adventure

This 30-minute multimedia presentation, combining Audio-Animatronic figures with film, is popular with all age groups. The technological highlight of the show is when the Ben Franklin robot actually walks upstairs to visit Thomas Jefferson. The entire presentation is packed with film montages, moving music, elaborate sets that rise from the stage, and painless history lessons.

Note: The America pavilion becomes quite crowded in the afternoon, but since it's located at the exact midpoint of the World Showcase Lagoon, it's impractical to skip it and work your way back later. If you're faced with a half-hour wait, enjoy the excellent Voices of Liberty preshow or have a snack at the Liberty Inn next door.

Wonders of China

See the previous listing for *O Canada!* on page 149.

Maelstrom

This Norwegian boat ride is a hit with kids. Your Viking ship sails through fjords and storms, over waterfalls, and past a threatening three-headed troll . . . all within four minutes. Riders disembark in a North Sea coastal village, where a short film is presented. Ride Maelstrom before 1 P.M. or just before park closing, when most people have lined up to await IllumiNations.

El Rio del Tiempo: The River of Time
There's rarely a wait at this charming boat ride, located inside the romantic Mexico pavilion. Reminiscent of It's a Small World in the MK, El Rio del Tiempo is especially appealing to younger riders.

GENERAL INFORMATION ON EPCOT CENTER RESTAURANTS

Among the families we surveyed, there was a great difference of opinion as to which Epcot restaurants are best. "We loved Alfredo's," wrote one family, "but the Coral Reef was a big disappointment. It was overpriced and you can get the same view for free upstairs at the Living Seas." "The Coral Reef was our absolute favorite," wrote another family. "Alfredo's, on the other hand, is a waste of time." (Alfredo di Roma and the Coral Reef are the most expensive, most popular—and most controversial—Epcot eateries. Perhaps because reservations are so hard to come by, diners enter with exalted expectations and leave either profoundly disappointed or convinced they've had a mountaintop experience.)

The following are some general tips for the obligatory Epcot dining experience.

• If you are staying on-site, you can make reservations for both dinner and lunch in advance, and such foresight may be necessary if you're aiming to get into the Coral Reef on a Friday night in July. If you're not staying on-site, make your reservations first thing in the morning at the WorldKey Information System inside the Earth Station under Spaceship Earth. Visitors who have no reservations sometimes get seated by simply showing up at the door, especially if they try a large restaurant, such as the Biergarten, or eat dinner very early.

• The Epcot dining experience doesn't come cheap. Dinner for a family of four will run about $60 without alcohol. But as throughout WDW, portions are very large, even on items from the kiddie menu. Two children can easily share an entrée; for that matter, so can two adults.

If you're trying to save money, remember that lunchtime selections are just as impressive as dinner, and the fare is much cheaper.

Many Epcot restaurants also offer an Early Value Meal between 4:30 and 6 p.m. The meal includes an appetizer, entrée, dessert, and beverage for about $15—an excellent deal at a restaurant such as Chefs de France, where a three-course dinner would more typically run about $35.

• Kids are welcome at any Epcot eatery, although some are more entertaining for youngsters than others. (See the following section for details.) High chairs, booster seats, and kiddie menus are universally available.

The World Showcase restaurants offer "Mickey's Child Deals" for about $4. The food is a nod to the country whose cuisine is being represented, i.e., skewered chicken in Morocco and fish and chips in the United Kingdom. But the entrées are smaller, less spicy, and look enough like chicken nuggets and fish sticks that the kids will eat them.

- Casual attire is OK anywhere in the park. It may seem strange to eat oysters with champagne sauce while wearing a Goofy sweatshirt, but you'll get used to it.

- The Epcot restaurants take their reservations seriously. If you show up at the Mitsukoshi at 12:45 for a 12:30 reservation, expect to be told "sayonara."

- Be careful when booking for France, which is home to two sit-down restaurants: Chefs de France, which is streetfront, and Le Bistro de Paris upstairs. Many visitors get these confused and risk losing their reservations by showing up at the wrong place.

- Be bold. Your hometown probably has good Chinese and Italian restaurants, but how often do you get to sample Norwegian or Moroccan food?

- If you want to save both time and money, stick to the fast-food places for meals—but make a reservation at a sit-down restaurant for a truly off time, say 4 P.M. or 10 P.M., and just have dessert. You can soak up the ambience for an investment of 30 minutes and 10 bucks.

FULL-SERVICE RESTAURANTS AT EPCOT CENTER

What is Norwegian food, anyway? Is the service so slow we'll miss IllumiNations? Is there anything to keep the kids entertained while the adults sip their sake? Read on for an overview of the suitability of the full-service restaurants for kids, and keep in mind that if you have fussy eaters in the family, all the full-service restaurants post menus outside their doors.

Note: See Section 8, "Disney World After Dark," for more information on the most romantic and adult-oriented of the Epcot restaurants.

Chefs de France

France
Suitability for kids: Moderate. It's fun to watch the crowds go by, but the tables are close and the waiters move at quite a clip, so there is no place for children to stand and stretch their legs. Older kids might be wowed by the atmosphere and the chance to order a *croquette de boeuf en brioche*—surely the classiest hamburger they'll ever wolf down.

Bistro de Paris

France
Suitability for kids: Low. This is one of the more romantic (and expensive) Epcot restaurants, with dim lighting and leisurely service. Try it on the night you leave the kids back at the Mouseketeer Club.

Rose and Crown Pub

United Kingdom
Suitability for kids: High, especially if you eat outside and can watch the FriendShips go by on the World Showcase Lagoon. Pub atmosphere, charming service, mediocre food.

Mitsukoshi Restaurant

Japan
Suitability for kids: High. Diners sit at large common tables while chefs slice and dice in a flamboyant fashion. If there's a Benihana in your hometown, you get the idea. The night we visited, ladies were circulating among the tables making origami souvenirs for the kids.

L'Originale Alfredo di Roma
Italy
Suitability for kids: Moderate. Most children like Italian food, but the restaurant is very crowded and service is slow.

Marrakesh
Morocco
Suitability for kids: Moderate. Exotic surroundings, and kids enjoy the belly dancers. The unfamiliarity of the food may pose a problem, but the children's portions are not as spicy as those served to the adults; so if the kids can be persuaded to give it a try, they'll find that roasted chicken tastes pretty much the same the world over.

Nine Dragons Restaurant
China
Suitability for kids: Moderate. There isn't much entertainment going on, but the service is fast and the staff is quite happy to accommodate special requests, as in "Can you hold the sweet-and-sour sauce on the sweet-and-sour chicken?" The ambitious menu here extends far beyond the typical Chinese fare at your favorite take-out place back home. Experimenting with an unknown dish such as red bean ice cream can lead to some very pleasant surprises.

San Angel Inn
Mexico
Suitability for kids: High. The service is swift and friendly, and kids can browse among the market stalls of the Mexico pavilion or ride El Rio del Tiempo while waiting for the food. One of the best bets in Epcot.

Biergarten

Germany

Suitability for kids: High. There's plenty of room to move about, as well as a rousing, noisy atmosphere and entertainment in the form of yodelers and an oom-pah-pah band.

Akershus

Norway

Suitability for kids: Moderate. There's a buffet, so you get your food fast and have the chance to see things before you make a selection. But most of the food is apt to be unfamiliar to the kids, and there's a lot of fish, so picky eaters may rebel. This is a fine spot for hearty eaters, because you can load up at the hot and cold buffet tables. Also a good chance to sample a variety of unusual dishes.

Le Cellier

Canada

Suitability for kids: Medium. Le Cellier is in the process of changing from a cafeteria to a sit-down restaurant. The menu features foods hearty enough to please a lumberjack—pork pie, meatball stew, and cheddar cheese soup. If the kids rebel against anything too unfamiliar, but the parents can't face another burger, head for the neutral territory of Le Cellier.

The Garden Grille Room

Land pavilion

Suitability for kids: High. Here you'll find easily recognizable American dishes, served family style, with some of the food grown in the greenhouses downstairs. The booths are large, which lets you stretch out, and the restaurant rotates, allowing diners to observe scenes from the Living with the Land boat ride below. Best of all, the characters, dressed in gingham and dungarees, circulate among the diners, and everyone is given a free straw hat to complete the down-home theme.

The Coral Reef Restaurant
Living Seas pavilion
Suitability for kids: High. One whole wall is glass, giving diners an unparalleled view of the Living Seas tank; and because the restaurant is arranged in tiers, every table has a good view of the fish.

DECENT FAST-FOOD PLACES AT EPCOT CENTER

Fast food is a somewhat relative term at Epcot, where long lines are the norm during peak dining hours. But the choices are far more varied and interesting than those in the Magic Kingdom. And the views are so charming—especially in Mexico, Japan, and France—that Epcot blurs the distinction between fast food and fine dining.

• The skewered chicken and beef at the **Yakitori House** in Japan are excellent, and the little courtyard outside has the feel of a Japanese tea garden.

Note: As is the case in many of the World Showcase eateries, a child's combination plate is more than adequate for an adult, especially if you'll be snacking in a couple of hours.

• The **Cantina de San Angel** in Mexico serves tortillas and tostadas at tables clustered around the lagoon.

• You'll find open-faced salmon or ham sandwiches and unusual pastries at **Kringla Bakeri og Kafe** in Norway.

• If your kids are suffering hamburger withdrawal, there's always the **Liberty Inn** at the American pavilion, the **Odyssey Restaurant** on the bridge connecting Future World to the World Showcase, or the **Electric Umbrella** near Innoventions.

• Pizza is available in the **Pasta Piazza**, also near Innoventions.

• If you find yourself in Future World at lunchtime and your party can't agree on a restaurant, visit **Sunshine Season** in the Land pavilion. The food court here has plenty of variety, including clam chowder, quiche, barbecue, stuffed potatoes, scooped-out pineapples filled with fruit salad, and killer chocolate-chip cookies.

• If it's raining, you'll probably want to avoid the outdoor tables for many of the fast-food places, so head for **Sunshine Season** in the Land pavilion, or the **Electric Umbrella** or **Pasta Piazza**, both near Innoventions. The **Odyssey Restaurant**, currently closed for renovation, is also a good indoor choice, and at certain times the characters appear here in the afternoon. Check the entertainment schedule.

• **La Maison du Vin** offers wine tastings throughout the afternoon and evening. The fee is minimal, and you get to keep the souvenir glass. A case of chardonnay is the last thing you need with you when you're riding Test Track, so if you find something you like, the bottles can be sent to Package PickUp for you to retrieve as you exit the park, or, if you're staying on-site, delivered directly to your room.

EPCOT CENTER EXTRAS

Special Shows

• Singers, dancers, jugglers, and artisans from around the globe perform throughout the World Showcase daily. Most of these presentations (which are detailed in the daily entertainment guide) are not especially oriented toward children—although kids over 7 will catch the humor of the World Showcase Players in the United Kingdom, who put on wacky farces with lots of audience participation.

• Sometimes very special performers, such as Chinese acrobats or stars of the Moscow circus, are showcased in Future World. These acts draw high ratings from kids in every age group.

IllumiNations

This display of laser technology, fireworks, syncopated fountains, and classical music is a real-life *Fantasia* and an unqualified WDW classic. Very popular, very crowded, and a perfect way to end an Epcot day, IllumiNations takes place on the World Showcase Lagoon, and the performance coincides with the park closing time. Try to watch from the Mexico or Canada pavilion, so you'll be able to beat most of the crowd to the exits afterward. (If you're staying at the Swan, Dolphin, BoardWalk, or Yacht and Beach Clubs and thus leaving via the "back door," try the benches in the America or Italy pavilion.)

Shopping

You'll see things in Epcot that aren't available any-where else in WDW: German wines, silk Chinese robes, a collection of piñatas that would put any Mexi-can marketplace to shame, and an entire shop devoted to English teas are all within strolling distance of each other. You don't want to end up carrying those hand-knit Norwegian sweaters and that Venetian crystal around the park with you, however, so if you make major purchases, either have them sent to Package PickUp near the front gate or, if you're staying on-site, have them delivered to your hotel.

AFTERNOON RESTING PLACES AT EPCOT CENTER

- Universe of Energy
- *Circle of Life* or *Food Rocks* in the Land pavilion
- *Honey, I Shrunk the Audience*
- *The Making of Me* in the Wonders of Life pavilion
- The American Adventure
- *Impressions de France*
- Any of the restaurants, since the service is leisurely at lunchtime

BEST RESTROOM LOCATIONS AT EPCOT

The restrooms within the Future World pavilions are always crowded, and those around Innoventions aren't much better. But there are places where you can take a relatively quick potty break:

- Outside the Odyssey Restaurant (Baby Services is also located here, so you can take care of everyone's needs with one stop).
- Behind Kringla Bakeri og Kafe in the Norway pavilion.
- Between the Morocco and France pavilions.
- Near the Group Sales booth in the Entrance Plaza (near the monorail—a good place to stop as you exit the park).
- Within Future World, the restroom near the Garden Grille Room is your best bet. In fact, many of the sit-down restaurants have their own restrooms, which are less crowded.

THE EPCOT DON'T-MISS LIST

- Spaceship Earth
- Body Wars and Cranium Command in the Wonders of Life pavilion
- Test Track
- *Honey, I Shrunk the Audience* and Journey Into Imagination
- The American Adventure in the America pavilion
- IllumiNations
- Innoventions

THE EPCOT WORTH-YOUR-WHILE LIST

- Universe of Energy
- The Living Seas

- *The Making of Me* in the Wonders of Life pavilion
- Living with the Land and *Food Rocks* in the Land pavilion
- Horizons
- Image Works in Journey Into Imagination
- El Rio del Tiempo in the Mexico pavilion
- *Wonders of China* in the China pavilion
- *O Canada!* in the Canada pavilion
- Maelstrom in the Norway pavilion
- *Impressions de France* in the France pavilion

THE SCARE FACTOR AT EPCOT CENTER

Test Track

You'll be blown away by this one. The ride is fast and wild, with lots of sharp turns and steep banks.

Final verdict: Most kids who pass the 40-inch height requirement will love the ride.

Maelstrom in Norway

This ride sounds terrifying: You encounter a three-headed troll, become caught in a North Seas storm, and narrowly miss going over a waterfall backward. The reality is much more tame than the description. Kids seem especially enchanted by the fact that you ride in Viking ships, and the much-touted "backward plunge over a waterfall" is so subtle that passengers in the front of the boat are not even aware of the impending danger.

Final verdict: Some preschoolers are put off by the darkness, the swirling mists, and the troll; fine for 7 and up.

Journey Into Imagination

This attraction, although one of the more child-oriented in Future World, does have a dark segment that explores the world of mystery.

Final verdict: Most kids like Figment and the peppy theme song, but if one of yours is a bit put off, one parent could always wait with him in Image Works while the rest of the family rides.

Universe of Energy

Again, preschoolers have a range of reactions. The dinosaurs bend fairly low over your passing theater car, dripping vines from their mouths. Most kids are such dinosaur junkies that they scream only when it's time to get off, but some children are genuinely frightened.

Final verdict: Probably fine for everyone, unless you have a very young child who has trouble distinguishing reality from illusion.

Body Wars in the Wonders of Life

The Disney PR people must love the word *plunge,* for this ride too is described as "plunging through the human immune system as you dodge blood cells and antibodies at breakneck speed in a race against attacking organisms that threaten to destroy your craft and you!" Makes you breathless just to read it!

Final verdict: Body Wars was rated highly among families responding to the survey—although a few people did mention that the visual effects gave them vertigo, and a few others were put off by the general theme of the ride. ("All that blood," moaned one father.) In general, the ride should be fine for kids over 7, but anyone prone to motion sickness should stay away.

Honey, I Shrunk the Audience

This one seems to gross-out more parents than kids. There is the mice-running-up-your-legs effect and the larger-than-life snake, but most kids were very enthusiastic about this show.

Final verdict: This is one of the more kid-pleasing attractions in all of Epcot. If your child does happen to be unnerved by the special effects, have him take off the 3-D glasses and sit in your lap. That way he won't see the images clearly and won't feel the tactile sensations.

6

★★★★★★★★★★★★★★★★★★★★★★

Disney–MGM Studios Theme Park

DISNEY–MGM STUDIOS

BACKSTAGE STUDIO TOUR

MICKEY AVENUE

THE GREAT MOVIE RIDE

VOYAGE OF THE LITTLE MERMAID

ANIMATION TOUR

TWILIGHT ZONE TOWER OF TERROR

SUNSET BOULEVARD

BEAUTY AND THE BEAST STAGE SHOW

STROLLER RENTAL

HOLLYWOOD BOULEVARD

MAIN ENTRANCE

HONEY, I SHRUNK THE KIDS ADVENTURE ZONE

ECHO LAKE

50'S PRIME TIME CAFE

SUPERSTAR TELEVISION

MONSTER SOUND SHOW

NEW YORK STREET

INDIANA JONES EPIC STUNT SPECTACULAR

HUNCHBACK OF NOTRE DAME STAGE SHOW

MUPPETVISION 3-D

STAR TOURS

GETTING TO THE DISNEY–
MGM STUDIOS THEME PARK

Compared to the MK, getting to MGM is a snap.

• Shuttle buses run approximately every 15 minutes from the Ticket and Transportation Center (TTC), Epcot, and all on-site hotels.

• If you're staying off-site and have a car, note that the MGM parking lot is small. If you get there at opening time, you can forgo the parking lot tram and walk to the front gate.

• If you're staying at the Swan, Dolphin, Board-Walk, or Yacht and Beach Clubs, you're a 10-minute water-taxi ride from the MGM gates.

YOUR FIRST HOUR AT MGM

• Once you're through the gate, one parent can handle stroller rental at Oscar's Super Service Station while the other picks up a map/entertainment schedule at Guest Services or Crossroads of the World.

Note: Unlike those at Epcot and in the MK, MGM strollers are the lightweight "umbrella" type and are easy to load onto the Backstage Studio Tour tram.

• If your kids are old enough and bold enough for a big-deal ride, go straight to the Twilight Zone Tower of Terror on Sunset Boulevard.

Younger kids? If an early show of the Voyage of the Little Mermaid is scheduled, you should head there the minute you enter the gate. Your entertainment schedule will tell you if an 8:30 or 9 A.M. show is planned.

- Pause at the Hollywood Junction Red Car Station, where Sunset Boulevard meets Hollywood Boulevard, to make reservations for either the SciFi Drive-In or the 50's Prime Time Cafe.

Note: These two popular eateries are often closed to reservations within 15 minutes of the park opening. If you're not staying at an on-site hotel and are thus unable to make your reservations by phone, it is imperative that you make them first thing in the morning at the reservations booth, where sample menus for all MGM restaurants are on hand.

- Board the Great Movie Ride.

- Board Star Tours.

- If you haven't had breakfast, check out the pastries at Starring Rolls.

MGM TOURING TIPS

- With the exception of Voyage of the Little Mermaid, save theater-style presentations such as SuperStar Television, the Indiana Jones Epic Stunt Spectacular, the Hunchback of Notre Dame Stage Show, and the Monster Sound Show for afternoon or evening. Tour continuous-loading attractions such as the Twilight Zone Tower of Terror, the Great Movie Ride, and Star Tours early in the day.

- MGM is the park where the newer Disney films are showcased, so parades and shows are constantly being updated. The *Aladdin* parade makes way for the *Toy Story* parade, and then *Hercules* comes through; *Pocahontas* leaves the Backlot Theater and *The Hunchback of Notre Dame* moves in, and so on.

Consult the entertainment schedule and map for the latest offerings, as the changes can be quite abrupt.

• Save the tours for after lunch or early evening.

• The Disney people post a gigantic blackboard at the end of Hollywood Boulevard, keeping visitors updated on approximate waiting times at various attractions. Consult it whenever you're in doubt about what to do next.

Note: If you're in MGM very early as a result of the "Surprise Mornings" program, the blackboard will also inform you which attractions are operative; the whole park doesn't open early for the surprise mornings, but at least four major attractions will be ready to ride.

• The entertainment schedule not only provides showtimes, but also gives you information on the Celebrity of the Day and what shows are taping. If any Disney Channel shows are in production on the day of your visit, Guest Services can tell you how to become a member of the studio audience.

Note: Many of the shows require that audience members be 12, and for some shows, 17.

• MGM is small and easily crisscrossed, so don't feel obligated to tour attractions in any particular geographic sequence. Those 4- and 5-year-olds who would need a stroller in the MK or Epcot can do without one here.

• If you miss an attraction such as the popular Indiana Jones Epic Stunt Spectacular in the afternoon, return in the evening. It's also easier to get tapped for Super-Star Television at one of the less-crowded evening shows.

• Also, after the dinner hour, popular restaurants such as the SciFi Drive-In sometimes accept walk-ins, especially if you're just dropping by for dessert. As at the other theme parks, the restaurants are still serving food after the park officially closes, so if you'd didn't make it into one of the big-deal restaurants earlier in the day, now's your chance.

MGM ATTRACTIONS

Twilight Zone Tower of Terror

The Twilight Zone Tower of Terror combines the spooky ambience of a decaying, cobwebby 1930s-style Hollywood hotel with sheer thrills. The clever preshow, for which Disney spliced together clips from the old TV series in order to allow the long-deceased Rod Serling to narrate the story, invites you to enter an episode of "The Twilight Zone." The story begins on Halloween evening, 1939, when five people boarded the hotel elevator: a movie star and starlet, a child actress and her nanny, and the bellboy. The hotel was struck by lightning, the elevator dropped, and the five passengers were permanently transported into the Twilight Zone. The next morning, the indicator on the elevator was found pointing to the nonexistent thirteenth floor, and the hotel has stood abandoned ever since.

After watching the preshow, guests are directed to a cage "freight" elevator, which ascends—you guessed it—13 stories. You are seated with a lap-bar, and each elevator holds about 20 people. On the way up, the elevator stops to reveal a hallway that literally vanishes before your eyes.

But it's the second stop that will get you. The elevator moves forward past a series of holographic images, the doors eventually opening onto a panoramic view of the park from more than 150 feet in the air. Then you free-fall. It takes only two seconds to hit the bottom, but it's a squealer—and then they haul you up and do it again. (The fall can be computer-programmed in several different ways, ranging from a teasing bungee-style drop, in which you are partially dropped and then relifted to a no-holds-barred plunge.)

The Tower can be crowded, but the line moves swiftly for this 10-minute ride. If you miss it in the morning, return in the evening for an even more intense experience.

The height requirement is 40 inches, and the Tower of Terror is generally too much for kids under 5.

The Great Movie Ride

Housed in the Chinese Theater at the end of Holly-wood Boulevard, the Great Movie Ride debuted as an instant classic. Disney's largest ride-through attraction, it loads steadily and fairly swiftly, but this 25-minute ride draws large crowds and is best toured either early in the morning or in the last hour before the park closes.

Note: Most of the waiting area is inside the Chinese Theater; if you see a line outside, rest assured that there are hundreds more tourists waiting inside, and skip the attraction for the time being.

Each tram holds approximately 30 riders, and your tour guide provides an amusing spiel as you glide past soundstage sets from *Casablanca, Alien, The Wizard of Oz,* and other great films. The Audio-Animatronics figures of Gene Kelly, Julie Andrews, and Clint Eastwood are among Disney's best.

Things suddenly turn ugly as your car stalls and the movie scenes come to life. Depending upon which car you've boarded, you're about to be overrun by either a gangster on the lam from James Cagney or a desperado trying to escape John Wayne. Your tour guide may be gunned down or your tram taken hostage, but don't fret too much. In a later scene, drawn from *Indiana Jones and the Temple of Doom,* expect another stunning twist of fortune—just in time to reestablish justice and guarantee a happy ending.

Star Tours

Motion-simulation technology and a slightly jostling cabin combine to produce the real feel of flight in Star Tours, the MGM version of the highly acclaimed Disneyland ride. With the hapless Captain Rex at the helm, your crew is off for what is promised to be a routine mission to the Moon of Endor. But if you think this mission is going to be routine, you don't know diddly about Disney. "Don't worry if this is your first flight," Rex comforts visitors as they board. "It's my first one, too." One wrong turn later and you're ripping through the fabric of space at hyperspeed, headed toward combat with the dreaded Death Star.

George Lucas served as creative consultant, and the ride echoes the charming as well as the terrifying elements of his *Star Wars* series. The chatter of R2D2, C3PO, and assorted droids make even the queues enjoyable. Star Tours is the best of both worlds, with visual effects so convincing you'll clutch your arm rails, but actual rumbles so mild that only the youngest children are eliminated as potential crew members.

Note: As in Body Wars at Epcot, Disney attendants are happy to help families traveling with children under 3 break up their party so that everyone except the baby gets to ride.

Like the Twilight Zone Tower of Terror, this ride takes only 10 minutes from start to finish, so the lines move at an agreeable pace. It's still better to ride in the morning if you can.

SuperStar Television

Want to belly up to the bar at "Cheers"? Ride the range with the Cartwrights? Show up on "Home Improvement" or chat with Carson? You get your chance at the highly inventive SuperStar Television, where special effects integrate the actions of audience volunteers with footage from well-known TV shows.

To volunteer your services as an actor, show up at the preshow holding area about 20 minutes before the stated performance time. (Showtimes for SuperStar Television, the Monster Sound Show, and the Indiana Jones Epic Stunt Spectacular vary from day to day, so consult the trusty entertainment schedule.) If your kids would like to join the cast of "Gilligan's Island" or be interviewed by Howard Cosell, there's no secret to getting selected. Work your way to the front of the crowd and shamelessly wave your arms; they aren't looking for shy people here. Kids tapped to perform remembered SuperStar Television as the highlight of their MGM day. If you aren't chosen in one casting session, you can always exit the holding area without seeing the show and try again later.

Once you are selected, you're taken backstage for costuming and a brief rehearsal while the rest of the gang files into the 1,000-seat theater. Most volunteers respond ably, and the resulting 30-minute show is usually quite funny. Because of the large seating area, SuperStar Television is a good choice for midafternoon, but if you don't catch it then, try the evening shows, which are never crowded.

The Monster Sound Show

This theater is the smallest at MGM, so check the size of the line before you queue up to watch this "monster" movie featuring Chevy Chase and Martin Short. Audience volunteers add sound effects to the 15-minute film; and when the tape is rolled back, the mistakes are screechingly funny. Most kids love this show—and the SoundWorks exhibits as you exit are also a good way to kill some time. (Especially neat are the Phonic Funnies, which let you dub your own voice into films starring Snow White or Roger Rabbit.) The Monster Sound Show is generally a fine choice for afternoon.

The Magic of Disney Animation Tour

Don't be put off by the name. This 45-minute tour is fun, and the preshow starring Robin Williams and Walter Cronkite is hilarious.

After the preshow a guide leads you through the animation department, where you see Disney artists working on upcoming projects. An animator shows you some drawing techniques and answers questions. You end up in a separate theater, where you see a movie compilation of Disney animated classics.

This is a good choice for afternoon, assuming your kids are over 5 and can understand the significance of what they're seeing. If you don't mind missing the sight of animators at their desks, the evening tours are also a good choice since they're rarely as crowded. The tour is a long one, however, so don't start it unless everyone is relatively chipper and well-rested.

The Indiana Jones Epic Stunt Spectacular

Next to Star Tours and the Twilight Zone Tower of Terror, this is the favorite MGM attraction of teens and preteens. You may think the lines are the most spectacular part of the show, but, because the 2,000-seat theater is so huge, people standing as far back as the 50's Prime Time Cafe are usually seated. Line up about 20 minutes before showtime, and be aware that afternoon shows are sometimes a mob scene. If so, try it again during one of the last two seatings of the evening.

As in the other theater presentations, audience volunteers are chosen. (Your odds of being tapped seem to improve if you show up early and are near the front of the line.) Professional stunt people re-create daring scenes from the *Indiana Jones* series, and this 30-minute show is a great chance to learn how those difficult and dangerous stunts end up on film. The finale is spectacular.

The Backstage Studio Tour

The Backstage Studio Tour, which once took nearly two hours, has now been split into segments to make it more palatable to families with young kids. You can take the 45-minute backlot tour first, then stop and play in the Honey, I Shrunk the Kids Adventure Zone or take in one of the backlot shows before queuing up for the second segment of the tour: the Backlot Pass.

The tour begins with a stop at the special-effects water tank, where audience volunteers re-create a naval battle scene. Then you stroll through the props department before being loaded onto a tram that scoots you through wardrobe and past huge outdoor sets representing a typical small town and a large city. The highlight of the tram segment is a stop in Catastrophe Canyon, where you're caught in a flash flood, an oil explosion, and an earthquake. (If you're sitting on the left side, prepare to get wet.) Later you'll ride behind the Canyon and see how the disasters were created.

After you disembark from your tram, you'll be near the Honey, I Shrunk the Kids Adventure Zone and the Studio Catering Co. snack bar.

Note: Bring your stroller on the tram with you, since you'll disembark far from where you began.

The Honey, I Shrunk the Kids Adventure Zone

The Adventure Zone is based on the popular Disney movie of the same name. "Miniaturized" guests scramble through a world of giant Legos, nine-foot Cheerios, and spiderwebs three stories high. Kids are generally so entranced by all the tunnels and neat little hiding areas that many parents have had to go in to retrieve their tots—and then found that they don't want to leave themselves!

Children 2 to 5 can enjoy the Junior Adventurers area, with a downsized maze and slide where they can play in safety away from the rougher antics of the older kids. It is strongly recommended that toddlers stay out of the three-story spiderweb, which requires that you climb all the way through before exiting—a daunting task for little legs. Families with preschoolers must stay alert inside the Adventure Zone—when a child enters a tunnel or climbs to the top of a slide, it's often difficult to judge exactly where she'll emerge. Ergo, the attraction really should be retitled "Honey, I Lost the Kids."

This attraction is very popular with kids 8 and under. The only complaint? It needs to be about four times larger!

Backlot Show

A themed show runs several times a day in the street behind the Honey, I Shrunk the Kids Adventure Zone. In the past such luminaries as the Teenage Mutant Ninja Turtles and Ace Ventura have been featured; Disney changes the featured star to keep it fresh, and a picture-taking and autograph session follows the performance. Consult the entertainment schedule for showtimes.

Backlot Pass

Disney uses this section to hype whatever movie is presently in the theaters; as this book goes to press, sets and props from *101 Dalmatians* are on display, and the tour includes some fun segments wherein audience volunteers are inserted into the movie, and special effects are explained and reproduced. The tour is fairly long and can be boring for young kids. It's probably skippable—unless you're a *101 Dalmatians* junkie.

Voyage of the Little Mermaid

Using puppets, animation, and live actors to retell the beloved story of Ariel and Prince Eric, Voyage of the Little Mermaid remains one of the most popular shows at MGM. Come early or prepare for an hour-long wait.

The special effects in this 20-minute show are the best Disney has to offer; during the brilliant storm scene, you'll feel that you're really underwater, and the interplay among the cartoon characters and live actors is ingenious. Toddlers may find certain scenes too real for comfort, but everyone else is certain to be dazzled.

MuppetVision 3-D

Look for the hot-air balloon with Kermit's picture and you'll find the *MuppetVision 3-D* movie. The show combines slapstick with sly wit, and everyone from preschoolers to adults will find something to make them laugh. The 3-D glasses in themselves are a kick, and the 20-minute movie is charming, touching—and loud. Although *MuppetVision 3-D* tested highly among kids ages 2 to 5, some parents reported that kids under 2 were unnerved by the sheer volume of the finale.

Note: The preshow is nearly as clever as the main show. Be sure to watch the screens while you're waiting to be admitted into the theater.

The Beauty and the Beast Stage Show

Still red-hot after four years in production, this 30-minute show re-creates musical scenes from the film of the same name. Be at the theater at least 10 minutes before showtime to guarantee a seat, 20 minutes if you want to be near the stage. It's a good choice for afternoon.

Recognizing the enduring popularity of the production, Disney moved it to a large theater on Sunset Boulevard and provided enough shade to make the afternoon shows pleasant. The new Theatre of the Stars, modeled on the Hollywood Bowl, is the perfect setting for this Broadway-caliber show.

The Hunchback of Notre Dame Stage Show

Who is best qualified to tell the story of Quasimodo? Obviously, it's the gypsies who dwell in the Court of Miracles deep beneath the streets of Paris. By combining magic, music, and lots of audience participation, the gypsies create the set using coins, cloth, baskets, rugs, and other objects they've "found" on their travels.

The popularity of such MGM stage shows as Voyage of the Little Mermaid and Beauty and the Beast leaves Disney show producers with a dilemma: How do they keep topping themselves? In The Hunchback of Notre Dame Stage Show, they have opted not to make the special effects bigger, newer, and wilder, but rather to return to age-old magic tricks and illusions. In order to dazzle or confuse their audience, the gypsies do not rely on a pyrotechnic "pow," but rather on transforming one thing into something else: Puppets may change into live performers with the twirl of a cape, and Quasimodo's first bell-ringing appearance is especially dramatic. The best part is that in creating these effects, the "gypsies" use only technology that would have been available in the fifteenth century.

The Hunchback of Notre Dame Stage Show is in the relatively small Backlot Theater. In order to ensure a good seat, you'll need to show up at least 20 minutes early; make it 30 minutes if you want to sit close enough to the stage to be in shady comfort. There are snack bars nearby, and you can bring in food and eat during the show; a juggler/comedian keeps the crowd entertained while you wait.

Afternoon Parade

A themed parade featuring Disney's most current release runs every afternoon. The time (usually 1 P.M.)

and the route are outlined on the map. Stake out curb space 30 minutes in advance during the on-season. Because the parade route is short, the crowds can be 8 to 10 people deep, and no place on the route is substantially less crowded than another. Although short, the parades are popular and extremely well done.

Disney Channel Taping

On given days, Disney Channel shows may be in production on the MGM backlots. If so, a sign will be posted at the front gates, telling which show is taping and when, and instructing you to go to Guest Services if you want to be in the studio audience. Many shows require that audience members be at least 12, others as old as 17.

Watching a taping is time-consuming and involves a lot of sitting, so visitors on a tight touring schedule or those with kids under 12 are advised to skip the taping sessions.

MEETING THE CHARACTERS AT MGM

MGM is a great place to meet the characters. They appear more frequently than at Epcot or in the MK, there are fewer kids per square foot vying for their attention, and certain favorites—most notably the *Aladdin* characters, the Muppets, Beauty and the Beast, the Little Mermaid, Pocahontas, Hercules, and the Hunchback—appear only at MGM. Check the tip board or entertainment schedule for times; then get your camera ready and check out the following locations.

- A variety of characters greet visitors as they enter the park, usually around 8:30 or 9 A.M. The same characters return to the entrances around 3 P.M.

- An even larger variety of characters can be found on both Mickey Avenue and Sunset Boulevard from midmorning on. The shift changes about every 30 minutes, so keep checking.

- If Breakfast with Aladdin is scheduled at the Soundstage Restaurant, it offers your best shot at getting a picture and autograph with these popular characters. There is also currently a lunch buffet featuring the *Hunchback* and *Aladdin* gangs.

- The characters are often found in the Animation Courtyard just outside the Soundstage Restaurant.

- If a parade or ceremony is scheduled for the Celebrity of the Day, the characters will be there in full force. The 3 P.M. parade, although the theme changes, is also a sure bet for seeing characters.

- Periodically, the *Star Wars* crew can be found outside the Star Tours ride.

- The Muppets are sometimes "on location" outside *MuppetVision 3-D*.

FULL-SERVICE RESTAURANTS AT MGM

Although MGM, like the rest of WDW, is hardly a bastion of haute cuisine, the food here is fun, with a far greater variety than you'll find in the MK and more punch to the service. Make reservations by phone if you're staying on-site; otherwise, go to the Hollywood Junction Red Car Station reservations booth on Sunset Boulevard. Reservations are taken each morning for the 50's Prime Time Cafe, the SciFi Drive-In, Mama Melrose's Ristorante Italiano, and the Hollywood

Brown Derby. The reservations booth is a real time-saver, because you can make lunch and dinner reservations simultaneously and see sample menus from all of the restaurants.

As at Epcot, the food is expensive and the service slow, especially at peak dining hours. If you just want to see the inside of the SciFi Drive-In or 50's Prime Time Cafe, make your reservations for 3 P.M. or 10 minutes before the park is slated to close and just have dessert. Certain restaurants such as Mama Melrose's often run special deals where kids eat free. Beer and wine are available.

50's Prime Time Cafe

With its kitsch decor and ditsy waitresses dressed like June Cleaver, the cafe is almost an attraction in itself. Meatloaf, macaroni, milkshakes, and other comfort food are served in a fifties-style kitchen while dozens of TVs blare clips from classic sitcoms in the background.

"Hi, kids," says your waitress, pulling up a chair to the Formica-topped table. "You didn't leave your bikes in the driveway, did you? Let me see those hands." Assuming that you pass her clean-fingernails inspection, "Mom" will go on to advise you on your food choices. "I'll bring peas with that. Vegetables are good for you."

The camp is lost on young kids, who nonetheless love the no-frills food and the fact that "Mom" brings around crayons and coloring books, then hangs their artwork on the front of a refrigerator with magnets. But it's baby-boomer parents, who were raised on the sitcoms the restaurant spoofs, who really adore the place. The tacky Tune-In Lounge next door is decorated in exact replicas of the furniture my parents had in their den 45 years ago.

Much of MGM is dedicated to nostalgia, but it's nostalgia on a small and extremely enjoyable scale. You can fill up at lunch or dinner for about $8 per person, and the s'mores, so huge that they cover the pink Fiestaware plate, can be split by the whole family for dessert. (The dessert menu is on a Viewmaster!)

The Hollywood Brown Derby

Terrific Cobb salad as well as veal, pasta, and fresh seafood are served at the Derby, where, not surprisingly, caricatures of movie stars line the walls. Service, however, is extremely slow, making this a bad choice for families with young kids. Lunch for an adult will run about $10, dinner $15. Dining outside is a good option if the kids are rambunctious, but the inside decor is spiffy, too.

The Hollywood & Vine Cafeteria of the Stars

This large, attractive art deco cafeteria offers a wide variety of salads and desserts and an outstanding rotisserie chicken. The line moves fast and it's nice to see what you're getting. Lunch or dinner will be about $8, breakfast a bit less. (Breakfast is a popular meal here, with fruit plates, eggs and bacon, pancakes, and all the traditional breakfast foods; it's a good alternative to Starring Rolls if you want more than a pastry to start the day.) Reservations are not necessary.

The SciFi Drive-In

At least as campy as the 50's Prime Time Cafe, the SciFi Drive-In seats diners in vintage cars while incredibly hokey movie clips run on a giant screen and carhops whiz by on roller skates. Standard drive-in fare such as milkshakes and popcorn are on the menu, but more-elaborate entrées such as seafood salads and mesquite chicken are also offered. Kids adore the setting and give the SciFi high marks. (Even the food has cute names: A shortcake dessert is dubbed "When Berries Collide.") Dark and relatively quiet even at high noon, the SciFi an excellent way to refresh and regroup after a morning of vigorous touring. Adults should expect to pay about $10 for lunch and $15 for dinner and, once again, portions are enormous.

Mama Melrose's Ristorante Italiano

This restaurant is tucked away near the *Muppet-Vision 3-D* Plaza and serves "gourmet" brick-oven pizza and a wide variety of pasta dishes. Expect a rather wacky New York ambience—sometimes Mama herself turns up to inspect the premises—and fairly quick service. The pizzas are a reasonably cheap alternative for lunch; if everyone wants pasta, expect to pay about $10 a head. Occasional specials allow kids to eat free.

DECENT FAST-FOOD PLACES AT MGM

Soundstage Restaurant

The Soundstage Restaurant is in the Animation Courtyard and provides buffet dining, often with the characters from *Aladdin* or *The Hunchback of Notre Dame*.

The Backlot Express

Located near Star Tours, the Backlot Express lives up to its name and serves up burgers and chicken within minutes. This large restaurant is a good place to grab a bite during the most crowded hours of the day.

Dinosaur Gertie's

Kids can't resist this big green tyrannosaurus. Gertie's is the place to get ice cream while waiting in line for the Indiana Jones Epic Stunt Spectacular.

Starring Rolls

This is your best bet for a fast breakfast, as well as a great spot to pick up cookies, brownies, and pastries for an afternoon snack.

Echo Lake Produce or Anaheim Produce

Stop by one of these fruit stands if you're looking for a fast, healthy snack.

THE MGM DON'T-MISS LIST

- Star Tours
- The Great Movie Ride
- Indiana Jones Epic Stunt Spectacular
- Voyage of the Little Mermaid
- Hunchback of Notre Dame Stage Show
- Beauty and the Beast Stage Show
- SuperStar Television
- Twilight Zone Tower of Terror
- *MuppetVision 3-D*

THE MGM WORTH-YOUR-WHILE LIST

- Magic of Disney Animation Tour
- Honey, I Shrunk the Kids Adventure Zone
- Monster Sound Show
- Backstage Studio Tour
- The parade

THE SCARE FACTOR AT MGM

The Great Movie Ride

The ride begins innocently enough as you drift past re-creations of scenes from classic films. But everyone in my tram, no matter what their age, gave a collective gasp when one movie set "turned real" and our tram driver was killed in a 1930s-style gangland shoot-out. After collecting the jewelry of a couple of the riders, the gangster commandeered our tram for the rest of the ride. "Is this supposed to be happening?" wailed one boy who looked about seven, echoing the thoughts, no doubt, of many of the riders. (If your tram manages to elude the gangster, you'll be held up instead by a rootin' tootin' cowboy, who blows up the town bank in an explosion so real that even riders in the back of the tram feel the blast of heat.) Danger lurks throughout the ride in the form of the alien from the movie of the same name, as well as from *The Wizard of Oz*'s green-faced Wicked Witch of the West, who appears in a cloud of quite-convincing mist.

Final verdict: A couple of scenes are startling and intense, and this ride will have your family debating "How did they *do* that?" for weeks afterward. Although aspects may scare kids under 4, the fact that the tram driver eventually reappears does underscore the fact that it's all "just pretend."

Catastrophe Canyon

As part of the Backstage Studio Tour, you experience how artificial disasters are created in an outdoor set. Your tram shakes with an earthquake and narrowly misses being swept away by a flood.

Final verdict: The tour guide explains how it's all done. Most children find the Canyon the most fun part of the Backstage Studio Tour.

The Monster Sound Show

Despite the somewhat ominous-sounding title, this is really a funny film starring Chevy Chase and Martin Short, with volunteers from the audience providing sound effects.

Final verdict: Not scary at all.

Star Tours

The warnings posted at the entryway are a bit paranoid, for most kids love this attraction, especially if they've seen the *Star Wars* movie series.

Final verdict: Fine for kids over 5, unless they are prone to motion sickness. If so, skip this attraction— the flight-simulation technology is capable of persuading your stomach that you're really moving.

Voyage of the Little Mermaid

The storm sequence is very true to the movie that inspired it, with lightning, thunder, and overhead jets of water combining to convince viewers that they are "under the sea." In addition, the sea-witch Ursula appears onstage.

Final verdict: Unless your child is young enough to be frightened by noise, or was terrified by the storm scenes in the movie, he or she should be able to handle the show. A significant number of kids in the 2-to-5 age range named this their favorite MGM attraction.

MuppetVision 3-D

This show is funny but *loud*. Several parents reported that babies and toddlers were put off by the cannon explosions at the end of the film.

Final verdict: Fine for everyone except sleeping babies and toddlers who might be unnerved by the noise level.

Twilight Zone Tower of Terror

When I toured the Tower of Terror, I noticed any number of 5- and 6-year-olds having a ball. Interestingly, the kids who were frightened by the ride were crying before they even got into the elevator, i.e., it was the atmosphere that got them, not the plunge.

Final verdict: After repeatedly riding with kids of different ages, I've readjusted my thinking on the age recommendation. A hearty 5-year-old can handle this, assuming he passes the 40-inch height requirement.

7

★★★★★★★★★★★★★★★★★★

*The Rest of
the World*

PLEASURE ISLAND

Wildlife of a different sort abounds at the Pleasure
Island Nightclub Theme Park, whose motto is *It's New
Year's Eve every night!* This complex of clubs, restaurants, and shops comes alive at 7 P.M. each evening as
adults 18 and over pay one $19 admission price for un-
limited access to two dance clubs, two comedy clubs, a
country-music bar, a jazz club, and a seventies-style
disco. A different band performs each evening, winding down just before midnight, when a street party
culminates in the New Year's Eve countdown,
complete with champagne, fireworks, and confetti.

If you have a five-day World-Hopper pass, you're
entitled to free admission to Pleasure Island for seven
straight days from first use. (Even if you don't have the
five-day pass, you still shouldn't have to pay full
price—there are numerous discount coupons to be
found in the freebie magazines at your hotel. These
are the only Disney tickets that are regularly discounted.) And if you just want to see the shops and
restaurants of Pleasure Island, there is no admission
charge until 7 P.M., when the clubs open.

Although Pleasure Island is clearly geared toward
adults, some families do bring their kids. This is a wholesome, Disneyesque nightclub environment—no raunchy
material at the comedy clubs, drunks are discreetly
handled, and security is so tight that no one, even the lone
woman traveler, is ever hassled. So if for some reason you
are reluctant to leave your children at the hotel, Pleasure
Island is OK. If your kids are preteens and thus too old for
a sitter but too young for a nightclub, a 24-screen movie
theater lies right across the bridge from Pleasure Island.
You're also just a short stroll from the many shops and
restaurants of the Disney Village Marketplace.

PLEASURE ISLAND TOURING TIPS

• If you choose Pleasure Island for parents' night out, get an in-room sitter for the kids. Most hotel services close down at midnight, and if you stay for the fireworks and street party, you won't be back until after that. With an in-room sitter, the kids can go to bed at their usual hour. (If your hotel doesn't provide in-room sitting, call Fairy Godmothers at (407) 277-3724 before you leave home, or one of the other sitting services listed in Section 8, "Disney World After Dark," page 241.)

• Visit Pleasure Island after your least demanding touring day. There isn't much walking on the island, but dancing is murder on already puffy feet. Pleasure Island is a good follow-up to a day spent at Typhoon Lagoon or Blizzard Beach; since you won't be visiting a major park, you won't lose a day on your multiday pass.

• You won't be pressured to drink in the clubs; but if you do, you'll soon learn that the alcohol is expensive.

• Even if you don't dance, Pleasure Island is worthwhile. Nearby barstools let you watch the dancers, and the comedy clubs and live bands are very entertaining.

PLEASURE ISLAND TOURING PLAN

• Arrive about 7 P.M. Eat at one of the cool new restaurants at the Disney Village Marketplace—such as Wolfgang Puck's, Bongo's Cuban Cafe, the Rainforest Cafe, or Planet Hollywood.

• Take in the Comedy Warehouse first. (The dance clubs don't gear up until later.) This 30-minute show, a combination of improvisation and Disney spoofs, is proof positive that comedians don't have to be profane to be funny. And because so much of the material truly is improvised, some guests return to the Comedy Warehouse several times during the course of the evening, seeing an essentially different routine each time.

• Move to the Neon Armadillo across the street for country-western music with a live band. The free line-dancing classes are a blast, especially after all the participants have had a few "Electric Lemonades."

• For something completely different, try the Adventurers Club, a lavish, eccentric hideaway based on British hunting clubs of the 1930s. You won't be in the bar for long before you realize that some of your fellow patrons are actors . . . and the bar stools are sinking and the masks on the walls are moving. Every 30 minutes or so, a seemingly spontaneous comedy routine erupts among the actors; the seance routines are especially memorable. The biggest hoot is the twice-nightly New Members Induction Ceremony, during which hapless bar inductees are encouraged to learn the club salute, club creed, and all-purpose theme song.

Unfortunately, many people just walk in, peruse the bizarre decor of the place, and leave before they have a chance to really get into this particular brand of comedy. Give it time! The Adventurers Club is definitely worth an hour of your evening. There's nothing like this back home—unless you're from the Congo—and the club is a favorite among Orlando locals.

• Next stop by the Jazz Company, which features live music and draws an interesting crowd. The Jazz Company has a great selection of wine, many offered by the glass, and so many munchies that if you plan to spend a lot of time here, you may not need to eat dinner first. The tables are small, the music relatively subdued, and the clientele more mellow, making this the most romantic of the Pleasure Island clubs.

• At 8-Trax, polyester and disco are still king. It's fun to watch the thirtysomethings sitting in their beanbag chairs, valiantly pretending that they don't remember the words to old Bee Gees hits. The club occasionally spins back even farther in time to late-sixties psychedelia. Sometimes special guests—such as former cast members from "The Brady Bunch"—appear, adding even more camp to the atmosphere.

• Divide your remaining hours between the two dance clubs. The Rock 'n Roll Beach Club offers a live band and an informal pool-shooting, beer-drinking, resort-style ambience. Mannequins is darker and wilder and features canned music, strobe lighting, and a revolving dance floor.

• Be sure to be back outside for the street party (11 P.M. during the off-season, midnight during the summer and holidays) and countdown to New Year's. Flat-out bizarre entertainment can be found up and down the street, running the gamut from female body builders posing in bikinis, a velcro wall begging to be leapt against, and a Russian mime troupe.

• Then grab a cappuccino and sit in the cobblestone courtyard at D-Zertz. You may feel like dancing more, or you may decide it's time to head home to the kids.

PLANET HOLLYWOOD

Planet Hollywood restaurants are always fun, and the one in Orlando is no exception. The giant blue globe parked right beside Pleasure Island holds a terrific restaurant choice for the whole family. Adults will like the good, reasonably priced food and fast, friendly service. Kids love the decor: Props from a variety of movies pack the three-tier eatery, the bus from the movie *Speed* hovers overhead, and even the menus, printed with high-school graduation pictures of stars, are entertaining. Film clips run constantly on giant screens, and the whole atmosphere is heady and fun.

No reservations are taken, and the place can get packed at mealtime; two-hour waits are not uncommon at 6 P.M. Try it at off hours—Planet Hollywood is the perfect spot for a 4 P.M. dinner. Or, since the desserts are among the best in town, stop off for a late-night sweet spree as you're leaving Pleasure Island. (The ebony-and-ivory brownie is beyond comparison.)

Note: If you're interested in T-shirts and memorabilia, they're sold in a separate shop downstairs.

DISCOVERY ISLAND

Just a short ride across Bay Lake is thoroughly unmodern, uncrowded Discovery Island, an 11-acre zoological park. There you'll find walking trails, lush natural vegetation, beaches perfect for picnicking, and hundreds of varieties of animal life. This is not a full zoo, so don't expect to see elephants and zebra; birds and reptiles are the most plentiful animals. Of special interest are the trained birds at Parrots Perch and the Galapagos sea turtles at Tortoise Beach.

Discovery Island launches leave from the MK and Fort Wilderness Campground. If you have a five-day pass, which allows you unlimited access to the minor theme parks, you may enjoy taking a break at Discovery Island. In fact, if you're touring in the MK and would like to escape the bustle of the parks for a couple of hours, buy some fast food inside the MK, then take the launch to Discovery Island for an impromptu picnic. If you don't have a five-day pass, don't spend the time and money ($12 adults, $7 kids 3 to 9) to visit the island; there are undoubtedly similar zoological parks closer to home.

Several of the Wonders of Walt Disney World and Camp Disney programs developed by the Disney Institute are guided field trips to Discovery Island. If your kids have a real interest in nature, the seminars are very worthwhile, offering a behind-the-scenes look at the animal nursery and other things the typical park guest never sees.

RIVER COUNTRY

Billed as an "ol' swimming hole perfect for splashin' and slidin'," River Country was completely over-shadowed by the openings of Typhoon Lagoon and Blizzard Beach. But River Country remains a good choice for families with young kids or anyone who doesn't swim very well. This five-acre park never gets as crowded as Typhoon Lagoon and Blizzard Beach, which are literally 10 times larger. River Country draws far fewer preteens and teens, and the water level in the center of Bay Cove is only about chest-deep on an 8-year-old.

Bay Cove, the largest section of River Country, features swing ropes, two water slides, and White Water Rapids, an exhilaratingly bumpy inner-tube ride down a winding 230-foot-long creek. The nearby swimming pool offers two small but steep slides which shoot riders into midair; kids smack the water eight feet below with such force that they can barely stagger out of the pool and make it up the stony steps to try it again . . . and again. . . .

Younger kids will prefer the Ol' Wading Pool, a roped-off sandy-bottomed section of Bay Cove with four small slides cut into a wall of boulders, designed specifically for preschoolers; since older kids are kept out of this section and the slides empty into a mere 18-inches of water, parents can relax on the many lounge chairs scattered along the Ol' Wading Pool beach.

Again, the five-day pass lets you in gratis, but individual tickets are available at $16 for adults, $13 for kids—or buy a $20 (adult) or $14 (child) combo ticket for River Country and Discovery Island. River Country is a fine place to picnic, and there are a couple of fast-food stands on-site.

Whereas Typhoon Lagoon and Blizzard Beach can take up a whole day, a swift-moving 10-year-old can try out every attraction at River Country in two hours flat. For this reason, it's a good water park to drop in to when the theme parks are sweltering and everyone needs to unwind for a couple of hours.

If you're coming by car or taking a shuttle from the TTC, be aware that the River Country parking lot is quite far from the park. You'll catch a shuttle from the parking lot, drive through Fort Wilderness Campground, and be let out near the gates. Those coming from Fort Wilderness or those who have taken the launch from the Magic Kingdom to Fort Wilderness have only a short walk to the River Country entrance.

RIVER COUNTRY TOURING TIPS

• Although the oversized swimming pool is heated, making fall and spring swimming a delight, it's obviously impossible to heat the bay. River Country is sometimes closed during December, January, and February. Call (407) 824-4321 for details on hours of operation.

• If you don't have a five-day pass, buy your River Country admission tickets at either Guest Services at your hotel or at one of the major theme parks. As the park grows crowded, management sometimes abruptly suspends ticket sales but, if you already have a ticket in hand, they'll let you in.

• Families not returning to their hotels in midafternoon can use River Country to break up a day in the MK. Stow your bathing suits in one of the lockers beneath the Main Street Railroad Station in the morning; then, when the park heats up and fills up in the afternoon, exit the MK and take the launch marked *Campground and Discovery Island.* (The 15-minute boat ride is so pleasant that it almost constitutes an afternoon getaway in itself.) If you're staying off-site, this option is less time-consuming than returning to your hotel pool. After a few hours in the cool waters of River Country, you can hop back on the launch and be in the MK within minutes.

• Many families swear that the perfect time for a River Country visit is on a summer night; the park stays open until 8 p.m., but crowds thin about 5 p.m., meaning shorter waits for the slides and a nearly empty pool.

• Horseback riding is available near the River Country parking lot; if you're planning to try the trail rides during your Disney stay, it makes sense to combine the horseback riding with an afternoon at River Country.

For younger kids, the pony rides and Fort Wilderness petting farm are located right at the River

Country main entrance. The ponies are available from 10 A.M. to 5 P.M., cost $2 to ride, and are incredibly gentle.

• If you think obtaining a rental life vest will better qualify an unsteady swimmer for the slides and tube ride, forget it. The lifeguards have the final say over who is allowed to ride what, and a life vest often tips them off that a child really isn't capable of handling the major slides.

• If you enter River Country early in the morning, head for White Water Rapids first. This is the first attraction to draw lines.

• Remember that you're swimming in a lake, not a pool. The netting does a good job of critter control, but this is not the day to wear your new $90 white swimsuit.

TYPHOON LAGOON

Disney has dubbed its 56-acre Typhoon Lagoon "the world's ultimate water park," and the hyperbole is justified. Where else can you slide through caves, picnic with parrots, float through rain forests, and swim (sort of) with sharks? Typhoon Lagoon opened in 1989 as the largest water park in the world and was instantly so popular that it was hard to get in. The opening of the even bigger Blizzard Beach in 1995 has taken off a bit of the pressure, but it is still difficult to get in to Typhoon Lagoon during peak touring times.

Typhoon Lagoon occasionally becomes so swamped with swimmers that it closes its gates. On four separate days during Easter week 1996, the park became so crowded that no one was admitted after 10 A.M., to the great dismay of families who had put on their bathing suits, swabbed themselves with sunscreen, and prepared for a day in the pools. The moral is: If you're visiting during a holiday or during midsummer, plan to arrive at the water parks at opening time—or wait for evening.

For anyone with a five-day pass, Typhoon Lagoon is free for seven days following first use. Otherwise, admission is $26 for adults and $20 for children 3 to 9, entirely too much to pay for a morning of splashing around.

Typhoon Lagoon Attractions

Humunga Kowabunga

Two water slides propel riders down a mountain at 30 mph. No kids under 48 inches tall are allowed.

Note: If you're female, a one-piece suit is recommended. A young Disney employee informed me that the most desired duty in all of Typhoon Lagoon is to stand at the bottom of Humunga Kowabunga, helping riders out of the chute—apparently at least one woman per hour loses her swimsuit top during the descent.

Storm Slides

Three curving slides deposit riders in the pool below. Kids of any age can ride, but it's suggested that they be good swimmers, because, although the pool isn't deep, you do enter the water with enough force to temporarily disorient a nervous swimmer. Most kids 7 to 11 (and some younger) love these zesty little slides, but if you're unsure if yours are up to it, wait at the edge of the pool where the slide empties so you can help them out.

Note: Each of the three slides—the Rudder Buster, Jib Jammer, and Stern Burner—offers a slightly different thrill, although none is necessarily wilder than the others.

Mayday Falls

This is for white-water tubing enthusiasts. A Disney employee helps you load into the giant rubber tubes and gives you a gentle shove. What follows is a fast, giggly journey that makes you feel like you're about to lose your tube more than once. No kids under 48 inches are allowed.

Keelhaul Falls

This corkscrew tube ride is full of thrills. Kids under 48 inches are provided with a smaller tube, and lots of kids as young as 4 reported that they loved this ride.

Gangplank Falls

Slower, milder, but much bumpier than Mayday or Keelhaul, Gangplank Falls features four-passenger rafts in white water. This is a good choice for families with kids too young for the other white-water rides. Gangplank loads slowly, however, and the ride is short, so hit it early in the morning, especially if you think your kids will want to ride more than once.

Note: If the kids are small, sometimes more than four people are allowed into a raft.

Surfing Lagoon

Machine-made waves up to six feet high hit the beach of this 2.5-acre lagoon. The waves come at 90-second intervals and are perfectly designed for tubing and bodysurfing. Every other hour the pool is emptied of tubes, and the wave machine is cranked up to allow for bodysurfing. A foghorn blast alerts you to when a big 'un is under way. Although the Surfing Lagoon admits everyone, don't take small children too deep during the hours designated for bodysurfing: Every 90 seconds 400 shrieking teenagers will bear down upon your head.

Whitecap Cove and Blustery Bay

The Surfing Lagoon has two small, roped-off coves, where smaller waves lap upon toddlers and babies.

Castaway Creek

This is a meandering 2,000-foot stream full of inner tubes. Guests simply wade out, find an empty tube, and plop down. It takes about 30 minutes to encircle the rain forest, and there is a bit of excitement at one point, when riders drift under a waterfall. There are numerous exits along the creek, so anyone who doesn't want to get splashed can hop out before the falls. In general, this is a very fun, relaxing ride, appropriate for any age or swimming level.

Shark Reef

In this saltwater pool, snorkelers swim "among" exotic marine life, including sharks. The sharks are behind Plexiglas, of course, and not too numerous, so anyone expecting the casting call for *Jaws* will be disappointed. Most of the fun is in getting to view the brightly colored fish up close; if your kids are unsure, the underwater viewing area will give them a greater feel for what snorkeling is all about. Take them down to the viewing area first and let them observe the marine life and other snorkelers and then make up their own minds.

Note: The Shark Reef is a great, safe, controlled first snorkeling experience for kids.

Ketchakiddee Creek

This water playground is sized especially for preschoolers, with geysers and bubblers in the shape of crocodiles and whales, as well as slides and a small white-water raft ride. No one *over* 48 inches is allowed to ride, which is a pleasant change from most of the park rules; parents are encouraged to enter into the area to help their kids. Lifeguards are everywhere, and lots of chairs are set out nearby for adults.

Mt. Mayday Scenic Trail

This footpath leads almost to the top of Mt. Mayday, where the shipwrecked *Miss Tilly* is impaled, and offers great views of the slides and rides below.

BLIZZARD BEACH

Disney's third and largest water park opened in the spring of 1995. When word got out in the travel industry that Disney was opening another water park, there was great speculation as to the theme. Having already designed the ultimate country swimming hole and the ultimate tropical lagoon, what could the imagineers come up with this time?

A melting ski lodge, of course. Blizzard Beach is built on the tongue-in-cheek premise that a freak snowstorm hit Orlando and a group of enterprising businessmen built Florida's first ski resort. The sun returned in due time, and for a while it looked like all was lost—until someone spied an alligator slipping and sliding down one of the slushy slopes. Blizzard Beach was born. The snow may be gone, but the jumps, sled runs, and slalom courses remain, resulting in a high-camp, high-thrill ski lodge among the palms.

Blizzard Beach centers around snowcapped Mt. Gushmore. You can get to the top via either ski-lift or a series of stairs, but how you get down is up to you. The bold can descend the Summit Plummet or the Slush

Gusher, but there are medium-intensity flumes, inner-tube runs, and white-water rafts as well. The motif extends into every element of the park; there is a chalet-style restaurant, Plexiglas snowmen, and innumerable sight gags such as ski tracks running off the side of the mountain. The original skiing alligator has returned as the resort mascot—Ice Gator.

Blizzard Beach was built in response to Typhoon Lagoon's popularity and draws huge crowds. Come early in the morning or prepare for monster waits. A five-day World Hopper pass gets you in free for seven days following first use; otherwise, admission is $26 for adults, and $20 for children 3 to 9.

Blizzard Beach Attractions

Summit Plummet

The icon of the park, this slide measures a whopping 120 feet, making it the longest flume slide in the world, twice as long as Humunga Kowabunga at Typhoon Lagoon. A clever optical illusion makes it seem that riders are shooting out the side of the mountain into midair. The actual ride is very nearly as intense, with a 60-degree drop that feels more like 90. Top speeds on Summit Plummet reach 55 mph, much faster than Space Mountain—and you don't even have a seat belt. The height requirement is 48 inches. In short, this flume is not for the faint of heart.

Slush Gusher

This is another big slide—but with a couple of bumps to slow you down. Still a big-deal ride, Slush Gusher is akin in intensity to Humunga Kowabunga at Typhoon Lagoon.

Runoff Rapids

A separate set of stairs up the back of Mt. Gushmore leads you to these three inner-tube rides. You'll have a choice of tubes that seat one, two, or three people. (The family tubes are designed only for the two open slides. If you want to ride in the dark tunnel slide, you'll have to brave it alone.) The Rapids are great fun, and each path provides a slightly different thrill, so many people try it over and over. Bear in mind that you'll have to carry your own raft up the seven zillion stairs (157 to be exact!); visit early in the morning before your stamina fails.

Snow Stormers

This is a mock-slalom run which you descend on your belly while clutching a foam rubber "sled." The three slides are full of twists and runs that splash water back into your face. If you like, you can race the sledders in the other two tubes to the bottom. Snow Stormers is so much fun that, like the Runoff Rapids, hardly anyone does it just once.

Toboggan Racers

Eight riders on rubber mats are pitted against each other on a straight descent down the mountain. The heavier the rider, the faster the descent, so the attendant at the top of the slide will give kids a head start over adults. Not as wild as the Snow Stormers, this is a good choice for getting kids used to the feeling of sliding downhill on a rubber sled. The two rides share a mat pick-up station at the bottom of the mountain.

Teamboat Springs

The whole family can join forces here to tackle white water as a group. The round boats, which an attendant will help you board at the top, carry up to six people, and the ride downhill is zippy and fun, with lots of splashes and sharp curves. This is one of the best-loved rides in the park, drawing an enthusiastic thumbs-up from preschoolers to grandparents. Since parents and kids can share a raft, this is another good first ride to test young children's response before moving on to the Snow Stormers or Runoff Rapids.

Downhill Double Dipper

This latest addition to the park is an individual tube ride. You go through a water curtain and tunnel, emerge into a free-fall, and then exit through another water curtain. At one point in the ride, your tube is completely airborne. The Double Dipper is fun and addictive, but if your kids are young, test them on the nearby Runoff Rapids first.

Ski Patrol Training Camp

This special section is designed for kids 5 to 9. They can walk across icebergs, swing from T-bars, and test their mountaineering skills. There are medium-intensity slides as well. This is a welcome addition for families who have children too old for Tike's Peak but not quite up to the major slides.

Tike's Peak

This is the preschool and toddler section, with yet smaller slides and flumes, igloo-style forts, and a wading pool that looks like a broken ice-skating rink. A separate section for toddlers ensures that they won't be trampled by overenthusiastic 5-year-olds. There are nearby chairs and picnic areas for parents.

Chair Lift
The chair lift offers transportation to Summit Plummet, Slush Gusher, and Teamboat Springs and is also a fun ride in itself.

Melt Away Bay
Unlike the huge Surfing Lagoon at Typhoon Lagoon, this swimming area is relatively small and offers mild swells instead of big waves. Fed by "melting snow" waterfalls, the attractive pool area is surrounded by chairs and shady huts for relaxing.

Cross Country Creek
This lazy creek circles the park. All you have to do is wade in, find an empty tube, and climb aboard. Expect major blasts of cold water as you float through the "ice cave." (There are exits before the cave if this is just a bit too authentic for you.) It takes about 25 minutes to make a full lap, and this is a pleasant experience for any age.

TYPHOON LAGOON AND BLIZZARD BEACH TOURING TIPS

• The water parks draw a rowdy teenage crowd, which means young kids and unsteady swimmers may get dunked and splashed more than they like. If your children are very young, you might be better off at River Country—or staying in the children's sections (Ketchakiddee Creek or Tike's Peak), which are off-limits to older kids.

Kids 10 and up are allowed to visit the water parks without adults. Some families who are staying on-site send their preteens and teens to the water parks via bus while younger kids are napping in the hotel room.

- Because they're popular with locals as well as tourists, the water parks are extrapacked on weekends.

- In the summer, evenings are a better bet than afternoons. Call (407) 824-4321 or (407) 560-4141 for hours of operation.

- Many visitors arrive with their swimsuits on under their shorts and shirts, which does save time. It's also a good idea to bring your own towels, since towel rental is $1 per towel and they're small. There are plenty of lockers which rent for $5 with a refundable deposit. The locker keys come on rubberized bands that slip over your wrist or ankle, so you can easily keep them with you while in the water.

- Don't bother bringing your own snorkels, rafts, or water wings. Only official Disney equipment is allowed in the pools.
You can "rent" life vests for free, although a driver's license or credit card is required as a deposit. Snorkeling equipment can be picked up for no charge at Hammerhead Fred's near the Shark Reef at Typhoon Lagoon. An instructor runs you through the basics before letting you loose in the saltwater pool.

- Because you're constantly climbing uphill all day, half the time dragging a tube or mat behind you, the water parks are extremely exhausting. If you spend the day at a water park, plan to spend the evening touring passive attractions, like films or shows—or make this your parents' night out and leave the kids with a sitter.

- The water parks are a good place to picnic, although there are also several places to get fast food.

• If your kids have rubberized beach shoes with nonskid bottoms, be sure to throw them in your beach bag. The sidewalks can be slippery and the pavement can be hot.

• The Lost Kids Station at Typhoon Lagoon is across a bridge and so far from the main water areas that lost children are very unlikely to find their way there on their own. At Blizzard Beach it's at Shoeless Joe's rentals, also far from the swimming action. Instruct your children, should they look up and find themselves separated from you, to tell one of the Disney employees. (They all wear distinctive name tags.) The Disney people will escort the children to the Lost Kids Station, and you can meet them there.

Because both parks are full of mazes, with many sets of steps and slides, it's easy to get separated from your party. Have standard meeting places and times for older kids.

• There are two schools of thought on Typhoon Lagoon and Blizzard Beach: Should you go once and stay all day, or go several days for just a few hours at a time?

The advantages of going on only one day are that you save commuting time and, by getting there early in the morning, you can hit the major slides and raft rides before the crowds build. Disadvantages? That's a lot of water activity to cram into just one day.

The advantages of going on several days are that the water parks can cool you off and de-stress you after a morning in the theme parks. Most kids, especially those over 7, love the water parks so much that they'll want to come more than once; and if you have a five-day pass, cost is not an issue. Disadvantages? You have to go through the logistical hassles of parking and lockers more than once, and these parks are too

large to tromp around every day of your visit. Also, by
going every afternoon, you'll be arriving at the most
crowded times of the day, when long lines have formed
for major attractions. And during the summer, you'll
run the risk of arriving after the park has reached
peak capacity and been closed to visitors.

Note: If you don't have the five-day pass and are
thus having to pay $92 just to get a family of four
through the gates, your choice is a simple one: You
have to cram it all into one day or go broke.

Possible solutions are to select a day fairly early in
your WDW visit and make this your "big" trip to
Typhoon Lagoon or Blizzard Beach, the time when you
circle the park and try out everything. After that,
return on a couple of subsequent days and go to only
one attraction. Come back for an hour or two on Tuesday, for example, and spend the whole time in the lagoon
itself. On Thursday you can go directly to the slides. If
it's summer and crowds are a problem, consider
coming in early evening instead of the afternoon.

• Whichever touring method you choose, be sure to
visit a water park early in your WDW visit. Several
families reported that they saved this experience until
late in their trip and then found it was the highlight of
the whole vacation for their kids. "If we'd known how
great it was, we'd have come every day," lamented one
father. "As it turns out, we went to Blizzard Beach
only once—on the morning of the day we were due to
fly out."

• Typhoon Lagoon and Blizzard Beach are often
closed for refurbishing during January and February.
If you're planning a winter trip, call (407) 824-4321 to
make sure at least one of the parks will be open during
the week you plan to visit.

QUIZ: WHICH WATER
PARK IS RIGHT FOR YOU?

This quiz is designed to help you determine which of the three water parks—River Country, Typhoon Lagoon, or Blizzard Beach—is most appropriate for your family. Choose the answer that best describes your family's situation and/or collective opinion.

The most important feature in a water park is:
  A. the slides
  B. the waves
  C. the pools

The ages of our kids are:
  A. preteens and teens
  B. a mix—they're 4, 8, and 11
  C. preschoolers and toddlers

Long lines are:
  A. to be expected—this is Disney World, after all
  B. tolerable at the big-deal rides, but I like to get away from the crowd sometimes
  C. the last thing I want when I'm trying to relax

When we go to a water park, we like to:
  A. go early and stay all day
  B. show up in the evening and use the time to unwind
  C. just drop in for a couple of hours to cool off

I'd most like to lie by the pool with:
  A. who has time to lie by the pool?
  B. the latest Tom Clancy and a piña colada
  C. a big old shade tree and a slice of watermelon

As a family, we're looking for:
A. excitement
B. variety
C. relaxation

And the Answer Is . . .

Mostly *A*'s? Hit the slopes of Blizzard Beach.

Mostly *B*'s? There's a wave with your name on it at Typhoon Lagoon.

Mostly *C*'s? Wade into River Country.

THE DISNEY INSTITUTE

Educational may not be the first word that comes to mind when you think of Walt Disney World, but the Institute is aiming to change all that. The Institute was created specifically to give guests the chance to sample programs in animation, cooking, gardening, photography, tennis, and more than 80 other subjects. Guests can stay in a secluded, campus-like enclave and spend their days taking classes, enjoying the world-renowned performers who appear each evening, and working-out at the spectacular Sports and Fitness Center. Or you can drop in for a one-day class and sample a bit of what the Institute has to offer.

The Disney Institute opened in 1996 in what was once the Disney Village Resort, located near the Disney Village Marketplace and Pleasure Island. The accommodations are either townhouses with full kitchens and sitting rooms, or bungalows with minikitchens. The villas are clustered around a huge lake and the Institute village green. Guests can rent bikes or golf carts or simply walk to classes.

Although the laid-back small-town atmosphere provides much of the Institute's charm, the real draw is the programs. The classes are part of the package—you take as many or as few as you like, with no additional charge. Some classes are designed specifically for kids; others are created for parents and children to enjoy together. See "Camp Disney at the Disney Institute" in Section 1 on page 7 for details on programs for kids 7 to 10 and 11 to 15.

The instructors are the best in their fields, some of them Disney imagineers trained to lead guests through creativity exercises, storytelling, or computer animation "the Disney way." One of the comics from Pleasure Island may be your coach for improvisational acting, or an Institute chef may be on hand to show you the secrets of Mexican cuisine. There is an instructor for every 15 students, and many classes are even smaller, ensuring lots of individual attention.

You can either choose a package that emphasizes a specific skill, such as cooking, or opt for one of the "dabbler" packages, which allow you to try a little bit of everything. It's also OK to choose all your courses individually; the reservations system averages 45-minute phone calls, because the counselors are prepared to talk guests through all the available options.

Most guests request a catalog and preselect their courses, but if a program looks unexpectedly interesting once you arrive, the Institute is quite flexible. Counselors are on hand in the lobby to help guests drop or add programs. People often arrive in Orlando and get fired up to try something they'd never do at home—such as acting or rock climbing. The beauty of the Institute is that it encourages you to stretch your boundaries. Who knows what you might enjoy if you'll just give it a try?

Youth Central is the hang-out place for kids; it has its own kitchen, stereo, big-screen TV, computers, and billiards table. The Camp Disney programs meet and return here. Adults seem to congregate at the whirlpool in the spa area. Although Disney never announces the artist-in-residence in advance, there are several options for entertainment each evening— musical performances, comedians, plays, movies, lectures, and so on. The Institute is its own little world and security is tight, so parents and kids can do some things together and split up for others. The system is designed to encourage both family time and new friendships with Institute classmates.

The 38,000 square-foot Sports and Fitness Center is the cornerstone of the campus. You can either take classes or create your own fitness program using the dozens of beyond-state-of-the-art machines. There's also a full-service spa, a basketball court, and adjacent golf and tennis.

There are three-, four-, and seven-night packages available, some of which include dining in Seasons, the Disney Institute restaurant. With a different menu every night, Seasons is actually four dining rooms in one, the themes corresponding to the seasons of the year. One-day admission to a theme park is included in the package. For information or reservations, call 1-800-4-WONDER. For a free video call 1-800-654-8666.

DISNEY VILLAGE MARKETPLACE AND DOWNTOWN DISNEY

The Disney Village Marketplace has undergone serious expansion in the past few years and is now, along with Pleasure Island, Planet Hollywood, and the AMC theater complex, collectively referred to as "Downtown Disney." When Downtown Disney is complete, it will not only be Orlando's largest shopping and dining complex, but also home to the 1,650-seat Cirque de Soleil Theater, featuring the finest circus acts in the world.

The marketplace offers serious shopping, with twice the selection and half the crowds you'll find in the theme parks. The World of Disney, the largest Disney store on earth, is a sure bet for a variety of souvenirs. If you've been mentally shopping throughout your whole visit (I want the ESPN shirt for Sean, the Mickey salt-and-pepper shakers for Aunt Ruth, and a stuffed Quasimodo for Tracy), World of Disney is the perfect place for one-stop shopping and a good last-day wrap-up to your trip.

The Character Christmas Shoppe is another must-see. Team Mickey, featuring sporting equipment and clothes, is full of unusual souvenirs; a softball "autographed" by all the characters makes a special gift for a young athlete.

There has also been expansion to the restaurants. Newer additions include the Rainforest Cafe, which is a fun place for kids because birds and fish (real) and rhinos and giraffes (fake) surround your table while you eat. Check out the incredible barstools with their zebra and parrot legs. Like the Hard Rock Cafe and Planet Hollywood, the Rainforest Cafe is heavily themed, but since the theme is the jungle, even toddlers can get into the spirit.

You might also want to check out Bongo's Cuban Cafe, which is owned by Gloria Estefan and has the cool ambience of Miami's South Beach. Also new are Wolfgang Puck's Cafe and the House of Blues, which is partly owned by Dan Aykroyd, making Disney Village Marketplace the dining hub of the whole Walt Disney

World complex. The bonus is that people staying on-site without a rental car are no longer tied to the family-style restaurants of the theme parks. Catch a bus to Downtown Disney and you'll enjoy far more sophisticated food.

The marketplace has a small playground, train, and sand area to keep younger kids entertained; if kids 12 and older get restless, they can venture down to the dock at the Buena Vista Lagoon to rent one of the little water sprite speedboats. If you're staying off-site, the marketplace marina is your best option for boat rental. The cost is $15 per half-hour, and younger kids can ride with an adult. Although the boats appear to be flying, they really don't go very fast and are a fun, safe diversion for all ages. (If the whole family would like to get into the act, canopy boats also are available for rent. See "That Sportin' Life: On Water" on page 225.) The marina area is so engaging that I've spent hours roaming the marketplace, getting a jump on Christmas shopping, only to have my family greet me at the end of my spree with those astounding words, "What? You're finished *already?*"

DISNEY CRUISES

In the competitive world of cruise ships, everyone is making way for the Main Mouse. In February 1998 the Disney Cruise Line's first ship, *Disney Magic,* will begin sailing from Port Canaveral to Nassau and Gorda Cay, a private Bahamian island. (A second ship, *Disney Wonder,* will set sail in November 1998.) The full seven-day vacation package will combine a three- or four-day cruise with a stay at Walt Disney World, although you can opt to just take the cruise.

On-board entertainment will be nonstop. The characters, needless to say, are along for the ride, and the theater will showcase a different Broadway-style show each evening, based on a popular Disney movie (such as *Beauty and the Beast*). Want to hang with the kids? The ship will boast a family lounge, featuring both G-rated cabaret acts and game shows in which the audience can participate. There will also be an interactive sports club—the ESPN Skybox—where multiple screens will broadcast sporting events from around the world. The pool is divided into separate areas for children, adults, and those looking for "a more active water experience."

Feel like a little private time? The *Disney Magic* will have the largest number of children's counselors of any ship at sea. The staff will oversee age-specific activities for kids 3 to 12, as well as a teen club. The *Disney Magic* has more than 15,000 square feet of space devoted to the kids' clubs, so don't expect the cramped, depressing child-care centers you may have seen on other ships. Kids are encouraged to don costumes and participate in plays, treasure hunts, and theme parties. After choosing between drop-off child care or private baby-sitting in their cabin, parents can head for one of the three nightclubs or dine in Palo, the adults-only restaurant on the top deck, which offers a stunning ocean view.

The restaurants sound amazing, especially the Animator's Palate. As you enter, the room is black and white; and as you dine, the color of the room begins to change. Colors gradually appear in the character drawings on the walls, on the ceiling, and at your table, with synchronized light and sound accompanying every change in the spectrum. By the end of the meal, the whole room is filled with color. Sounds like the kids may be too entertained to eat.

On shore you can explore Nassau, where the shopping is great and kids can enjoy a horse-drawn carriage ride. (Young kids not up to a day in the market stalls can stay on the ship in the care of the youth counselors.) At Castaway Cay, which is bound to be your favorite stop, you'll enjoy a whole day of beach activities. If your family has never snorkeled, this is a perfect opportunity to learn; the water is clear and warm, and the pace of the instruction is keyed toward beginners.

In short, the Disney cruise sounds like a great plan for a family who needs to "do it all" in the course of a one-week vacation; there is time for the adults to relax alone, get a massage, or have a quiet meal without the kids. And there are also plenty of activities for the whole family. Families whose kids vary in ages are especially sold on the cruises, because the fact that kids are divided into tight age categories makes it equally likely that both your 13-year-old and your 3-year-old will have a new friend by the end of the first day. Let's face it: Nothing is more relaxing than a trip where everyone is happy!

So, are you willing to pay for this bliss? The cost of a cruise is based on the time of year (holidays are the most expensive), length of cruise (the four-day cruise, which includes a whole day at sea, is obviously a bit more than the three-day cruise), and the level of cabin or stateroom you choose. Those in the large staterooms will be staying at the Grand Floridian or another of Disney's luxury resorts during the Orlando leg of the trip; those in smaller, inside cabins will be staying at the corresponding midpriced resorts.

Because you're in your cabin so little during one of these action-packed vacations, cruise veterans advise buying only the level of cabin you need to bunk your crowd comfortably, and to use your savings on shore excursions, such as a snorkeling package. All the rooms are new and nice, so it's just a matter of how much space you're willing to pay for. A cruise for a family of four will cost about $4,000, although obviously many variables affect the bottom line. Call 1-800-511-1333 for more information and specific prices.

DISNEY EXTRAS: PARADES, FIREWORKS, DINNER SHOWS, CHARACTER BREAKFASTS, AND HOLIDAY SPECIAL EVENTS

Don't pack your schedule too tightly. Disney works many wonderful extras into the day, and it would be downright criminal to miss them.

Parades

If you love a parade, you've come to the right place. Included in the festivities are the following:

- Afternoon parade in the MK, usually at 3 P.M.
- The electrical nighttime parade in the MK, which runs at both 9 and 11 P.M. during the busy season and on weekends during the off-season.
- Electrical Water Pageant, visible from the beaches of the Seven Seas Lagoon from 9 to 10:20 P.M. nightly.
- The MGM parade, which features whichever movie Disney is currently hyping. Usually at 1 P.M., but

showtimes vary, so check the daily entertainment schedule.

- Special parades are sometimes planned at Epcot and MGM. Consult the entertainment schedule for times.
- Mind-blowing holiday parades at Easter, Fourth of July, and Christmas.

Note: The nighttime parade in the MK is always amazing—but it runs only periodically during the off-season, so call (407) 824-4321 to see which evenings during your visit the parade is scheduled and make sure you plan to stay in the MK until closing on that date. If you're going in the summer, when two parades run, remember that the 11 P.M. parade is never as crowded as the 9 P.M. one.

Fireworks

A 5- to 10-minute display is seen in the sky above Cinderella Castle at 10 P.M. nightly during the on-season. Just before the fireworks begin, you'll see one of the Magic Kingdom's niftiest—but least advertised—little extras: Tinkerbell's Flight. A young gymnast, dressed in tights and zestily hacking the air with a magic wand, slides down a wire suspended from the top of Cinderella Castle to a rooftop in Tomorrowland.

Fireworks close the day year-round at Pleasure Island and during the on-season at MGM.

IllumiNations

Don't miss this laser, fountain, light, and music extravaganza at closing time each evening at Epcot. See "IllumiNations" in Section 5, page 159, for more information.

Dinner Shows

All dinner shows should be booked before you leave home by calling (407) 939-3463. Reservations are accepted at the time you book your room for on-site guests, 60 days in advance for off-site guests, and are especially crucial for the Hoop-Dee-Doo Musical Revue. The on-site dinner shows are as follows:

Hoop-Dee-Doo Musical Revue

The Revue plays three times nightly (5, 7:15, and 9:30 P.M.) in Pioneer Hall at Fort Wilderness Campground. You'll dine on ribs and fried chicken while watching a hilariously hokey show that encourages lots of audience participation. Prices are $37 for adults and kids over 12, $19.15 for kids 3 to 11.

Polynesian Luau

You'll enjoy authentic island dancing and not particularly authentic island food at this outdoor show at the Polynesian Village Resort. The two seatings are at 6:45 P.M. and 9:30 P.M. Prices are $33 for adults and kids over 12, and $17 for kids 3 to 11.

A better choice for families with young kids is Mickey's Tropical Luau, which features the characters and the Polynesian dancers and is presented at 4:30 P.M. Prices are $31 for adults and kids over 12, and $15 for kids 3 to 11.

The All-American Backyard Barbecue

This new outdoor show takes place right across from Pioneer Hall at Fort Wilderness, where the Hoop-Dee-Doo Musical Revue plays. You'll get all-you-can-eat barbecue with classic picnic fixins', while you watch dancing and singing. The Disney characters will be on hand. The show runs Tuesday, Wednesday, and Thursday nights only, with times varying with the season, so call (407) WDW-DINE for complete information. Prices are $35 for adults, $25 for kids 3 to 11.

Note: If you're staying off-site and don't want to return to the WDW grounds in the evening or if you've waited too late to book a Disney show, be advised that Orlando is chock-full of engaging family-style dinner shows which can be easily booked on the afternoon of the show. See "Off-site Dinner Shows for the Whole Family" in Section 10, page 323, for details.

Character Breakfasts

The character breakfasts take at least a couple of hours and probably should be skipped if you're on a tight touring schedule or are watching your pocketbook carefully. But families who stayed at WDW for four or five days gave the breakfasts very high marks, especially if they scheduled them near the end of their stay, when the kids had had plenty of time to warm up to the characters. Families who schedule their character breakfast on the last day of their visit also note that it then doesn't "mess up the day" so badly, since the last morning of your trip is usually broken up anyway by the 11 A.M. check-out time at most Orlando hotels.

The food is pedestrian at the character breakfasts, but who cares? Since it takes a while to eat and meet all the characters (usually six or seven circulate among the diners), either come early or, if you're able to make a reservation, try to book the first seating of the day. Prices generally run about $14 for adults, $8 for children. The more-elaborate Sunday brunches are also more expensive: about $19 for adults, $11 for kids.

Many of the Disney hotels host continuous-seating buffets. Most of the time, reservations are not accepted for the buffets; but during the busiest seasons, you can book in advance. To confirm times and prices and see if advance reservations are being accepted for the time you'll be visiting, call (407) 939-3463 before you leave home.

Note: The times, prices, and locations of the character breakfasts are constantly changing, so be sure to confirm the following information before you leave home.

Disney Character Breakfast Buffets

- *The Contemporary Resort.* 7:30 to 11:30 A.M. at Chef Mickey, featuring the "classic" characters, such as Mickey, Minnie, Pluto, and Goofy.

- *The Polynesian.* 7:30 to 11 A.M. at the Ohana Restaurant. Minnie is your hostess for this tropical-themed buffet featuring the classic characters.

- *The Grand Floridian.* 7:30 to 11 A.M. at 1900 Park Fare. The crew from *Mary Poppins* is featured.

- *The Beach Club.* 7:30 to 11 A.M. at Cape May Cafe. Goofy is your host; expect the classic characters in nautical attire.

- *Wilderness Lodge.* 7:30 to 11 A.M. at Artist Point, usually featuring the *Pocahontas* characters, although sometimes it's Goofy, Pluto, and Chip 'n Dale in western garb. Ask when you make your reservations.

- *Disney's Old Key West.* 7:30 to 10:15 A.M., Wednesday and Sunday only. This show features Pooh, Tigger, and the gang. Reservations are recommended.

Note: Although locale and theme vary, there is always at least one character breakfast at the Disney Village

Marketplace, such as Breakfast with Captain Mickey at Fulton's Crab House. If you're staying off-site and a marketplace location would be more convenient to you than breakfast at an on-site hotel, call (407) 939-3463 to see what's available during the time you're visiting.

Character Breakfasts Within the Theme Parks

- *In the Magic Kingdom.* Once Upon a Time Breakfast at King Stefan's Banquet Hall in Cinderella Castle, 8 to 10 A.M. The characters from *Cinderella* are featured. Theme park admission is required. *Note:* During busy seasons, a separate breakfast is sometimes offered at the Crystal Palace.
- *At MGM.* Breakfast and lunch in the Soundstage Restaurant, 8:30 A.M. to 4 P.M., featuring the *Aladdin*'s Genie and Jafar, and Meeko and Governor Ratcliffe from *Pocahontas.*

Note: Disney originally planned the in-park breakfasts to be seasonal, but they've proven so popular that they're now available year-round. Policy on reservations fluctuates, so call (407) 939-3463 before you leave home to see if you can book a theme park breakfast in advance.

Dinner with the Disney Characters
If your family isn't much for breakfast, you can also see the characters in the evening.

- *1900 Park Fare in the Grand Floridian.* A character buffet is offered from 5 to 9 P.M. at $22 for adults and kids over 12, $11 for kids 3 to 11.
- *The Liberty Tree Tavern in the MK.* A patriotic dinner with the characters dressed in Revolutionary War–era costumes. Make reservations in advance by calling (407) 939-3463.

Jolly Holiday Packages, Featuring Mickey's Very Merry Christmas Party

Walt Disney World is at its most magical during the holidays. Hours are extended, special parades and shows debut, and a meet-the-characters show and party runs on selected evenings. If you fantasize about seeing it snow on Main Street, this is your chance. Tickets for Mickey's Very Merry Christmas Party should be purchased in advance, or are included in a Jolly Holidays Package, an all-inclusive holiday deal. Call (407) W-DISNEY for details.

It is quite possible to celebrate Christmas at Disney without getting caught in the crush. The decorations go up just after Thanksgiving, and the special shows, packages, and holiday parties begin soon thereafter. A family visiting early in December can see all the special stuff—except, of course, for the Christmas Day parade—without having to face the harrowing holiday crowds. If school schedules rule out an early-December trip, note that the week before Christmas is slightly less hectic than the week between Christmas and New Year's.

When my family visited last Christmas, we were agog at the hotel decorations. Aladdin's hometown of Agrabah was reconstructed out of gingerbread at Port Orleans; the Yacht and Beach Clubs offered the gingerbread villages of the Little Mermaid and Belle. The on-site hotels hosted fun parties for their guests, with visits from Santa, stockings for the children, eggnog and cookies, and Victorian carolers giving a homey feel to a hotel holiday.

Each hotel has its own themed trees as well: a nautical tree for the Yacht Club, starfish and seashells at the Beach Club, Native American teepees and animal skulls at Wilderness Lodge—and the sweeping pink poinsettia tree at the Grand Floridian is a classic. The themed decorations are so drop-dead fabulous that Disney offers actual Christmas tours of the resorts, which are popular with Orlando locals. So if you're visiting WDW between Thanksgiving and New Year's, be sure to save some time just to check out the lobbies of the on-site hotels.

THAT SPORTIN' LIFE: ON WATER

Most on-site hotels have lovely marinas with a variety of watercraft to meet the needs of every age group.

The two major recreational lagoons in WDW are the Seven Seas Lagoon, which is in front of the MK and serves Fort Wilderness and the MK resorts, and the Buena Vista Lagoon at the Disney Village Marketplace. In addition, the Yacht and Beach Clubs share a lagoon with the Swan and the Dolphin; and the Caribbean Beach Resort, Coronado Springs, Port Orleans, and Dixie Landings all have their own canals, lagoons, and watercraft.

Because rates at WDW are raised frequently, it's not a bad idea to confirm prices in advance. In the on-season, reservations are a good idea. You can make them from your hotel room.

Note: You do not have to be a guest of an on-site resort to rent the boats, although the marina will ask for either a resort ID or a WDW ticket, along with a current driver's license for the larger boats. If you're staying off-site and don't want to bother commuting to an on-site hotel, try the Disney Village Marketplace, where water sprites and canopy boats are available.

• *Boat Rental.* The Disney fleet includes water sprites ($15 per half-hour), sailboats ($11 per half-hour), pontoons ($33 per hour), pedal boats ($6 per half-hour), and canoes ($6 per hour). The most popular are the water sprites, those zippy little speedboats you see darting around the Buena Vista and Seven Seas Lagoons. Drivers must be 12 years old, although kids of any age will enjoy riding alongside Mom or Dad.

• *Water-Skiing.* A boat, a driver, and full equipment can be rented at Fort Wilderness, the Polynesian, the Grand Floridian, and the Contemporary marinas. The cost is $82 per hour for up to five people. Reservations can be made 14 days in advance by calling (407) 824-2621.

• *Fishing.* Angling is permitted in the canals—but not in the lagoons or lakes—around Fort Wilderness Campground. Rods and reels are for rent at the Bike Barn, and you can either drop a line from shore or take a canoe or pontoon boat deeper into the canals. Guided two-hour expeditions leave three times a day, and up to five people can be accommodated for a $148 fee, which includes the boat, the guide, the equipment, and snacks. Make reservations up to 14 days in advance by calling (407) 824-2621.

Note: If your kids just want to play around with the idea of fishing, you can drop a line for catfish at Ol' Man Island at Dixie Landings. Guests of Dixie Landings and Port Orleans also have their own fishing excursions available. Call (407) 934-5409 for details.

• *Parasailing.* If you're up—way up—for something different, you can parasail high above the Seven Seas Lagoon. The cost is $48 per person, and riders must be at least 42 inches tall. Kids can ride in tandem with a parent, but they'll still have to pay.

Rides leave daily from the Contemporary Resort marina and reservations must be made in advance. Call (407) 824-1000, ext. 3586.

• *Swimming.* All the WDW hotels have private pools, but the Swan and Dolphin pools are the best for serious swimmers, because they have lanes reserved for laps. The newer resorts—the Yacht and Beach Clubs, Wilderness Lodge, Coronado Springs, the BoardWalk, Port Orleans, and Dixie Landings—boast elaborately themed pool areas, some of which almost qualify as mini–water parks.

THAT SPORTIN' LIFE: ON LAND

• *Tennis.* Several on-site hotels (the Contemporary, the Grand Floridian, the Yacht and Beach Clubs, the Disney Institute Villas, the Swan, and the Dolphin) have courts that can be reserved 24 hours in advance. Call (407) 824-3578 for details. The tennis courts at Fort Wilderness and Disney's Old Key West operate on a first-come first-served basis.

There is considerable variation in fees. A court costs $10 an hour at the Contemporary, $15 at the Grand Floridian, Swan, and Dolphin; but tennis is free at Disney's Old Key West and the Yacht and Beach Clubs. If you'd like private lessons or to participate in a clinic, consider staying at the Contemporary, which has lessons for $50 per hour, $30 for a half-hour. (You can get a $50 package that allows the entire family court time for the duration of your stay.) The Contemporary also runs clinics, which include videotaped analysis of your play by the club pro. Call (407) 824-3578 for details.

The Grand Floridian, though not the tennis haven that the Contemporary is, also offers lessons at $50 an hour.

• *Golf.* There are now five courses on the WDW grounds, with greens fees running about $100 for WDW hotel guests, about $115 for those staying off-site. With such prices, anyone planning to golf a lot should consider the World Adventure or some other package. (Magic Kingdom Club members also get price breaks.) Or play in the early evening, when twilight fees drop to as low as $50.

The five courses are the Palm and Magnolia, which are fairly demanding and located near the MK; the Lake Buena Vista Course, which is near the Disney Institute Villas; and Osprey Ridge and Eagle Pines, which share the Bonnet Lakes Golf Club. Beginners and kids are better off at the nine-hole Oak Trail near the Magnolia, which is a walking course with fees of $24 for adults and $12 for kids under 17. (Two adults can get a reduced rate of $32, and two kids can play for $16.)

To reserve a tee-off time or arrange for participation in a golf clinic, call (407) 824-2270. WDW guests can make tee-off and lesson reservations up to 30 days in advance; those staying off-site can (and should) make reservations seven days in advance.

• *Miniature Golf.* A welcome addition to Disney's slate of family-oriented activities are two 18-hole miniature-golf courses across the street from Disney–MGM Studios. Fantasia Gardens is fun to look at, because of the fountains and whimsical statuary of characters from the classic movie *Fantasia,* but the course itself is fairly challenging, with caves, tunnels, and moving obstacles.

The second course, Fantasia Fairways, is a miniature of a real golf course, with sand traps, water hazards, and roughs. The holes are up to 100 feet long, but you play them with a putter. It's difficult enough to drive a veteran golfer to curses, so it's probably not a good choice for kids.

The courses can be crowded, but different enough from the miniature-golf course back home to justify the time and money spent. Fantasia Gardens is open until midnight, and the crowds thin out considerably after 9 P.M. Prices are $9 for adults, $8 for kids.

• *Running.* Jogging trails traverse the grounds of nearly every WDW hotel. Consult Guest Services for a map. Fort Wilderness has a 2.3-mile exercise trail complete with posted period stops for chin-ups, sit-ups, and a host of other tortures. The sprawling Caribbean Beach Resort and Wilderness Lodge Campground, with its invitingly shady trails, are also good choices for runners.

• *Horseback Riding.* Guided trail rides leave the Fort Wilderness grounds five times a day. Surprisingly and disappointingly, children under 9 are prohibited, even though the horses are gentle and the pace is slow. The cost is $17, and reservations can be made up to 14 days in advance. Call (407) 824-2832 before you leave home for reservations and information.

If younger kids really want to saddle up, short pony rides are offered from 10 A.M. to 5 P.M. during the on-season at the petting farm at Fort Wilderness for $2. No reservations are necessary, but to verify that the ponies are available on the day of your visit, call (407) 824-2832.

• *Health Clubs and Spas.* The Contemporary, Grand Floridian, Swan, Dolphin, Yacht and Beach

Clubs, Coronado Springs, and Disney's Old Key West all have health clubs. The cost is $10 per visit or $8 per visit if you'll be there more than three days—well worth it when you consider that most of the health clubs have whirlpools and saunas, a nice wrap-up to a day spent walking around the theme parks. Most of the health clubs are for the exclusive use of the hotel's guests, but the facilities at the Contemporary, Swan, and Dolphin are open to all on-site guests.

If working out is really important to you, stay at the Disney Dolphin, whose Body by Jake health club is the most complete, hands-down. The equipment is state-of-the-art, the class schedule is varied, and you can even book a session with a personal trainer.

Another option is a stay at the Disney Institute. The Sports and Fitness Center there is one of the most complete in Florida, with an amazing variety of machines; full tennis, golf, and basketball facilities; and daily classes in everything from boxing to yoga. Limited use of the facilities is currently available on a daily basis, although this is subject to change when the Institute is full. Call (407) 827-1100 for details.

There are also full spa facilities at the Grand Floridian and Disney Institute. An aromatherapy massage can be a lifesaver on day four of a seven-day trip.

• *Cycling.* Bikes ($6 an hour or $10 a day) or tandems ($7 an hour) can be rented at the Disney Institute Villas, the Bike Barn at Fort Wilderness, or at Dixie Landings, Port Orleans, Disney's Old Key West, the Wilderness Lodge, and the Caribbean Beach Resort.

ESPN CENTER

Sports enthusiasts will applaud the opening of the ESPN sports club as part of the BoardWalk complex near Epcot. The center contains a broadcast and production facility (meaning athlete celebs are often on hand) and the ultimate sports bar, featuring—and I'm quoting—"the best ballpark cuisine from around the country." This bold claim translates into sandwiches, salads, and burgers, all sized for hearty appetites; try the Bloody Mary chili. And just so you won't miss a single play, 70 TVs carrying games and sport-related shows blare constantly—even in the bathroom!

There's a shop and arcade next door. Most fun of all are the interactive virtual-reality games; you can swap shots with your favorite tennis pro or have all the excitement of playing in the NFL, with none of the bruises.

DISNEY'S WIDE WORLD OF SPORTS

This new multimillion-dollar complex will house competitions, tournaments, and vacation-fitness activities with facilities to accommodate 25 different sports. Beginning this year it will be the spring-training home of the Atlanta Braves and it is already the training site for the Harlem Globetrotters. As the facility is completed in stages, expect Disney to play host to a wider variety of tournaments and sports festivals.

It worked for rock stars, models, and movie actors, so why not athletes? The All Star Cafe is due to open at the sports complex as this book goes to press. Operated by the same savvy gang that run the Planet Hollywood chain, All Star Cafe's investors include

Shaquille O'Neal, Joe Montana, and Andre Agassi. When completed, the restaurant will be three stories high, chock-full of athletic memorabilia, and with non-stop big-screen viewing of sporting events and ball games. The menu is causal, the atmosphere loud, the souvenirs funky.

COMING SOON: DISNEY'S ANIMAL KINGDOM

Disney is doing everything it can to keep information about its fourth theme park under wraps. The park is obviously devoted to animals, both living and mythic. At the center will be the 14-story Tree of Life, an exhibit about ecology, which will serve as a park icon much like Spaceship Earth does at Epcot. Animal Kingdom will be laid out much like the Magic Kingdom is: divided into six sections, radiating from a central hub. The lands are: Africa Beach, Bradley Falls, Asia, Dinoland, Genesis Garden, and Dragon's Cave. A body of water called Discovery River will run through the park, leading visitors from one land to another.

In drawings you see a tram going across a river full of crocodiles, and another picture shows a dragon breathing fire at a passing boat. Real animals are showcased alongside Audio-Animatronic fantasy beasts, creating a park that is partly zoological and partly mythological.

Here's what you can expect: The park is billed as Disney's largest—more than 500 acres, compared with 107 for the MK, 300 for Epcot, and 157 for MGM. Most of the space is undoubtedly for animal habitats, such as the projected 100-acre African savanna; other large, open areas will be for guests to explore in boats, trains, and jeeps. The park will house more than 1,000 live animals representing 200 different species. More information will be available—and a rise in ticket prices will undoubtedly occur—as Animal Kingdom gets closer to its spring 1998 debut.

8

★★★★★★★★★★★★★★★★★★★

Disney World
After Dark

DISNEY AFTER DARK: WITH THE KIDS

Is there life in WDW after 8 P.M.? Sure there is. The crowds thin, the temperature drops, and many attractions are especially dazzling by dark. Orlando is actually a kiddie version of Las Vegas—a town that naps but never sleeps—where miniature golf courses and McDonald's stay open all night. During peak seasons the major theme parks stay open until midnight, so it's easy to have fun at night. But, needless to say, the particular kind of fun you'll have depends on whether or not the kids are with you.

Evening Activities for the Whole Family

The Evening Parade in the MK

SpectroMagic is the current incarnation of Disney's ever-popular Main Street Electrical Parade, blending lasers, lights, and fireworks for a dazzling display. SpectroMagic runs every night during the on-season, but only on selected evenings during the off-season. In the busiest weeks, there are two showings: the 11 P.M. is rarely as crowded as the 9 P.M.

Note: Whatever it's called at the time you visit, the parade is a must-see. If you're visiting during the off-season, plan your schedule to ensure that you'll be in the MK on one of the evenings it's slated to run.

The Electrical Water Pageant

If you're staying on-site, the Electrical Water Pageant may actually float by your hotel window; it is staged on the Seven Seas Lagoon, which connects the Polynesian, Contemporary, Grand Floridian, and Fort Wilderness resorts. Times do vary with the season, but generally the Pageant is visible at 9 P.M. from the Polynesian, 9:20 from the Grand Floridian, 9:45 from Fort Wilderness, and 10:05 from the Contemporary. (Call Guest Services at your hotel for exact showtimes.)

If you're not staying on-site, simply ride the monorail to the resort of your choice. The Electrical Water Pageant plays every night, even during the off-season. Although a much shorter and less elaborate show than SpectroMagic, nothing can beat the effect of multi-colored lights twinkling on dark water. Besides, by 9 P.M. most kids would rather sprawl on a beach than camp on a curb.

Movies

If you're staying on-site, check out the offerings in the theater of the Contemporary Hotel. Two different Disney classics show each night at 7 and 9 P.M. Movies are also shown at the evening campfire at Fort Wilderness (with Chip 'n Dale in attendance); and in many Orlando hotels, the Disney Channel is available 24 hours a day.

The 24-screen AMC theater adjacent to Pleasure Island is a good place to park older kids and teens while parents try out the clubs. Call (407) 827-1300 to see what's playing.

Arcades

It's no secret that kids flip for arcades, especially the mammoth Fiesta Fun Center in the Contemporary Resort. Even hard-core pinball junkies are bound to find games they've never seen before. The most state-of-the-art games are at the BoardWalk arcade adjacent to the ESPN center.

Downtown Disney

The Disney Village Marketplace and Pleasure Island stores stay open past the park closing times. Some families wait to shop until late at night, and the restaurants here serve past 10 P.M. as well.

IllumiNations at Epcot

IllumiNations can be viewed from anywhere around the World Showcase Lagoon at Epcot closing time. With fireworks, laser lights, stirring music, and choreographed fountains spurting in three-quarter time, IllumiNations is a definite must-see.

Fireworks

A rousing fireworks display can be seen from anywhere in the MK about 10 P.M. during the on-season. The show is short but exciting, and at holiday times a more extensive fireworks extravaganza is presented. Be there a few minutes earlier to witness Tinkerbell's Flight.

Fireworks also close Pleasure Island each night, and MGM is currently signing off with an elaborate display called Sorcery in the Sky.

The Rides at Night

Those attractions with the two-hour lines at noon are far more accessible by night, so it's worth revisiting any ride you passed up earlier in the day. In the MK, Big Thunder Mountain Railroad is much more fun in the dark; Splash Mountain feels like a totally different ride, and Cinderella's Golden Carousel is especially magical at night.

At Epcot it is almost always easy to tour Journey Into Imagination and see *Honey, I Shrunk the Audience* after 7 P.M. (In fact, any Future World attraction is easily boarded during the dinner hour, when everyone heads out to dine in the World Showcase.) At MGM, try SuperStar Television or the Indiana Jones Epic Stunt Spectacular; not only are the shows less crowded, but volunteer wannabes stand a better chance of being chosen during the evening shows, especially at SuperStar Television.

Night Swimming

Blizzard Beach, Typhoon Lagoon, and River Country all run extended hours in the summer, and the crowds are far thinner after 5 P.M. It stays hot in Orlando well into a summer evening, and, since you don't have to worry about heat exhaustion or sunburn, many families with young kids actually prefer evening swimming. Hotel pools stay open very late as well, some until after midnight.

Miniature Golf

Fantasia Gardens, across the street from Disney–MGM Studios, is far less crowded after 9 P.M.

DISNEY AFTER DARK: WITHOUT THE KIDS

Why would any decent parent seek a sitter while on a family vacation? Consider this scenario:

Meaghan's sucking the inside of her mouth. Loudly. Mom keeps making everyone stop while she readjusts the strap of her shoe to accommodate the blister she picked up halfway around the World Showcase Lagoon. You spent $148 to get through the gates of Universal Studios, specifically to ride those highly publicized high-tech rides you've heard so much about, and Devin spends the entire afternoon feeding quarters into the same arcade game that's in the mall back home. Dad has been singing the first line—and only the first line—of "Zip-A-Dee-Doo-Dah" since Thursday. You've asked to see the kiddie menus from nine different restaurants in nine different Epcot countries, and you end up at the American pavilion fast-food joint because Kristy won't eat anything but a hotdog. It's 108 degrees in the shade, this trip is costing $108 an hour, and that infernal sucking sound is getting on the last nerve you have left. In short, you have third-day-itis . . . and it's only the second day of your trip.

Although it may seem un-American or even sacrilegious to suggest building time apart into the middle of a family vacation, the truth is that everyone will have more fun if occasionally you break up the group for a while. Even the most devoted families aren't accustomed to being together 24 hours a day—for every meal, every ride, every potty stop. Every minute.

Many Orlando hotels have responded with programs designed to get the kids involved with other kids so that parents can have some peace and privacy. Kristy can eat her hotdog, Meaghan can give herself hickeys, and Devin can play Cosmic Invaders 77 straight times without parental glares. The adults can dare to order a meal that will take three hours to enjoy and linger over their coffee. Everyone returns refreshed and recharged, with some happy stories to tell, and you can start the next day actually glad to be together again.

If you decide to schedule a parents' night out during your trip, you'll soon learn that Orlando offers an array of child-care options. Several of the on-site hotels have full-fledged kids' clubs, and where else on earth can your child be bedded down by a real-life Mary Poppins? At the off-site hotels, there is a large range in cost and quality among the offered programs. Many off-site programs are free to hotel guests (at least during certain hours), which can mean big savings for parents.

The key point is to make your plans before you leave home, either by selecting a hotel that has a kids' club or by arranging for an in-room sitter. If you suddenly get an urge for fine dining at 4 P.M. on a Saturday in July, it will be hard to find a sitter. But if you've checked out your options in advance, it's a breeze.

In-Room Sitters

You'll need to arrange for an in-room sitter if any of the following conditions apply.

- *You Have a Child Under the Age of 4.* Very few of the organized kids' clubs admit children younger than 4, and most require that they be potty-trained.

- *You Plan to Be Out After 12 A.M.* Most kids' clubs close down at midnight, some as early as 10 P.M. Parents headed for Pleasure Island or Church Street Station, where the action doesn't begin to heat up until 10 P.M., need in-room sitting.

- *Your Kids Are Exhausted.* If you know in advance that you plan to employ an all-out touring schedule, or your children fall apart after 8 P.M., hire an in-room sitter who can put them to bed at their usual time. Most of the kids' clubs at least try to put preschoolers down in sleeping bags by 9 P.M., but this can involve moving them, and possibly waking them, when parents return.

- *You Have a Big Family.* Even with the add-on per-child rate, you'll come out cheaper with an in-room sitter than trying to book four kids into the Neverland Club.

If you decide you'll need in-room sitting, begin by contacting your hotel. Many are happy to arrange the sitting for you through one of the licensed and bonded agencies serving Orlando hotels, and this saves a bit of hassle. Guest Services personnel are also apt to give you a good recommendation on which service to try; if guests aren't pleased with a sitter or a service, the hotel is undoubtedly the first to hear about it.

Want to make your own arrangements? For guests staying on-site, KinderCare provides trained sitters for all the Disney hotels, if you call (407) 827-5444 at least eight hours in advance. The rate is $9 an hour, $11 an hour for two kids, and there's a four-hour minimum.

At least six independent agencies dispatch sitters to the off-site hotels, but the following two have received especially high marks from our readers:

Super Sitters   (407) 382-2558

ABC Mothers   (407) 857-7447

These services stay busy during the summer months, so it's not a bad idea to book them before you leave home. Rates are typically about $8 an hour with a four-hour minimum and an extra-child charge of $1 an hour per child. A $5 transportation fee is also common, meaning that in-room sitting for two kids for four hours would run $41—not a cheap option, but for many parents it's well worth the cost.

The independent agencies can be quite inclusive, with service available 24 hours a day, seven days a week. For families willing to pay the extra bucks, sitters will take the kids out to a fast-food place for supper or even to area attractions. One resourceful divorced father took his two daughters along on a business trip to Orlando, and while he sat in meetings a Super Sitter trotted the girls around the theme parks.

KinderCare Child-Care Center

KinderCare offers a "learning while playing" developmental program for children ages 1 to 12. The setup is similar to the hundreds of KinderCares nationwide. It's a daytime program; you drop off the children at the facility, which is on the WDW grounds, and pick them up a few hours later. Call (407) 827-5454 for details. The center primarily exists for the use of Disney employees, but visiting children are accepted on a day-by-day basis as space permits. You do not have to be a guest at an on-site hotel to use the service, and the cost is $8 an hour or $36 for a 10-hour day.

On-site Kids' Clubs

The following on-site hotels have kids' clubs:

BoardWalk	939-5100
Contemporary	824-1000
Dolphin	934-4000
Grand Floridian	824-3000
Polynesian	824-2000
Wilderness Lodge	824-3200
Yacht and Beach Clubs	934-8000

In general, the clubs run in the evening for kids 4 to 12. The clubhouses are well stocked with Disney-themed toys as well as computers, video and arcade games, and big-screen TVs. The cost is $4 an hour, and reservations are required. (Not much advance notice is needed, but you can make reservations by contacting Guest Services at the appropriate hotel. On-site guests get first crack at the available slots, but if the clubs don't fill up, space is available to off-site visitors as well.) The clubhouses are open from 4:30 until midnight, and cookies and milk are served at bedtime. Kids must be potty-trained—even Mary Poppins has her limits.

The Polynesian offers a twist: a "dinner theater" for kids 4 to 12 in the Neverland Club, which includes a full meal and entertainment. Animals and birds are often brought over from Discovery Island, a character drops by, and the evening is wrapped up with ice cream and games. The cost is $8 per child per hour, with a minimum three-hour visit. The Neverland Club is open 5 P.M. until midnight. Call (407) 824-2170 for reservations. Several families surveyed specifically mentioned what a swell evening this was for their kids. One father vividly described how his timid and stranger-shy 4-year-old was so won over by the drop-in visit from Alice in Wonderland that she screamed and clung to the Neverland Club doorframe when her parents returned to pick her up!

Note: Prices, policy, and planned entertainment change continually at the kids' clubs, so confirm all the above information when you make your reservations.

Off-site Kids' Clubs with Fees

Several off-site hotels have their own versions of kids' clubs, with big-screen TVs, Nintendo games, and wading pools to entertain the children while parents do the town. Most of these programs run only at night. Generally, it is not required that you be registered at the hotel in order to take advantage of the program, although this policy can change during busy seasons when the programs are filled. The typical cost is $6 an hour with a $3 add-on for each sibling.

Another advantage of these hotels is that they have fine-dining establishments right on the premises: Haifeng and Atlantis at the Renaissance, Hemingway's at the Hyatt Regency Grand Cypress, and Arthur's 27 at the Buena Vista Palace are outstanding restaurants with leisurely, adult-paced service. The Hilton is near Pleasure Island and Downtown Disney, which has a wealth of good restaurants. An evening of purely adult dining provides a nice break from the typical vacation restaurant experience, where you frantically color pictures of Pluto and juggle sugar packets in an effort to keep the kids entertained until the food arrives. All of the hotels mentioned are equipped to either escort the kids to the resort coffee shop for a simple meal or order in room service so the kids can eat while the parents dine out.

At various times the hotels have offered special deals, such as three hours of complimentary child care for parents dining in the hotel's flagship restaurant. This perk seems to come and go, and 24-hour notice is always required, so call to check. Even if you wind up having to pay for the service, this is a good option if you feel a bit nervous about leaving your children back at your hotel with a strange sitter. By dining at a hotel with on-site child care, you have the security of knowing that the kids are in the same building. It also softens the blow of the kids' being left behind, since they're "going out," too.

A hotel that provides daytime as well as evening child care is the Hyatt Regency Grand Cypress. (The Hyatt is known throughout the hotel industry for the quality of its children's programs.) Daily during summer and during some holidays as well, Camp Hyatt offers kids 5 to 12 a wide range of outdoor and craft activities. Kids 3 to 5 are welcome in the Childcare Center, a less-structured program, and the cost for either Camp Hyatt or the Childcare Center is $6 an hour. (In-room sitting for kids under 3 can be arranged.) The staff is on duty from 8 A.M. to 10 P.M. during the on-season, so parents can take in a round of golf at the resort's outstanding course, play tennis, or simply relax by the dramatically landscaped pool. If you need child care during dinner hours, both Camp Hyatt and the Childcare Center are operative during the evening on weekends.

But the Hyatt doesn't stop there. Rock Hyatt, oriented toward teens, gives your 15-year-old the opportunity to hang out with her own kind after a stressful day of having to be nice to her younger brothers. Rock Hyatt is free and runs on Friday and Saturday nights year-round.

For more information on the kids' clubs call:

Buena Vista Palace	(407) 827-2727
Hilton at Disney Village Hotel Plaza	(407) 827-4000
Hyatt Regency Grand Cypress	(407) 239-1234
Renaissance Resort	(407) 351-5555

Off-site Kids' Clubs Without Fees

Parents who'd like to go out more than once during their vacation, or whose kids just enjoy being around other children, should look for a hotel with a complimentary kids' club. Interestingly, this is not one of those times when you get what you pay for; one might think that free child care means a lackluster program, but just the opposite is true. Hotels that are committed enough to families to provide a free kids' club are also committed enough to do the job right. The Holiday Inn Sunspree at Lake Buena Vista, Embassy Suites at exit 27 off I-4, and the Delta Orlando all have hotel mascots, a program that combines outdoor fun with restful activities, and beeper service to keep you in contact and give you additional peace of mind. And, since most of the activities for the kids are free, you're shaving as much as $40 off the cost of a parents' night out.

These perks are not reflected in the cost of the rooms, either. The Holiday Inn Sunspree and Delta Orlando start as low as $99 a night; and with suites starting as low as $160, Embassy Suites is a reasonable option for families needing more space.

Note: The programs are free unless food is served or a craft is made. All the hotels listed will arrange to feed kids between 6 P.M. and 9 P.M. if parents wish to dine on their own. The cost for supplying the meals is usually about $8, and the food is always something that kids like, such as pizza or tacos, generally followed by make-your-own ice-cream sundaes. At some programs, such as at the Delta Orlando or Embassy Suites, the kids learn to tie-dye T-shirts or other fairly involved crafts. If out-of-the-ordinary supplies are required, that cost is passed along to parents. As with the food, however, the hotels try to keep the costs reasonable, usually around $6.

For details call:

Delta Orlando	(407) 351-3340
Embassy Suites	(407) 239-1144
Holiday Inn Sunspree	(407) 239-4500

DINING WITHOUT THE KIDS

Certain on-site restaurants are more enjoyable without children, so once you've found a sitter, reserve a table for two at one of the following fine establishments.

At Epcot Center

Chefs de France or Bistro de Paris

Chefs de France features nouvelle cuisine, meaning the sauces are lighter and the preparation simpler than traditional French fare. This is still heady stuff: grouper with lobster sauce, roast duckling with prunes, or salmon-and-tarragon soufflé. The atmosphere is elegant and understated, and the service is unrushed. Chefs de France is definitely one of the most expensive eateries in Epcot: Dinner for two runs about $100.

The Bistro de Paris upstairs is just as expensive and just as good. Although the atmosphere is still lovely—high ceilings, brass, and etched glass abound—and the service still attentive, Bistro de Paris represents hearty, casual French dining. Waiters are more than willing to advise you on selections and, as is true at Chefs, it's impossible to go wrong with any of the desserts.

Romance factor: B for Chefs de France, which is "on the street"; *A* for Bistro de Paris, which is quieter and darker.

Marrakesh

Ready to take a walk on the semiwild side? The music, architecture, and menu in the Moroccan restaurant are truly distinctive, proving beyond a doubt that you aren't in Kansas anymore. You'll be served lamb, couscous, and honeyed chicken by waiters in floor-length robes while belly dancers weave among the tile tables. (The effect of these dancers on husbands is somewhat akin to the effect meeting Mickey has on toddlers: They're stunned while it's happening, but later remember the experience fondly.)

Romance factor: C. The tables are very close together, lots of families bring the kids, and the place can become quite loud.

San Angel Inn Restaurante

The menu here goes far past the tacos and enchiladas most Americans consider Mexican food, and the atmosphere is unparalleled. The restaurant overlooks El Rio del Tiempo, the boat ride that encircles an Aztec pyramid beneath a starry sky. The darkness of the Mexico pavilion, which simulates midnight even at high noon, and the murmur of the *rio* are hypnotic. Throw in a couple of margaritas and you may never leave.

The *molé poblano* and any of the grilled seafood dishes are consistently good. The friendliness of the service makes the San Angel a good choice even when the children are along.

Romance factor: B

L'Originale Alfredo di Roma Ristorante

The Alfredo in question is the gentleman who created fettuccine Alfredo. This is the most popular restaurant in the World Showcase, usually the first to book up despite the fact that it seats 250 people. The restaurant in itself is entertaining: You can watch through a large window as the cooks crank out pasta; the walls are adorned with clever trompe l'oeil murals; and the waiters provide impromptu concerts, ranging from mildly bawdy Italian folk songs to passionate concerti di Verdi.

Most diners, however, have kids along, making the place a little too loud and crowded for romance.

Romance factor: C

The Coral Reef Restaurant

Tucked away under the Living Seas pavilion, this Future World restaurant is also expensive, about $100 for dinner for two.

Unfortunately, the Coral Reef is less romantic than the World Showcase restaurants. The room is simply too large to feel cozy and, as at Alfredo's, most families bring their kids, figuring—and rightly so—that little Nathaniel and Erica can stay busy watching the skin-divers while Mom and Dad crack a lobster.

Romance factor: C

Outside Epcot Center

Victoria and Albert's

For a very special evening, there is one place in WDW so elegant and so removed from the classic Disney image that you'll never feel sticky fingers creeping over the top of the booth behind you. Kids are never seen at Victoria and Albert's in the Grand Floridian, where harp music plays, candles flicker, and ties and jackets for men are required.

Where Disney has built a reputation on providing pleasure to the masses, this 50-seat restaurant proves there is also room in WDW for highly individualized service. When Henry Flagler built the railroad that opened Florida to the oil magnates of the late 1800s, Queen Victoria and Prince Albert sat upon the British throne. Now, in one of those "only Disney would go to such trouble" details, all hosts and hostesses in the restaurant call themselves Victoria or Albert.

Your menu will have your own name handwritten on the top; waiters describe the selections for the evening, and the chef often circulates among the tables. At the end of a six-course meal, guests are presented with long-stemmed roses, Godiva chocolates, and their menus. This is the most expensive restaurant in WDW, hands down—the prix fixe dinner is $125 per person—but it's so special that you'll be talking about it for years to come. On the evening we visited, the salad was a floral arrangement in a crouton vase—until Victoria tapped the side of the crouton, releasing the greens into a fan-shaped pattern on the plate; and the coffee service was more elaborate than a Japanese tea ceremony. Call (407) 824-2391 for reservations, or make arrangements through Guest Services.

Note: Victoria and Albert's is the only full-service restaurant in WDW that is not included in the World Adventure or any other package dining plans.

Romance factor: A+

The California Grille

This restaurant, located atop the Contemporary Resort, became so popular so fast that Disney is still reeling. One clue to the quality: Disney executives lunch here. Not only does the California Grille offer a marvelous variety of cuisine with stylish preparation, but the views from the top of the Contemporary are unparalleled, especially during the Magic Kingdom fireworks display. Call (407) 824-1576 for reservations.

Romance factor: B

Outside Walt Disney World

Excellent dining abounds beyond the Disney World gates, and many of the fancier restaurants are in hotels. **Dux** in the Peabody offers an intimate environment, unusual seafood and game selections, and an outstanding list of California wines, many available by the glass. **Arthur's 27**, the rooftop restaurant of the Buena Vista Palace, has an award-winning menu and a reputation for consistent quality in both service and food. The huge Hyatt Regency Grand Cypress, a gorgeous destination in itself, is also home to **Hemingway's**, offering the outstanding cuisine typical of the Hyatts and an atmosphere so lush and tropical it isn't typical of anything at all.

If you venture past the hotels, you'll find there are plenty of places in Orlando that offer good food at reasonable prices with friendly, unpretentious service. The majority of Orlando restaurants are informal. **Pebbles**, in the Crossroads of Lake Buena Vista, serves up Key West–style food in a casual atmosphere and is a good choice if you're going to nearby Pleasure Island after you eat.

Dining of a campier sort can be found at **Church Street Station**, a dining and shopping complex in downtown Orlando. **Rosie O'Grady's** and **Lilly Marlene's** dish up tasty but casual food, huge specialty drinks, and live music. Late in the evening, Church Street becomes a giant party, with patrons moving from one establishment to the next, sampling the various entertainment and bar munchies.

Planet Hollywood is also a popular place to party— either with or without the kids. The opening of **Bongo's Cuban Cafe** and **House of Blues** in Downtown Disney are bound to draw a late-night crowd. And nothing's quite as funky as the **Hard Rock Cafe**, adjacent to Universal Studios. But these places rev up late at night, so if you want to get in the true spirit, hire an in-room sitter and eat at 11 P.M.

9

★★★★★★★★★★★★★★★★★★★

And Another Thing . . .

BARE NECESSITIES: STROLLERS, BABIES, PREGNANCY, SPECIAL NEEDS, AND FIRST-AID

Strollers

• All kids under 3 need a stroller, for napping and waiting in line as well as riding.

• For kids 3 to 6, the general rule is: Strollers are a must at Epcot, nice in the MK, and not really necessary at MGM, where the park is smaller and a lot of time is spent in sit-down shows.

• Strollers rent for $6 a day, so if you'll need one every day, consider bringing your own from home. But if you have an older child who will need a stroller only at Epcot, rental isn't a bad option.

• If you plan to spend time at more than one park, you don't have to pay twice: Keep your receipt and show it for a new stroller when you arrive at the next park.

• The MK and Epcot strollers are sturdy, drop back to form a completely flat bed, and can hold two kids in a pinch. The MGM strollers are the lightweight, easily collapsible "umbrella" type.

• Tie something like a bandanna or a balloon to your stroller to mark it, thus reducing the probability it'll be swiped while you're inside Peter Pan's Flight. As one mother observed, "Otherwise honest people seem to think nothing about stealing a stroller, but stop when they see they might be taking a personal possession as well."

• Stroller stolen anyway? In the MK check in at the Trading Post in Frontierland, or Tinkerbell's Treasures in Fantasyland. At Epcot you can get a new stroller at the World Traveler Shop located between France and the United Kingdom. Return to Oscar's Super Service at MGM. So long as you've kept your receipt, there's no charge for a replacement stroller.

• If at 8 A.M. your 5-year-old swears she doesn't need a stroller, but at noon she collapses in a heap halfway around Epcot's World Showcase, head for the World Traveler Shop between France and the United Kingdom. The World Traveler is also the place to rent a stroller if you're coming from the Swan, Dolphin, BoardWalk, or Yacht and Beach Clubs and thus using the "backdoor" entrance.

• If you have an infant, bring a stroller from home. The rental strollers in the MK and Epcot are too large and too hard for babies who can't sit at all.

• Likewise, if you're staying at one of the more sprawling resorts, such as the Caribbean Beach Resort, Dixie Landings, Fort Wilderness, All-Star Sports, or All-Star Music, bring a stroller from home. It's likely to be quite a trek from your room to the pool or shuttle stop.

Baby Services

Rockers, bottle warmers, high chairs, and changing tables are all found at the Baby Services centers; and diapers, formula, and jars of baby food are for sale. The centers are an absolute haven for families traveling with a very young child. (One mother reported that the attendant on duty was even able to diagnose a suspicious-looking rash on her toddler as a reaction to too much citrus juice, evidently a common Florida malady. She later took the child to a doctor and learned that the attendant had been right on the money.)

In the MK, Baby Services is beside the Crystal Palace at the end of Main Street. It's inside the Guest Services building at MGM, and near the Odyssey Restaurant at Epcot.

Diapers

Diapers are available at the following locations:

- Baby Services centers
- Stroller-rental shops
- The Emporium on Main Street in the MK
- Celebrity 5 & 10 at MGM

The shops don't waste shelf space on mundane products, so you'll have to ask. Changing tables are available in most ladies' restrooms and now—finally—in some men's restrooms as well. You can always use the Baby Services centers to change infants, and there are potty chairs for toddlers as well.

Breast-feeding

WDW is so casual and family-oriented that you shouldn't feel self-conscious about discreetly nursing in the theaters or restaurants. Some shows, like the Hall of Presidents in the MK or *Impressions de France* at Epcot, are dark, quiet, and ideal for nursing. Others, like the Country Bear Vacation Hoedown in the MK or the Monster Sound Show at MGM are so loud that the baby will probably be too distracted.

If you're too modest for these methods or your baby is easily disturbed, try the rockers in the Baby Services centers.

Pregnant?

I've personally toured WDW twice while pregnant and not only lived to tell the tale, but honestly enjoyed both trips. A few precautions are in order:

• Make regular meal stops. Instead of buying a sandwich from a vendor, get out of the sun and off your feet at a sit-down restaurant.

• If you aren't accustomed to walking five or six miles a day—an average WDW trek—begin getting in shape at home. By taking 30- to 40-minute walks, beginning a couple of months before your trip, you'll be less likely to get sore or poop out once you're at WDW.

• Dehydration is a real danger. Drink lots of fluids and keep a juicebox in your tote bag for emergencies.

• This is definitely an occasion when it's worth the money to stay on-site. Return to your room in midafternoon to put your feet up.

• If staying on-site isn't feasible, the Baby Services centers have rockers and are a good place for mothers-to-be to take a break. And the parks are full of benches—sit down when you can.

• Standing stock-still can be much more tiring than walking, so let your husband stand in line for rides. You and the kids can join him just as he's about to enter the final turn of the line.

• Once you're inside the holding area for theater-style attractions, such as the Country Bear Vacation Hoedown or Universe of Energy, find a bench and sit down. If the benches are taken (and chivalry is apparently dead), sit on the floor near the wall and don't stand up when the Disney attendant gets on the loud-speaker and asks everyone to move into the theater; all the people in the holding area will be admitted into the theater, so it's pointless to get up now and all mob the turnstiles at once. Let everyone else go ahead and then amble through. (This is a good strategy for anyone who is utterly exhausted, pregnant or not.)

- Most important of all, check out restroom locations in advance. (See the "Best Restroom Locations" listings in Sections 4, page 126, and Section 5, page 160.)

Special Needs

- Wheelchairs can be rented at any stroller-rental stand, and most attractions are accessible by wheelchair. (Epcot has a few of those three-wheel motorized wheelchairs for rent, which can be very convenient, considering the miles you'll cover in a typical Epcot day.) Attendants are happy to help guests with special needs board and disembark from rides.

Once they're in the theme parks and ready to ride the attractions, guests in wheelchairs board through their own gates and are often able to avoid waiting in line altogether.

If someone in your party is in a wheelchair, be sure to request a copy of the *Guidebook for Disabled Guests,* either when you order your tickets in advance or at the wheelchair-rental booth. It's a specific guide to how each ride should be boarded.

- A tip from frequent visitors: If you're traveling with someone in a wheelchair, it's emphatically worth the money to stay on-site. Disney does an excellent job of offering disabled guests a number of transportation options. The ferry and monorail are wheelchair-accessible, but, if needed, you can request a van with a motorized platform. The resorts offer rooms with specially equipped bathrooms and extrawide doors; and life jackets for the handicapped are available at resort pools and water parks.

The Polynesian gets high marks from readers with special needs, but for those seeking a less expensive option, the All-Star Resorts have several rooms designed to meet the needs of the handicapped for $79 a night.

• Portable tape players and cassettes for sight-impaired guests are available, as are TDDs for the hearing-impaired. Check with Guest Services in the theme parks.
Deaf guests have a designated phone line to call for park information: (407) 827-5141.

• All on-site hotels are equipped to refrigerate insulin.

• Finally, a word of reassurance: If you're traveling with someone who has a chronic health problem or disability, rest assured that WDW is one of the most stress-free vacations you could have planned. Because WDW is frequently visited by children sponsored by the "Make a Wish" foundation and other programs like it, the personnel at WDW are accustomed to dealing with a wide variety of challenges and have proven themselves able to accommodate visitors who are quite seriously ill. The key is to make everyone at both your hotel and within the theme parks aware of your presence and the possibility that you'll need special assistance. Then relax. These people will help you in every way they can.

First-aid

Next to the Crystal Palace in the MK is the first-aid clinic, staffed by two nurses. Epcot has a first-aid clinic located beside the Odyssey Restaurant; MGM's is in the Guest Services center. Although most patients suffer from minor problems such as sunburn, motion sickness, and boo-boos, the clinics are also equipped to handle major emergencies and, when necessary, ambulance service to an area hospital.

It's worth remembering that any medical problem that could arise at home could also occur in the midst of a vacation. I've received letters from people who have had broken bones, fainted from the heat, and come down with chicken pox while in Orlando. Their general advice to others is: *Seek medical help the minute you even suspect there may be a problem.* Waiting only makes the solution more painful and more expensive.

Should you suffer a medical emergency, take comfort in the fact that the Disney people have received ringing endorsements for their response in times of crisis. One mother who developed an eye infection from a scratched cornea reported that the nurse at the Epcot first-aid clinic, immediately recognizing the severity of the problem, arranged for her transport to Sand Lake Hospital so she could see an ophthalmologist. "We had only a long weekend," the mother wrote, "and I would have felt horrible if the kids spent it in a hospital waiting room. But as it was, the nurse handled everything, and my husband and children were able to remain in the park while I was treated. My husband kept phoning in to the nurse for updates, and I met up with them back at Epcot a couple of hours later, looking like Long John Silver."

Another mother wrote, "When our 8-year-old son developed a (repeat) ear infection in the middle of the Magic Kingdom, we went to the first-aid clinic. There a sweet nurse gently examined him, contacted his doctor back in Ohio to get his regular prescription, and gave him Tylenol for his immediate relief. By the time we arrived back at our rooms at Port Orleans, the prescription was there, and by the next morning Nicky was back on his feet and ready to go."

A woman who suffered a miscarriage while staying at an on-site hotel also offered the highest praise to the staff there, both for their swift medical response and their emotional support.

General First-aid Tips

• If someone begins to feel ill or suffers an injury in the parks, head straight for the first-aid clinic. If they can't fix it, they'll find someone who can.

• Likewise, all on-site hotels and most off-site hotels have physicians on call 24 hours a day. Contact Guest Services or call (407) 396-1195 between 8 A.M. and 10 P.M. for in-room health care. Turner Drugs in Orlando, (407) 828-8125, will deliver to any on-site hotel room (and many off-site ones) 24 hours a day. There's a $5 charge for delivery, with a surcharge between 10 P.M. and 8 A.M.

• For minor health problems, visit the Medi-Clinic at the intersection of I-4 and Route 192, or the Lake Buena Vista Clinic, which will pick you up at your hotel room between 8 A.M. and 8 P.M. For more serious illnesses or injuries, head for the emergency room at Sand Lake Hospital.

• No matter where you're staying, of course, in a true emergency you should call 9-1-1.

HOW TO GET UP-TO-DATE INFORMATION

For information before you leave home:

• Write to:

Walt Disney World Guest Information
P.O. Box 10040
Lake Buena Vista, FL 32830-0040

- Subscribe to *Disney Magazine.* You'll receive eight quarterly issues (a two-year subscription) for $16.95.

   Disney Magazine
   P.O. Box 37263
   Boone, IA 50037-2263

- Subscribe to *Mousetales,* the unofficial newsletter of WDW. The cost is $12.95 per year.

   Mousetales
   P.O. Box 383
   Columbus OH 43216

- Want to get information online? The WDW home page is at www2.disney.com/DisneyWorld/index.html. Disney's home page at www.disney.com has links to all the Disney Web sites worldwide.

For information once you check in to your hotel:

- Both on- and off-site hotels provide informational materials upon check-in. Study the maps and brochures your first evening.

- On-site hotels provide continuous information about park operating hours, special events, and touring tips on your room TV, including an especially helpful program, called "Disney Nights," about dinner theaters, evening parades, and special shows.
   Resorts in the Disney Village Hotel Plaza have similar services on channel 7, and some of the large off-site hotels have their own entertainment information channels, which keep you up-to-date not only on Disney but all Orlando-area attractions.

- Magic Kingdom radio is 1030 AM. Epcot is 810 AM. Tune in as you drive into the parks.

- Guest Services in both on-site and off-site hotels is equipped to answer most questions.

• If you still have questions, call (407) 824-4321. You'll go through minutes of button-pushing torment, but eventually a real live person will come on the line to tell you what time Epcot closes on May 7, the price of Minnie's Revue for a 10-year-old, and how tall you have to be to ride Splash Mountain.

For information once you're in the parks:

• Check with Guest Services, which is located near the main entrance of all three major theme parks.

• At Epcot there are terminals for the WorldKey Information System (which operate like those located inside the Earth Station under Spaceship Earth) in the Germany pavilion and on the bridges that connect Future World to the World Showcase. You'll have access to a Disney employee within seconds.

• Flag down the nearest person wearing a Disney name tag. The "cast members" at the theme parks are remarkably helpful and well informed.

SAVING TIME

• Prepare as much as you can before you leave home. You should purchase theme park tickets, reserve rental cars, and book shows or special dinners long before you pull out of your driveway. Every call you make now is a line you won't have to stand in later.

• Visit the most popular attractions before 11 A.M. or after 5 P.M.

• Eat lunch either at 11 A.M. or after 2 P.M. This system will have you eating while everyone else is in line for the rides, and riding while everyone else is eating.

• It also saves time—and money—to make lunch your big meal of the day. Most families opt to eat a large breakfast and dinner and just a snack at lunch; go against the crowds by eating your big meal in early afternoon, when restaurant meals are cheaper and the parks are too hot and crowded for effective touring anyway.

• Split up. Mom can make the dinner reservations while Dad rents the strollers. Mom can take the 9-year-old to Space Mountain while Dad and the 4-year-old try out the Tomorrowland Speedway. Security in WDW is very tight, so preteens and teens can tour on their own, meeting up with the rest of the family periodically.

• Be aware that once you cross the Florida state line, there is an inverse relationship between time and money. You have to be willing to spend one in order to save the other. One family proudly listed such cost-saving measures as staying 30 miles outside of Orlando and cooking every meal themselves. They concluded by stating that it took them six days to tour the three major parks, something most families can manage comfortably in four days. Considering the high cost of admissions, it's doubtful that they saved very much money at all and they certainly wasted time.

• If you have three days or less to tour, it is imperative that you go during the off-season. What you can see in three days in November would take six days in July.

• Don't feel you have to do it all. If you study this guide and your maps before you go, you'll realize that not every attraction will be equally attractive to your family. The World won't come to an end if you skip a few pavilions.

- The full-service restaurants within the theme parks can be very slow. If you're on a tight touring schedule, stick to fast food or sidewalk vendors and order a pizza at night when you get back to your hotel room.

- If you're staying on-site, make all your dining reservations by phone.

SAVING MONEY

Saving money at WDW is somewhat of an oxymoron, but there are certainly ways to minimize the damage.

- Purchase a Magic Kingdom Club Gold Card. A two-year membership qualifies you for savings of up to 20% at Disney hotels during certain seasons of the year, as well as discounts on theme park tickets, meals, souvenir purchases, and a host of other benefits.

- If the cost of flying the whole family to Florida and then renting a car is prohibitive, consider renting a van in your hometown and driving to Orlando.

- Eat as many meals as possible outside of the parks. If you have a suite, fixing simple meals there is clearly your most economical option. Many Orlando hotels offer free breakfasts to guests, and there are numerous fast-food and family chain restaurants along International Drive and the I-4 exits.

- If you'd like to try some of the nicer Epcot restaurants, book them at lunch, when prices are considerably lower than dinner. Many Epcot eateries also offer an Early Value Meal from 4:30 to 6:30 P.M. And remember that restaurant portions are huge—even the kiddie meals. Consider letting two family members share an entrée.

- Children's value meals run about $3 at the fast-food places and $4 at the sit-down restaurants. Kids sometimes eat free at certain establishments, such as Mama Melrose's at MGM and Marrakesh at Epcot. Signs announcing the restaurants that offer this deal are well posted.

- Except for maybe an autograph book or T-shirt, hold off on souvenir purchases until the last day. By then the kids will really know what they want, and you won't waste money on impulse buys.

- Bring film, blank videotapes, diapers, and sunscreen from home. All these things are available in the parks, but you'll pay dearly for the convenience.

- The All-Star Resorts, Caribbean Beach Resort, Port Orleans, Dixie Landings, Coronado Springs, and Fort Wilderness Campground offer the most economical on-site lodging. Off-site, there are several Comfort Inns and Days Inns along I-4 and International Drive, most offering shuttle service to the parks.

- If you're driving to Orlando and not arriving until afternoon or evening, don't reserve your on-site room until the second day of your visit. It's silly to pay for a whole day of Grand Floridian amenities if you'll be checking in at 10 P.M. Instead, stop your first night at a budget hotel, rise early and check out the next morning, and then go straight to your on-site hotel. There you can unload your bags, pick up your tickets and resort ID, and go on to the theme parks, checking in when you return in the evening.

- If you park-hop in your car, save your parking receipt so you'll have to pay the $6 only once. Likewise, be sure to save stroller receipts.

• If you plan to try any of the minor parks, such as Typhoon Lagoon, Blizzard Beach, or Pleasure Island, buy the five-day World-Hopper pass. Without it, you'll have to pay for each minor park separately, which adds up fast. Some families reported that they went to one of the water parks every day during their WDW stay—a treat that is easy with a five-day pass but totally unfeasible otherwise.

• Call the Orlando Visitors Bureau at 1-800-255-5786 before you leave home and request a Magic Card, which entitles you to savings on restaurants, area attractions, and many off-site hotels. The Bureau will also send you a Vacation Planner booklet, with lots of discounts for off-site hotels, restaurants, and dinner shows. If you belong to the Entertainment Club, stay at one of the hotels listed in the back, which offer 50% price breaks to members.

• The dinner shows are expensive, costing a family of four about $130, and even a character breakfast can set you back $40 or more. If your budget is tight, skip these extras and concentrate on ways to meet the characters inside the parks.

• Employees of many of the companies that have exhibits inside of WDW, such as General Electric and Exxon, are entitled to discounts and benefits similar to those of Magic Kingdom Club cardholders. (Employees of the federal government also qualify for these price breaks.) Most companies don't publicize this benefit, but if yours does sponsor an exhibit inside WDW, contact the personnel office well before you leave home and see if any discounts are offered on park admissions or on-site lodging.

• Disney park admission prices have skyrocketed, with four substantial raises in the past two years; buy your tickets when you make your hotel reservations, and you'll be protected in case Disney decides it's time for another "adjustment."

MEETING THE DISNEY CHARACTERS

Meeting the characters is a major objective for some families, and a nice diversion for all. If your children are young, prepare them for the fact that the characters are much, much larger than they appear on TV and are often overwhelming in person. I once visited WDW with a 20-month-old whose happy babble of "my Mickey, my Mickey" turned into a wary "no Mickey, no Mickey" the minute she entered the MK gate and saw that the mouse in question was a good six feet tall. Kaitlyn's reaction is not atypical; many kids panic when they first see the characters, and pushing them forward only makes matters worse. The characters are trained to be sensitive and sensible (in some cases, more so than the parents) and always wait for the child to approach them. Schedule a character breakfast on the last morning of your visit; by then cautious youngsters have usually warmed up.

Many kids enjoy getting character autographs, and an autograph book can become a much-cherished souvenir. You also might want to prepare the kids for the fact that the characters don't talk. As many as 30 young people in Mickey suits might be dispersed around the parks on a busy day, and they can't all be gifted with that familiar squeaky voice. So the characters communicate, pretty effectively, through body language.

Also be aware that because of the construction of their costumes, the characters can't always see too clearly what's beneath them. Donald and Daisy, for example, have a hard time looking over their bills, and small children standing close by may be ignored. If it appears that this is happening, lift your child to the character's eye level.

It's easier to see the characters at MGM than in the MK. The newer characters—those from *Hercules, The Hunchback of Notre Dame, Toy Story, Pocahontas, Aladdin, Beauty and the Beast,* and *The Little Mermaid*—appear almost exclusively at MGM, and the character-to-kid-ratio is vastly better there than in the MK. Even if your kids insist on spending every day in the MK, the chance to see Ariel or Belle at MGM may just lure them away from the MK rides.

Times and places to meet the characters are listed on the map and entertainment schedule you pick up upon entering the park. Each park also has a chalk-board stating when the characters appear. Meeting the characters in the theme parks is free, but it can get pretty wild. If you want to be assured of a good picture, either head for Mickey's Toontown Fair or schedule a character breakfast.

ON A DIET?

Vacation dieting is always tough, and fast food abounds in WDW, which makes it even more difficult. But Disney's executive chef, Edwin Wronski, and his staff are making an effort to offer more choices for healthy eating by reducing the amount of oil used when frying, and substituting yogurt for cream in sauces and salads. Increasingly, fresh fruit (instead of mayonnaise-laden salads) is served, vegetables are steamed, and meats are broiled.

Restaurants that serve meals meeting the low-fat standards set by the American Heart Association are indicated on your map with a red heart. Chefs at many restaurants—most notably the Nine Dragons in the China pavilion at Epcot—are quite willing to adapt recipes, serving sauces on the side and leaving out forbidden ingredients.

Fruit stands can be found on Main Street and in Liberty Square in the MK, near Echo Lake and on Sunset Boulevard at MGM, and between the China and Germany pavilions at Epcot. They make it easier for families on the move to select grapes or watermelon instead of chips or ice cream and also provide juice instead of the omnipresent theme park soft drink.

PICKY EATERS

• Try the cafeterias: the Crystal Palace for lunch and dinner in the MK (it is presently used for character breakfasts) and Hollywood & Vine at MGM. The food court in the Land pavilion at Epcot also offers lots of options.

• Several of the on-site hotels run buffets in the interest of moving people in and out fast, but they're also a draw for families who can't agree on what to eat.

• Nearly all of the theme park restaurants offer such standards as peanut butter and jelly, albeit at $4 a sandwich. If a kiddie menu isn't posted at the door, ask the host if you can see one before you're seated.

• Kiddie meals, based on the McDonald's Happy Meal concept, are turning up all around the theme parks and hotel restaurants for about $3. You get either a burger, hotdog, chicken nuggets, or a sandwich in a cartoon-covered box, along with fries, a drink, and a prize.

BEST BREAKFASTS IN WALT DISNEY WORLD

Wasn't it Archimedes who said, "Give me a good breakfast and I can move the world"? The following meals will at least set you up for an active morning of touring.

- Mickey-shaped pancakes for kids are available at the food courts of all the on-site hotels.

- Try heart-shaped waffles with powdered sugar at Kringla Bakeri og Kafe in the Norway pavilion at Epcot.

- Pastries are available throughout WDW, but are especially good at the Boulangerie Patisserie in the France pavilion at Epcot, Starring Rolls at MGM, and the Main Street Bakery in the MK.

- Kids love the Lady and the Tramp character waffles at Tony's Town Square Cafe on Main Street in the MK.

- The absolute best is banana-stuffed French toast at the Coral Isle Cafe at the Polynesian Resort. Worth a special trip!

If for you the best breakfast is a fast breakfast, be aware that all of the on-site hotels have a food court or coffee shop that opens extremely early. On those mornings when the kids are moving slowly, one parent can always go for juice, cereal, and muffins and bring the tray back to the room. (At the All-Star Resorts, they even send around a mobile pastry-and-juice cart.) If you're staying off-site, hit one of the drive-thru eateries on your way into the park.

Sunday brunch buffets are big business in Orlando— one reason why the theme parks tend to be blissfully uncrowded on Sunday mornings. The off-site hotels are fiercely competitive when it comes to their Sunday buffets, each trying to outdo the others in terms of selection and the size of the spread. If you're in the mood for something special and rather elegant, the Hyatt Regency Grand Cypress is widely considered to have the biggest and best buffet of them all.

THINGS YOU DON'T WANT TO THINK ABOUT

Rain

Go anyway. Short of an all-out hurricane, Disney attractions are open as usual and crowds will be thin. If you get caught in one of those afternoon cloudbursts so common in Florida summers, rain ponchos are available for about $5 in most of the larger shops. Although hardly high fashion, they're better (and safer) than trying to maneuver an umbrella though crowds while pushing a stroller.

Lost Kids

Obviously, your best bet is to not get separated in the first place. Savvy families have standard meeting spots. *Note:* Everyone designates Cinderella Castle or Spaceship Earth, one reason why those places are always mobbed. Plan to catch up with your crowd at a more out-of-the-way locale such as the flower stall on Main Street or the gardens beside the Canada pavilion.

If you do get separated and your kids are too young to understand the idea of a meeting place, act fast. Lost-kid logs are kept at the Baby Services centers at the major parks; more important, Disney employees are well briefed about what to do if they encounter a lost child, so the odds are good that if your child has been wandering around alone for more than a couple of minutes, he or she has already been intercepted by a Disney employee and is on the way to Baby Services. In real emergencies—if the child is very young or is handicapped, or if you're afraid he's been nabbed— all-points bulletins are put out among employees. So if you lose a child, don't spend a half-hour wandering around looking. Contact the nearest Disney employee immediately and let the system take it from there.

Note: The one glitch in the system is that sometimes lost kids are so interested in what's going on around them that they don't look lost, and thus no Disney employee intercepts them. Take a couple of minutes to explain to young children that if they get separated from you, they should tell someone wearing a Disney name tag. The Disney employee will call the child's name in to Baby Services and, assuming you've contacted Baby Services to report the child as missing, the attendant there will tell you where the child is.

Closed Attractions
Because WDW is open 365 days a year, there is no downtime for refurbishing and repairing rides. Thus at any given time, as many as four attractions throughout WDW may be closed for repairs. If an attraction your family eagerly anticipated is closed, it can be heartbreaking. Call (407) 824-4321 before you leave home to find out which attractions are scheduled for maintenance during your visit. That way if Space

Mountain or Star Tours is closed, at least you'll know before you get to the gate. There's still a slight chance that a ride will be malfunctioning and temporarily closed when you visit, but the Disney people are so vigilant about repairs this happens only very rarely.

Auto Breakdowns

If you return to the parking lot at the end of the day to find your battery dead or your tire flat, walk back to nearest tram stop. WDW roads are patrolled continuously by security personnel, who can call for help. If it's any consolation, 12,000 visitors locked their keys in their cars last year at WDW, so the security people are used to it.

An Exxon station is located near the toll plaza at the MK entrance. Although prices are high, the station does provide towing and minor repairs in an emergency. If the car can't be swiftly repaired, don't despair—the day isn't lost. WDW personnel will chauffeur you to any of the theme parks or back to your hotel.

By far the most common problem is forgetting where you parked. Be sure to write down your row number when you leave your car in the morning. Although Pluto 47 seems easy to remember now, you may not be able to retrieve that info 12 brain-numbing hours later.

Running Out of Money

The Sun Bank, which has branches all around Walt Disney World, gives cash advances on MasterCard and Visa, provides refunds for lost American Express or Bank of America traveler's checks, and exchanges foreign currency for U.S. dollars.

Crime

Florida has received some very bad press over the past several years because of crimes against tourists. It's worth noting that the vast majority of these problems have occurred in the Miami area, several hours south of Orlando, and Orlando itself remains a relatively safe haven for tourists.

Nevertheless, use common sense, especially in trying to avoid the most common crime: theft. Make use of the lockers so that you won't have to carry valuables or new purchases around the parks; take cameras and camcorders onto the rides with you; and be extra-cautious in the water parks, where you may be tempted to leave your wallet on your lounge chair while riding the waves. It's far better to either wear one of those waterproof waist pouches in the water or rent a locker, returning to it whenever you need money. The locker keys are on elasticized bands that slip around your wrist, so there's no hassle in hanging on to them.

Two much more serious crimes were highly publicized a few years ago: a break-in and rape at an on-site hotel, and a kidnapping from within one of the major parks. The kidnapping turned out to be part of a custody battle and not a random crime, but reports like this remind us that there's always a chance we'll encounter violence while vacationing. Don't let paranoia ruin your trip—statistically, Orlando is a pretty safe town—but do keep your wits about you, making sure that hotel doors are bolted, rental cars are locked, and that you stick to major roads while exploring. Most important, be sure your kids know what to do if they get separated from you.

BEST SOUVENIRS

For serious shopping, head to the World of Disney at the Disney Village Marketplace, which has a little bit of everything. If you're looking for a more unusual souvenir, consider the following specialty items.

• Boldly colored T-shirts featuring the flags of Epcot countries are available at Disney Traders, near the mouth of the World Showcase Lagoon.

• Autograph books can be purchased nearly anywhere on the first day of your trip. The signatures of the more-obscure characters such as Eeyore or the Queen of Hearts are especially prized.

• World Showcase Passports can be purchased at the Port of Entry, as well as from vendors all around Epcot. Kids can collect a stamp and handwritten message from each World Showcase nation they visit.

• Characters in vehicles, purchased at the small trinket shops near the stroller rental stands, are the perfect size for a toddler's chubby fist. Mickey rides a moveable crane, Minnie a pink roadster, Donald a locomotive, and so on. At just $3 each, they're one of the few souvenir bargains to be found at WDW.

• An outstanding selection of Disney watches can be found at Uptown Jewelers on Main Street in the MK. Check out the Goofy watch—it runs backward.

• Consider a piñata from the Mexico pavilion at Epcot

• Character Christmas ornaments can be found in the Character Christmas Shop at the Disney Village Marketplace.

• Planet Hollywood T-shirts are available in a separate shop downstairs from the restaurant.

• Endor Vendors, adjacent to the Star Tours ride at MGM, offers a slick selection of movie memorabilia, made all the hotter by the theatrical rerelease of the trilogy.

• Also at MGM, old movie posters and other campy knickknacks from Hollywood's golden era are sold at Sid Cahuenga's One-of-a-Kind.

• Character cookie cutters or presses that stamp Mickey's visage onto toast and pancakes are available at Yankee Trader in Liberty Square in the MK. A Disney-themed breakfast on your first Saturday home is a nice way to fight those postvacation blues.

• There's a cool Hollywood Tower Hotel gift shop complete with bathrobes, towels, ashtrays, and "I survived" T-shirts as you exit the Twilight Zone Tower of Terror.

• Get character-themed athletic gear at Team Mickey in the Disney Village Marketplace. You'll find some items here that you won't see anywhere else, such as Mickey golf balls, softballs, and basketballs, and Little Mermaid ballet tights.

• All the on-site hotels have their own T-shirts, a nice variation from the shirts you see in the parks.

• And, of course, mouse ears have a sort of retro-chic. Get your name stitched on at the Mad Hatter in Fantasyland in the MK.

FAVORITE TEEN AND PRETEEN ATTRACTIONS AT WDW

The following attractions received the highest approval rating from the WDW visitors we surveyed, ages 11 to 16.

In the Magic Kingdom

- Space Mountain
- Splash Mountain
- Alien Encounter
- Big Thunder Mountain Railroad
- The Mad Tea Party

At Epcot

- Test Track
- *Honey, I Shrunk the Audience*
- Body Wars
- IllumiNations
- The American Adventure
- Innoventions

At MGM

- Twilight Zone Tower of Terror
- Star Tours
- Indiana Jones Epic Stunt Spectacular
- The Monster Sound Show

In the Rest of the World

- Blizzard Beach
- Typhoon Lagoon
- water sprites
- Planet Hollywood
- Pleasure Island

CLASSIC DISNEY PHOTO OPS

You can rent 35mm cameras at any of the Kodak Camera Centers for a nominal fee. Film and two-hour photo developing are widely available throughout WDW. Needless to say, the prices of both are higher than at home, but it's good to know you can get more film fast if you go into a photo frenzy.

Consider buying one of those waterproof disposable cameras and going wild at Blizzard Beach and Typhoon Lagoon.

Note: The employees at the Camera Centers are generally knowledgeable about photography and are a good source of advice if you've borrowed a big-deal camera from Aunt Lizzie and can't figure out how to advance the film.

For those postcard-perfect shots, Kodak has well-marked Photo Spot locations throughout all the major parks. But if, like most parents, what you really want to focus on is your kids, try the following locations.

In the Magic Kingdom

- The Dumbo ride just before takeoff. Once he rises it's just too hard to get a good angle on the riders.
- With Cinderella in the downstairs waiting area of King Stefan's Banquet Hall.
- With Mickey, of course, in his Toontown tent.

At Epcot Center

- In front of the entrance fountains or the neat anti-gravity fountains at Journey Into Imagination.
- Leaning against the railings inside the Land pavilion, with hot-air balloons in the background.

At MGM

- Halfway through the Backstage Studio Tour, there's a break for bathrooms, snacks, and pictures à la *Who Framed Roger Rabbit?* The kids can even pose beneath the steamroller that nearly did in the Toontown gang.

- At the Honey, I Shrunk the Kids Adventure Zone, you have lots of fun options, but most families seem to like the camp of posing inside a nine-foot-high canister of Kodak film.

- With your waitress-mom at the 50's Prime Time Cafe or in your SciFi Drive-In car.

- With the gossip columnist, budding starlets, autograph hounds, or other "streetmosphere" players on Hollywood Boulevard.

- Measuring your footprints against those of the real-life stars in the concrete courtyard of the Great Movie Ride.

CAMCORDER TAPING TIPS

Camcorders can be a hassle to carry on the rides, but it's way too risky to leave them in the stroller while you're inside the attractions. Consider taking your camcorder with you on only one day, preferably the last day of your trip when you're revisiting favorite attractions—that way you'll leave with a "WDW Greatest Hits" tape.

• If you do plan to take your camcorder with you frequently, make use of the lockers beneath the Railroad Station in the MK and near the main entrances of all three major parks. Lockers are a necessity if you'll be riding Space Mountain and Big Thunder Mountain Railroad, where you'll risk jarring the machine, or Splash Mountain, where there's a very good chance it'll get wet.

• Don't pan and zoom too much, because fast camera moves disorient the automatic focus—not to mention the viewer. If you're taping the kids, say, on the teacups, use the wide-angle setting and keep the camera stationary. Attempting to track them in close-ups as they spin past is beyond even a pro.

• Camcorders can be rented at the Kodak Camera Center on Main Street in the MK or at the Camera Center near Spaceship Earth at Epcot. Rental is $25 a day, and a refundable deposit of $300 is required. (The deposit is generally taken on a credit card, and the imprint is destroyed when you return the camera undamaged.)

• If you rent or borrow a camera, familiarize yourself with the machine before you begin to actually take pictures. Your kids may never forgive you for shooting their entire SuperStar Television appearance with the lens cap on.

• If you use narration, such as "We're in Frontierland now, looking toward Big Thunder Mountain Railroad," be sure to speak loudly. The background noise of the parks will muffle your words.

• Camcorder taping is allowed inside attractions, even many of those that prohibit flash photography.

• Be sure to capture events such as parades, character shows, and theater-style attractions—for example, the Country Bear Vacation Hoedown or the Indiana Jones

Epic Stunt Spectacular. These are especially fun to watch once you're home.

• Remember to ask each time you board the monorail if the driver's cab is vacant. Sooner or later you'll get the chance to ride up front, and one bonus is the chance to photograph the panoramic views of the parks as you enter.

TIPS FOR EXTRA-CROWDED TIMES

If your schedule is such that you simply have to go Easter week or in the dead of summer, the following tips will make the trip more manageable.

• Stay on-site. You'll have the advantage of the "Surprise Mornings" program, and you won't have to hassle with the traffic jams that paralyze Orlando during the on-season. It's also very helpful to be able to make dining reservations in advance.

• Allow an extra day—or two. First of all, you won't be able to see as much in a single day as you would if you were going at a less crowded time. Second, your family will tire more easily when the crowds are thick, and you'll need longer rest periods to recuperate. Many families schedule an entire day off from touring in the middle of the week, and this is really helpful when you're going in the busy season.

• You *must* be at the parks when they open. By 10 A.M. you'll be facing hour-long waits at many rides and the parks may even close to arriving guests.

• Read the sections on each park and choose the two or three attractions you most want to see. Focus on them and be aware that when you're touring at a

crowded time, you probably won't be able to "see it all."
Just make sure that what you do see is the best.

TIPS FOR BIG FAMILIES

If you're seeing WDW with a really big brood, the
following tips—all offered by family reunion veterans—
might make things run more smoothly.

• Staying on-site makes splitting up much easier,
since you can rely on the WDW transportation system
instead of the family car. This is especially vital if you
have a wide variation in age, stamina, or risk-tolerance
of the family members.

• The best on-site options for large families include
the trailers at Fort Wilderness, Disney's Old Key West,
the Disney Institute Villas, and the new BoardWalk
Villas.

• Rent a pager at Guest Services of your hotel or one
of the major theme parks. Because big groups tend to
scatter, a pager can be invaluable for getting everyone
reassembled when it's time to eat or head for home.
Lacking this, you can also leave messages for each
other at Guest Services.

• Have everyone wear the same color T-shirt or hat
each day. A tour operator passed along this tip, which
makes it much easier to spot "your people" in a sea of
faces.

• If the adults plan to head out for a night, an
in-room sitter is generally less expensive than drop-off
child care when more than three kids are involved.

10

★★★★★★★★★★★★★★★★★★★

*Life Beyond
Disney:
Universal
Studios,
Sea World,
and Other
Orlando
Attractions*

UNIVERSAL STUDIOS

Should You Visit MGM or Universal Studios?

Proving once again that imitation is the sincerest form of flattery, Universal and Disney-MGM opened studio theme parks a scant 18 months apart. Both parks offer mind-blowing technology, and there is a real split of opinion among the families surveyed as to which is better. In general, families with children under 11 preferred MGM. A quick scan of some of the attractions that MGM has added since opening—*MuppetVision 3-D*, Voyage of the Little Mermaid, Beauty and the Beast Stage Show, the Honey, I Shrunk the Kids Adventure Zone, and the Hunchback of Notre Dame Stage Show—shows that Disney is making a concerted effort to gear MGM more toward younger kids. Universal Studios, in contrast, is best known for high-thrill adventures such as Kong-frontation, Jaws, and Back to the Future, which scare the socks off of preschoolers but delight preteens and teens.

With a $39 adult admission fee and a cost of $31 for kids 3 to 9, Universal is nearly as expensive as MGM, but many area hotels offer slightly discounted tickets, and anyone flying down on USAir, the official airline of Universal Studios, gets a price break as well. Families surveyed also noticed that Universal seems less crowded than MGM. It is generally conceded at Disney that MGM was too small the day it opened, and although management has tried to control the crowds by keeping MGM open later at night than originally planned, the park can still become claustrophobic. Universal Studios is larger, and major attractions are spread out geographically, so—with the exception of the area around the main entrance—few sections of the park ever become unbearably crowded.

Universal does a good job of controlling crowd flow by breaking many presentations into stages. At Alfred Hitchcock, for example, a group of visitors is admitted into the first theater while the previous group is in theater two, and the group that entered before them is in the third phase of the show. This means that although the total presentation time is 40 minutes, a group is let into the first theater to begin the cycle every 15 minutes, dramatically reducing waiting time. Universal also presents several shows—the Animal Actors Stage Show and the Wild West Stunt Show, for example—in theaters so enormous that large groups can be seated at once, ensuring that even on the most crowded days anyone arriving at the theater 10 minutes before showtime can see the show.

In regard to how well the parks manage their own technology, the nod has to go to MGM. Universal has been plagued with attraction breakdowns since the week it opened, and in the early days many visitors requested refunds after highly publicized rides either malfunctioned or were closed for hours at a time. (The Jaws ride was shut down completely due to the frequency of malfunctions, but reopened, at last, in 1994.) Although Universal has made great strides since those early months, glitches are still fairly common, so be forewarned that some attractions may be shut down for an hour or two on the day you visit. On the day my family toured recently, Murder She Wrote, E.T. Adventure, and Earthquake were all closed down at different times during the course of an eight-hour period. It makes you appreciate the smooth competence of Disney more than ever.

Nonetheless, Universal packs some major punches, and Back to the Future, E.T. Adventure, Kongfrontation,

Jaws, the Funtastic World of Hanna-Barbera, and Earthquake match or surpass anything offered at WDW. So which is better—Universal or MGM? Since at this time each park is small enough to be comfortably toured in a day, there's no reason not to see both and draw your own conclusions.

YOUR FIRST HOUR AT UNIVERSAL STUDIOS

• The new parking garage is in New Jersey (seems that way, anyhow), so arrive at least 30 minutes before the main gate opens. Call either 363-8230 or 363-8000 the day before you plan to visit to confirm hours of operation.

• After getting your tickets, you'll wait in a small holding area for about 10 minutes. Hanna-Barbera characters such as Woody Woodpecker and the Flintstones often circulate among the crowd to pose for pictures and sign autographs.

• Generally, guests are allowed through the main turnstiles about 10 minutes before the official opening time. If a Nickelodeon Studios show is taping on the day you're visiting, it will be indicated on a sign outside the main turnstile, along with directions on how to get tickets.

Note: Watching a taping is time-consuming. If your kids are young and will be skipping many of Universal's scary attractions anyway, you'll have the time. But if your children are older and you'll be trying to cram all the big rides into your day, it's unlikely you'll want to devote two hours to viewing a taping.

• After entering the main turnstiles, early-arriving visitors are allowed partway down Plaza of the Stars and Rodeo Drive, the two major streets in Universal Studios. If you want to see Back to the Future, Jaws, or E.T. Adventure first, go down Rodeo Drive as far as you're allowed. If you'd rather see the Funtastic World of Hanna-Barbera, Kongfrontation, or Earthquake first, go down Plaza of the Stars until you're stopped by the ropes. Families who haven't had breakfast can stop for a pastry at the Beverly Hills Boulangerie before the ropes drop.

• Once the ropes drop, go directly to the Funtastic World of Hanna-Barbera. Because of its proximity to the main entrance, this attraction draws large lines from 10 A.M. on and must be visited early. After you've saved Elroy, try to convince the kids not to linger too long in the interactive play area behind the Hanna-Barbera ride. You can always come back again in midafternoon, but now you need to move on to the other big-name attractions as quickly as possible.

• If your kids are old enough, ride Kongfrontation, Jaws, and Back to the Future in rapid succession. (At this time of day, you shouldn't encounter any waits of longer than 15 minutes.) If your kids aren't up to the high-intensity rides, head toward E.T. Adventure, then the water ride in Fievel's Playground.

• If you have tickets for a Nickelodeon taping, it's probably time to head back toward the Nick Studios gate. If you're not planning to watch a taping, you're undoubtedly worn down from the impact of the rides and are ready for a break. Visit a theater-style attraction such as Ghostbusters, Terminator II in 3-D, the Horror

Makeup Show, the Wild West Stunt Show, Murder She Wrote, or the Animal Actors Stage Show next.

UNIVERSAL STUDIOS TOURING TIPS

• The same basic plan you used in the Disney theme parks applies here: You need to visit the major attractions—Kongfrontation, Back to the Future, E.T. Adventure, Jaws, Earthquake, and the Funtastic World of Hanna-Barbera—either early in the morning or in the evening. Take in the theater-style attractions in the afternoon.

If you miss one of the major continuous-loading attractions in the morning, hold off on it until two hours before the park closes. Midday waits of up to 90 minutes are common at popular attractions like Kongfrontation, but the crowds do ease off a bit during the dinner hour; and by the time the crowds have moved to the lake to watch the Dynamite Nights Stunt Spectacular, the lines at major attractions are much shorter.

• A bulletin board located across from Mel's Drive-In keeps you posted on upcoming showtimes and the approximate waits for continuous-loading attractions. Because Universal is big and spread out, crowd movement is uneven, so the board is definitely worth perusing on a crowded afternoon; you may find there's a 40-minute wait at Kongfrontation but a mere 5-minute wait at Earthquake.

• If you plan to see Universal in one day, it's unlikely you'll have time for a midafternoon break, such as returning to your hotel or visiting a water park. But the numerous theater-style attractions at Universal offer plenty of chances to rest up, and small kids can nap.

• If the kids burn out from too much riding or sitting, Universal offers a pleasant alternative to arcades—although, needless to say, the park has those too—in the form of the carnival midway in the Amity Beach section of the park. This section, modeled after the New England seacoast village that was beset by the great white star of *Jaws,* is rarely crowded. The kids can throw balls in a peach basket or try their luck at hoops while munching candy apples and popcorn. Playing the midway is like stepping back into a different era and is a nice mental break from all the pizzazz of the rides.

Fievel's Playground offers the same sort of escape for kids under 8. As in the Honey, I Shrunk the Kids Adventure Zone at MGM, however, the playground can become unbearably crowded, especially around the popular water ride, which can draw lines so long that a 40-minute wait is not uncommon in midafternoon.

• The theaters that hold the Horror Makeup Show, Alfred Hitchcock, Terminator II in 3-D, and Murder She Wrote are high capacity, so even if the lines in midafternoon look discouraging, odds are you'll still be seated. Consult the entertainment schedule that you receive with your ticket, or check the chalkboard at the attraction entrance for showtimes, and then put one parent in line about 20 minutes before the show is due to start. The other can take the kids for a drink or bathroom break. If you all opt to wait in line together, be aware that Universal has placed trash cans all through the queue areas of the high-capacity attractions in acknowledgment of the fact that visitors on a tight touring schedule may well be eating or drinking in line.

Likewise, the outdoor theaters for the Animal Actors Stage Show, Beetlejuice's Graveyard Revue, and the Wild West Stunt Show are huge. So long as you're through the gate 10 minutes before showtime, you'll get a seat.

• If you plan to see the Dynamite Nights Stunt Spectacular on the lake (which shows at the park closing time), be there at least 20 minutes before showtime. Unlike IllumiNations or the fireworks that close the Disney parks, the show is a boat race and subsequent explosion which take place at water level, so unless you're actually standing lakeside, you won't see much.

• Headed toward Back to the Future or another intense attraction? Universal employees are prepared to help families traveling with a baby or toddler to do a "baby swap" so that everyone can ride.

Universal employs height restrictions on only one ride—Back to the Future—and even then kids need to be only 40 inches or taller. (But just because any kid big enough to sit up is allowed on Jaws or Kongfrontation, that doesn't mean it's a good idea to take them; consult the ride descriptions for information on the special effects.) Other attractions such as E.T. Adventure and the Funtastic World of Hanna-Barbera provide separate stationary seating for kids under 40 inches, thus allowing families to go through the attraction as a group.

• Universal is currently offering value passes, which allow visitors to take in Sea World, Wet 'n Wild, and Busch Gardens as well. If you'll be spending lots of time in central Florida, the passes are cheaper than paying for the tickets separately.

UNIVERSAL STUDIOS ATTRACTIONS

Back to the Future

Flight-simulation technology makes a quantum leap forward—or is it backward?—in Back to the Future, which has drawn rave reviews since opening. After being briefed by Doc Brown (played by Christopher Lloyd of the movie series) in a preshow video that bad-boy Biff has sabotaged his time-travel experiments, you'll be loaded into six-passenger Deloreans. What follows is a high-speed chase back through the prehistoric era. The cars bounce around, but it's the flight-simulation techniques that are the real scream-rippers—far more intense than those provided by Disney's Star Tours or Body Wars. Passengers who can bear to glance away from the screen will notice that as many as 12 Deloreans, arranged in tiers, take the trip simultaneously, making Back to the Future a sort of ultimate drive-in movie.

At one point in your trip through the prehistoric era, you're even swallowed by a dinosaur, making the ride much too much for most kids under 7, although technically anyone over 40 inches is allowed to board. If your child does want to try it, brief him or her that the majority of the effects can be erased simply by closing your eyes— which is not a bad tip to keep in mind yourself if you're prone to queasiness. For those with strong stomachs, however, the ride is pure pleasure, still one of the hottest things in Orlando after nearly seven years in operation— high praise in a town that takes its fun seriously.

Earthquake

After a preshow hosted by Charlton Heston, visitors travel through two separate theaters, where they learn how special effects and stunts were done in the *Earthquake* movie. (The special effects and intricate models of San Francisco are somewhat of a revelation to most kids, since few have seen the original movie, which was made 23 years ago.) In the second preshow, audience volunteers are drafted to play quake victims, which is great fun for the kids who are chosen.

Note: Several Universal attractions, most notably Earthquake, Alfred Hitchcock, and Murder She Wrote, require that visitors move from theater to theater in the course of the presentation. It helps the lines outside the attraction move steadily, but is tough on families lugging a sleeping child. If your youngster dozes off during one of the preshows of the theater-style attractions, it is easier to hold her than attempt to put her down, since you'll undoubtedly be moving on within a few minutes.

After the preshows, you'll be loaded into your subway car for the ride itself. Earthquake is a very short ride and less intense than the hype may have led you to believe. Most kids will hold up just fine through the rumbles, fires, floods, and train wrecks, and, as one mother wrote, "It's fun to feel it really happen instead of watching it on a screen." And it's even more fascinating to watch the water recede, the concrete mend itself, and the fires implode when the ride is over!

Kongfrontation

You'll go head-to-head with one of the fiercest monsters in movie history in the justifiably popular Kongfrontation. The long "underground" queue area, meant to emulate the subways of New York, sets the mood with TV cameras overhead reporting that the ape is loose and on a rampage. You'll eventually be loaded onto trams (which carry about 30 riders) and lifted above the fiery streets of a city under siege. Riders will confront Kong up close twice, coming near enough to inspect his 4-foot fangs and feel the hot blast of banana breath in their faces. This is one real-looking ape, and the ride is simply too intense for toddlers. Some parents of kids as old as 8 reported that the combination of the darkness, the bursts of flames, and, of course, the mega-ape had their kids clutching their arms and ducking their heads.

Older kids love the ride, of course, and rate it extremely highly—especially the impressive finale where Kong grabs your tram and "drops" you back onto the street. (The actual fall is only about 6 feet; this attraction relies heavily on its atmospheric effects to scare riders.) As your wounded tram limps to a halt, you'll learn that your close brush with disaster has made the evening news. A video camera inside your car filmed your reaction to the drop, and the tape is replayed on a TV monitor above your head, adding a novel close to a powerfully fun ride.

Note: The Universal people are no dummies; every major attraction empties through a gift shop selling memorabilia from the movie or TV show on which the attraction is based. You can pick up a Jetsons T-shirt after riding the Funtastic World of Hanna-Barbera, hats with fins after riding Jaws, and an ashtray from the Bates Motel as you exit Alfred Hitchcock. At Safari Outfitters, adjacent to Kongfrontation, you can pose clutched in the fist of King Kong himself for a family souvenir shot; the pictures are developed immediately, and at $5 per pose it's a fun and reasonably priced memento.

The Funtastic World of Hanna-Barbera

This attraction features a high-speed cartoon flight-simulation chase and is very popular with kids in every age group.

The premise of the ride is established in the brief preshow, when you learn that Dick Dastardly has kidnapped Elroy Jetson and that it is up to you, along with Yogi Bear and Boo Boo, to rescue him. You'll go into another room to be loaded into cars that seat six to eight passengers. Since the cars will be lurching a bit during the movie, children under 40 inches tall, pregnant women, anyone with back or neck problems, or those who are just plain gutless are ushered to stationary seats at the front of the theater.

The flight-simulation effects make you feel like you're really flying, and most kids squeal with delight as they meet up with other well-known Hanna-Barbera characters, such as the Flintstones and Scooby Doo. Needless to say, Elroy is safely back with his family by the end of the ride. After Yogi brings you in for a rather rough landing, you go on to the interactive area, where you can make a choir of birds sing by stepping on a huge piano and color your own cartoon via computer.

Note: Like Alfred Hitchcock and the other attractions along the Plaza of the Stars, huge lines form by 10 A.M. as late-arriving visitors walk through the front gate and queue up to the first attractions they see. Visit the Funtastic World of Hanna-Barbera first thing in the morning, both to avoid the crowds and to use the ride as a gauge for how well your kids will handle the more intense flight-simulation ride, Back to the Future.

Terminator II in 3-D

Universal's latest action show, Terminator II in 3-D combines 3-D effects, live actors, and movie clips. (The best special effect is the way the live actors seem to emerge from the movie screen onto the stage and then later run back "into" the movie.) The show is fast, loud, and violent—just like the film series it's based on—with the action fairly difficult to follow unless you're familiar with the *Terminator* movies.

Due to the size of the theater, Terminator II in 3-D is relatively easy to get in to, so it is best saved for the afternoon.

E.T. Adventure

This charming ride is as technologically impressive and atmospherically seductive as anything at MGM, but, because there's nothing scary about it, the entire family can enjoy it as a group.

The attraction begins with a brief preshow featuring Steven Spielberg and E.T., after which you file through a holding area and—somewhat mysteriously at the time—are required to give your name in exchange for a small plastic "interplanetary passport." Then you move into the queue area, which winds through the deep dark woods and is so evocative that it even smells and sounds like a forest. (Universal in general does a bang-up job of setting the mood in the queue areas; Kongfrontation has many visitors in a lather of nerves before they even board the ride, and E.T. Adventure is designed to make you feel small and childlike.)

After handing your "passport" to the attendant, children under 40 inches tall or anyone elderly, heavy, pregnant, or otherwise unsteady are loaded into flying gondolas. Others get to ride bicycles, and the lead bike in each group has E.T. in the front basket. You rise up and fly over the forest in an effective simulation of the escape scene in the *E.T.* movie. After narrowly missing being captured by the police, you manage to return E.T. to his home planet, a magical place populated by dozens of cuddly aliens.

The ride closes on a stunning note, for as you sail past E.T. for the final time, he bids you farewell by name. When you give your name to the attendant before you enter the queue area, your name is computer-coded onto the plastic passport. As you hand over the passport and mount your bicycle, the passports are fed into a computer. The ride thus "knows" who is riding which bicycle, enabling E.T. to say "Good-bye, Jordan, Good-bye Leigh, Good-bye Kim . . ." as your family flies past.

Note: Unfortunately, this personalized "good-bye" system is the most frequently malfunctioning part of the ride, so I wouldn't mention it to the kids at all. That way, if it works, everyone is extra-delighted, and if it doesn't, the ride is still an upbeat experience.

Alfred Hitchcock: The Art of Making Movies

You pick up 3-D glasses in the holding area, but only part of the film that follows requires them. This rapid-fire montage of classic scenes from Alfred Hitchcock thrillers will go right over the heads of most kids, who aren't familiar enough with the movies to tense up when they see that *Psycho* shower curtain. The brief 3-D effect, however, is a thrilling adaptation from a scene in *The Birds;* and you don't have to be a Hitchcock buff to get chills down your spine as those ravens appear to be coming right off the screen toward you.

After the movie, you are directed into a separate theater, where audience volunteers illustrate how the infamous shower scene in *Psycho* was shot. This part may be too scary for younger children. If one of the kids would like to see the 3-D movie but skip the *Psycho* portion, inform the attendant, who will let you walk straight through the second theater and into the interactive area, where you can play with the props until the rest of your party joins you.

The interactive area is interesting, giving guests a chance to try out action special effects. And if you miss the Bates Motel Gift Shop on your way out, Mother will be very upset.

Jaws

As the people of Amity Beach learned, that darn shark just won't stay away.

Although closed down for more than two years due to malfunctions, Jaws is now back online in a big outdoor set. The shark rises from the water several times quite suddenly, the unseen boat before you "gets it" in a gruesome way, and there are also grenade launches, explosions, and a fuel spill. There's tremendous splashing—especially on the left side of the boat—and most of the boat captains throw themselves totally into the experience by shrieking, shouting, and firing guns on cue. It all adds up to one action-packed boat ride.

Kids 7 to 11 gave Jaws a strong thumbs-up, and the ride was also popular with many kids under 7. The fact that you're outdoors in the daylight, however, diminishes the intensity; the really brave should wait until evening—the "Shark in the Dark" effects are much more scary.

Note: Interestingly enough, Universal invested $50 million on the ride, which is more than six times what Steven Spielberg spent on the original 1975 movie.

The Gory, Gruesome, and Grotesque Horror Makeup Show

A witty pair of young actors illustrate certain makeup effects onstage, but you'll also see clips from *The Exorcist* and *The Fly* as well as an astounding man-to-beast transformation scene from the little-known *An American Werewolf in London.* Although the movie clips and general gore level are too intense for preschoolers, most kids over 7 can stomach the show which is, in the final analysis, an informative illustration of how special effects have become more and more realistic over the years.

The Animal Actors Stage Show

If your children are strung out from a combination of 90-degree heat, 3-D birds, and man-eating dinosaurs, the Animal Actors Stage Show will offer a welcome change of pace. The show features apes, birds, and Benji-clone dogs, and takes place in a large open-air arena. Kids in both the 4-to-7 and 7-to-11 age groups rated the animals very highly—and adults love the show, too. This attraction is fun to videotape and watch again at home.

Murder She Wrote Mystery Theater

This amusing show, which allows the audience to select the outcome of an episode of the well-known TV series, has been overlooked and somewhat underrated by the crowds, who rush past it on their way to the theme rides. Fans of the TV series will find the attraction especially engaging—they even get to choose a dinner date for their beloved Angela Lansbury—but the presentation is so wittily presented and encourages so much audience participation that almost everyone ends up having fun.

As at most of the theater-style Universal attractions, you move from theater to theater as you edit the show, add sound effects, and ultimately select the outcome of the episode. Although kids under 7 won't get most of the jokes, kids 7 to 11 will enjoy the attraction more than you'd guess, especially if they're chosen to come up on stage and help with the sound effects, a possibility that becomes more likely if you sit near the front of the theater.

The Wild West Stunt Show

Funny, fast moving, and full of surprises, this show ranks at the top of the list with kids 7 to 11 and rates highly with kids under 7 as well. The shoot-'em-ups, fistfights, and explosions are played strictly for laughs, and sometimes the comedy tends to overshadow how dangerous these stunts really are. This is a good choice for the whole family, and, like the Animal Actors Stage Show, it's fairly easy to get in to even in the crowded parts of the afternoon.

Fievel's Playground

Fievel's Playground is a cleverly designed play area filled with western-style props, including a harmonica that plays notes as kids slide down it, a giant talking Tiger the cat, canteens to squirt, cowboy hats to bounce in, spiderwebs to climb, and a separate ball pit and slide area for toddlers.

The centerpiece of the playground is a 200-foot water ride in which kids and parents are loaded into "sardine cans built for two" and swept through a sewer. The ride is zippier than it looks, will get you soaking wet, and is so addictive that most kids clamor to get back on again immediately. The water ride is very popular and loads slowly, so by afternoon the lines are prohibitive. If you come in the morning, it is possible to ride several times with minimal waits, but by afternoon one ride is all you can reasonably expect.

Note: Fievel's Playground often opens an hour or two after the main park. If you ride the big-deal rides and then show up at the playground at the opening time indicated on the entertainment schedule, you'll be able to try the water ride without much of a wait.

Fievel's Playground is great fun, and most kids could happily stay for an hour or two. The only drawbacks are that, like the Honey, I Shrunk the Kids Adventure Zone at MGM, it needs to be much, much larger; and Universal unwisely admits preteens and teens, whose rowdy play makes the area downright unsafe for younger kids, especially in the afternoon when the playground is crowded. How about a few reverse height restrictions, guys?

A Day in the Park with Barney

Designed to appeal to Universal's youngest guests, A Day in the Park with Barney is actually an enclosed, parklike setting with pop-art colored flowers and trees. Barney appears several times a day in a song-and-dance show, and there is also an indoor interactive play area designed for toddlers. This play area is far cooler and calmer than Fievel's next door, and the nearby shop and food stand are never crowded.

Universal has located all the stuff for very young children close together. If you have preschoolers, hang an immediate right on Rodeo Drive after you enter the park and follow the signs to E.T. Adventure. The Animal Actors Stage Show, A Day in the Park with Barney, E.T. Adventure, and Fievel's Playground are all located within close proximity to one another, so a family with kids under 7 can set up base here for the afternoon.

Rocky and Bullwinkle Live

This seasonal stage show features not only Rocky and his "enormoose" friend Bullwinkle, but also Dudley Do-Right, Snidely Whiplash, and the notorious Boris and Natasha (who have headed for Hollywood, since jobs are getting hard to find in the spy business). The distinctive style of humor of the late Jay Ward is in truth so sophisticated that many of the jokes will go right past the kids. The production is enjoyable on several levels, however, and the kids will giggle at the pure silliness of the situations while the adults smirk at the satire and in-jokes. The characters hang around after the show for autographs and pictures, and Rocky and Bullwinkle both arrive and depart via a bright blue prop plane, which rolls through the streets of the park, stirring up a bit of excitement.

Rocky and Bullwinkle Live runs only during summer and major holidays. The show takes place outdoors and is completely exposed to the sun, so afternoon performances can be sweltering. Come to the first show of the day or wait until evening.

Beetlejuice's Graveyard Revue

A rock 'n' roll dance show starring Dracula, the Wolfman, Phantom of the Opera, and Frankenstein and his Bride, the Revue is very popular with the 7-to-11 age group and teens—although the show is so goofy and upbeat that younger kids certainly won't be frightened by the ghouls.

This is a high-tech performance featuring pulsating lights, fog machines, synchronized dancing, and wry renditions of rock classics. (My personal favorite is the Bride of Frankenstein's version of "You Make Me Feel Like a Natural Woman.") The theater is huge, and this 15-minute show plays frequently throughout the day, so getting in isn't too tough—work it in to your schedule whenever it happens to suit you.

Lucy: A Tribute

Fans of "I Love Lucy" should take a few minutes to walk through this exhibit. It houses memorabilia from the famous TV show, which includes scale models of the Tropicana and the Ricardos' apartment, clothes and jewelry worn on the show, personal pictures and letters from Lucy and Desi's home life, and the numerous Emmys that Lucille Ball won over the years. The "California Here We Come Game" is a treat for hard-core trivia buffs. By answering questions about episodes of "I Love Lucy," game participants get to travel with the Mertzes and Ricardos on their first trip to California. They lost me somewhere in the desert, but perhaps you'll do better.

The Nickelodeon Tour

After being labeled somewhat of a drag by reviewers and families, this tour has been revamped and is now much more fun. Even if you opt to skip the taping of a Nickelodeon Studios show, your kids will enjoy the 45-minute walk-through tour. You'll see the sets of shows they'll immediately recognize, perhaps get a glimpse of a show in production, and then move on to the popular Game Lab, where audience volunteers play games and one lucky kid is slopped and glopped in the best Nickelodeon tradition. Kids 7 to 11 rated the tour very highly, as did younger kids who were familiar with the Nick line-up.

Note: Even if you don't plan to take in the tour or a taping, drop by the Nick Studios entrance and check out the Green Slime Geyser, which periodically erupts and spews into the air an unearthly colored substance about the consistency of pudding. The bathrooms in the Nickelodeon section have green slime soap in the dispensers; for some preschoolers, this is the highlight of the trip.

SHOWS AT UNIVERSAL STUDIOS

Showtimes are listed on the entertainment schedule. It's worth your while to take in at least a couple.

If you're trying to do the whole park in a day, it's a good idea to plan your meals around the musical shows, such as eating your noontime burger at Mel's Drive-In while the Hollywood Hi-Tones croon ballads from the '50s, or taking in a bit of Irish folksinging at Finnegan's Bar and Grill along with your evening meal of shepherd's pie and ale. It's like a free dinner show!

The most well known of the Universal Studios shows is the Dynamite Nights Stunt Spectacular, which is staged at closing time every evening. The show is Universal's answer to the popular Indiana

Jones Epic Stunt Spectacular at MGM and involves a high-speed boat chase that ends in a fiery explosion. Be aware that you must stake out your position early. One of the best vantage spots is on the small pavilion in front of the Animal Actors Stage Show—if you don't mind getting splashed, that is.

BEST FOOD BETS AT UNIVERSAL STUDIOS

The fastest fast food is simply to purchase a hotdog from one of the many vendors scattered throughout the park, but you'll be missing much of the fun if you eat on the run for all three meals. Universal has many appealing dining choices and, in general, the food is tastier and less pricey than that in the Disney theme parks. Not only is there a good selection, but they keep the lines moving, even during lunchtime on busy summer days.

In addition, because most families have a one-day ticket and are trying to cram all of Universal into 12 straight hours of touring, few break up the day by leaving the park. That means you'll need to rest up in the afternoon or risk having the kids—and maybe the parents—collapse in tears of exhaustion at 6 P.M. A late lunch or early dinner is advised; it will get you off the streets during the hottest and most crowded time of day and give everyone a chance to rest and regroup before heading on to those attractions you missed earlier. Some of the restaurants listed accept reservations at the door, which is a good idea if you'll be dining at peak hours.

The Hard Rock Cafe

What's there to say? The Hard Rock Cafes, found in major cities all over the world, are justifiably famous for their funky atmosphere, raucously friendly service, and tasty, unassuming food. The one in Orlando is the largest of all, with a correspondingly large collection of pop memorabilia; even the guitar-shaped building is fascinating. (Note the pink Cadillac crashing into the front of the facade.) Hard Rock T-shirts and sweatshirts are highly valued souvenirs, especially among status-conscious teenagers and preteens. It would be a shame to visit Universal and not take in the Hard Rock.

The problem is when to go. The Hard Rock Cafe does not take reservations, and large crowds are the norm from midafternoon on. If you have young kids along, the best bet is to eat an early lunch around 11 A.M., when the cafe isn't so crowded that you can't get up and look around. Another crowd-busting option is an early dinner around 4 P.M.

Others swear that the Hard Rock gets better and better as they day wears on and that it's impossible to truly get into the spirit of the place before dark. If adults in your party would like to linger over drinks and listen to the music, this is a good option for a parents' night out.

Note: You can enter the Hard Rock Cafe from Universal Studios or from a separate parking lot, so you don't need a Universal Studios ticket to enter the restaurant. The Hard Rock is, in fact, popular with Orlando locals, which is one reason why it is always hard to get in.

If you just want to buy a Hard Rock T-shirt, you can purchase it downstairs without entering the restaurant.

Finnegan's Bar and Grill

Friendly, informal, and with the added bonus of live music during peak dining hours, Finnegan's is a great place to rest up and pig out. It's dark inside, too, even on the most blistering summer afternoons, and kids can stretch out and nap in the booths.

Lombard's Landing

If you crave a fancier meal, such as prime rib or fresh pompano, Lombard's Landing is a beautiful restaurant in the Fisherman's Wharf section of San Francisco. The service is leisurely and the atmosphere a bit more elegant than most of the park restaurants, so opt for Lombard's only if your kids can be counted on to behave reasonably well (or sleep) through a 90-minute meal. Lombard's Landing becomes quite crowded at dinner, so a late lunch or midafternoon meal is a better bet. Reservations are recommended.

Cafe la Bamba

A good choice for Mexican food, with margaritas and live music on the patio during the lunch and dinner hours.

Studio Stars

Big eaters in the party? Studio Stars runs lunch and dinner buffets (adults $10, children $5), which are a good choice if you crave more than a burger but still want to get your food quickly.

Mel's Drive-In

Unquestionably the place to go for fast food, Mel's offers home-style burgers and fries, served up with fifties-era music and a bevy of car hops on roller skates. The drive-in is based on the one in the film *American Graffiti,* and even kids far too young to remember the movie, much less the decade being spoofed, will fall for the tabletop jukeboxes and the vintage cars parked outside. If you plan ahead and arrive about 15 minutes before showtime, you can claim one of the outside tables and catch a performance of the Hollywood Hi-Tones, an excellent a capella group, while you eat.

Louie's

A nice spot for a fast Italian dinner, especially if you're headed for the nearby Dynamite Nights Stunt Spectacular, Louie's offers spaghetti for kids at a reasonable $3 and a choice of hearty pasta favorites for adults.

Best Places for a Snack

Schwab's Pharmacy

We can't promise you'll be discovered here as Lana Turner allegedly was, but the milkshakes are made the old-fashioned way and are absolutely delicious.

San Francisco Pastry Co.

If you need a break after riding Earthquake or Jaws, stop off for a brownie, a kiwi tart, or a fantastic flan. (The Key West flan with lime is the best!)

Chez Alcatraz

Sweets aren't your thing? You can always sit by the dock of the bay here in the San Francisco district and enjoy a crab or shrimp salad. Just don't leave your food if you go back for a napkin—those seagulls circling overhead mean business.

CLASSIC UNIVERSAL STUDIOS PHOTO OPS

Universal offers a wealth of great photo opportunities, surpassing the Disney parks in the sheer variety of campy locales for an unusual family snapshot. Your kids would look great in any of the following locations.

- Perched on the hood of one of the brightly colored vintage cars permanently parked outside Mel's Drive-In.

- With their heads inside the mouth of the great white shark strung up in the Amity Beach section.

- Vamping and camping it up with Mae West, Charlie Chaplin, the Blues Brothers, or any of the other Hollywood stars who roam Rodeo Drive.

- In front of the Bates Motel, near the Hard Rock Cafe.

- In front of the globe and fountains outside the main turnstile.

- In front of the Green Slime Geyser beside the Nickelodeon Studios entrance.

- For $5 you can pose on a bike with E.T., beneath the mouth of a T-Rex, or in the grip of King Kong. Just stop by E.T.'s Photo Spot, the Jurassic Park booth, or Safari Outfitters as you exit Kongfrontation.

- Kodak sponsors the Trick Photography Photo Spots scattered throughout the park, although the most elaborate are in the "boneyard" of props on Plaza of the Stars. By placing your camera in the indicated spot and arranging your family in front of specially scaled props, you can turn the kids into the crew of a NASA space shuttle or photograph them in front of the Hollywood Hills.

FAVORITE TEEN AND PRETEEN ATTRACTIONS AT UNIVERSAL STUDIOS

Most of the visitors 11 to 17 rated Universal as "grosser and wilder" than MGM, and in this age group that's a compliment. Attractions especially popular with teens and preteens include the following:

- Kongfrontation
- Back to the Future
- Terminator II in 3-D
- Jaws
- Alfred Hitchcock: The Art of Making Movies
- The Gory, Gruesome, and Grotesque Horror Makeup Show
- Dynamite Nights Stunt Spectacular
- Beetlejuice's Graveyard Revue

And, not surprisingly, this age group considered a visit to the Hard Rock Cafe an essential wrap-up to a perfect day at Universal Studios.

UNIVERSAL STUDIOS DON'T-MISS LIST

- The Funtastic World of Hanna-Barbera
- Kongfrontation
- E.T. Adventure
- Back to the Future
- Jaws
- The Animal Actors Stage Show—if your kids are under 10
- The Wild West Stunt Show
- Fievel's Playground—if your kids are under 10

UNIVERSAL STUDIOS
WORTH-YOUR-WHILE LIST

- Earthquake
- Alfred Hitchcock: The Art of Making Movies

- Murder She Wrote Mystery Theater
- The Horror Makeup Show
- Terminator II in 3-D
- Dynamite Nights Stunt Spectacular
- The Nick Tour—if your kids are under 10
- Rocky and Bullwinkle Live
- A Nickelodeon taping—if one of your child's favorites is in production on the day you visit
- A Day in the Park with Barney—if you have preschoolers along

YOUR LAST HOUR AT UNIVERSAL STUDIOS

• If you want to see the Dynamite Nights Stunt Spectacular, find a spot around the lagoon at least 20 minutes before showtime. Benches are everywhere, so after you stake out a good spot, one parent can go back for snacks so you can enjoy a picnic while you wait for the show.

• If you don't care to see the lagoon show, you'll find that it draws so many people to one spot that it's now much easier to get into rides like Kongfrontation or Jaws, which may have been swamped all day. The Jaws ride is much more atmospheric at night, so if you're brave enough, make it your last stop.

• As you work your way toward the exit, many characters such as Ace Ventura, the Blues Brothers, and the Hanna-Barbera cartoon gang will be circulating among the crowds. If you haven't gotten pictures or autographs earlier, now's your chance.

- Some of the shops and restaurants stay open 20 to 30 minutes past the official park closing time. If the exits seem glutted, stop for a drink or check out the shops until the crowd disperses.

- Forget about slipping into the Hard Rock Cafe for a nightcap as you leave. Eleven thousand other people have the same good idea.

THE SCARE FACTOR AT UNIVERSAL STUDIOS

The shows and tours are family-oriented and fine for everyone, but some of the big-name attractions are too frightening for preschoolers.

Universal imposes very few height restrictions and thus gives parents little guidance. Kids under 40 inches are banned from Back to the Future and are required to use special seating on E.T. Adventure and the Funtastic World of Hanna-Barbara; but beyond these minimal restrictions, parents are the ones who decide who rides what.

Any child old enough to sit on his own can ride Jaws, Earthquake, and Kongfrontation. Universal seems to set the rules based on how physically wild the ride is—and none of the rides listed bounces you around too much. But they're psychologically scary, and a visit to Kongfrontation or Alfred Hitchcock may lead to more bad dreams than even the wildest roller coaster. Although individual reactions vary from child to child—my own son has adored Kongfrontation since he was four—read the ride descriptions and consult the following list to help you decide.

Attractions Fine for Anyone

- The Funtastic World of Hanna-Barbera—especially if you choose the stationary seats
- E.T. Adventure
- The Animal Actors Stage Show
- Murder She Wrote Mystery Theater
- Earthquake
- Lucy: A Tribute
- Rocky and Bullwinkle Live
- Beetlejuice's Graveyard Revue—unless the child is afraid of loud noises
- Fievel's Playground, including the water ride
- A Day in the Park with Barney

Attractions Best for Kids 7 Years or Older

- Kongfrontation
- Back to the Future
- Jaws
- Alfred Hitchcock: The Art of Making Movies
- The Gory, Gruesome, and Grotesque Horror Make-up Show
- Terminator II in 3-D

SEA WORLD

Opened in 1973, Sea World is best known as the home of Shamu and the killer whales. Sea World's claim to fame is its lineup of three standing shows: the Shamu Show, the Dolphin Fest, and the Sea Lion and Otter

Show. These three classics are funny, fascinating, and
very worthwhile. See them if you do nothing else.

All the shows take place in enormous open-air
theaters, so touring Sea World is as simple as consulting
your map for showtimes and being at the theater
about 15 minutes early. Clever preshows, such as the
mime at the Sea Lion show and the silly Shamu quiz,
make the waiting bearable. (And as you enter Shamu
Stadium, be sure to take a snapshot of the kids on top
of the whale statue.)

Note: Be forewarned that if you opt to sit in the
"splash zone"—the first 10 rows of the stadium—
Shamu's good-bye wave will leave you not just
splashed, but drenched straight through to your underwear. Kids enjoy the blast of saltwater, but if you're
touring off-season, or catching a nighttime show, it
may be wiser to sit farther back and laugh at the
unwary tourists down by the tank.

Other shows are updated on a rotating basis. There
is generally a water-skiing show, acrobatics, films,
musicals, a Polynesian revue, and a laser light show.
Work these in as your schedule permits; they are well
done, but not as essential as the three Sea World
classics mentioned previously.

Sea World is also known for its fascinating standing
exhibits, such as the Penguin Encounter, where you
can observe the tuxedoed charmers both above
and below the ice floe—and witness their startling
transformation from awkward walkers into sleek
swimmers.

Note: Check the entertainment schedule for feeding
time, when the trainers slip about on the iceberg with
buckets of fish, and the penguins waddle determinedly
behind them. The birds ingest the fish in one amazing

gulp, and you can stand on the top observation level and watch for as long as you like.

If your kids are too cool to like cute, try the Terrors of the Deep exhibit, where you'll encounter sharks, moray eels, and barracudas at close quarters. The California sea lions are at the Pacific Point Preserve. In Key West at Sea World, you'll find Florida's own endangered species—the manatee—as well as sea turtles, dolphins, stingrays, and other species indigenous to the Florida Keys. There are also underwater viewing tanks, where you can observe many of the animals up close. These continuous-viewing exhibits do not have specific showtimes and can be visited at your leisure as you circle the park.

In 1995 Sea World added Wild Arctic, an exhibit dedicated to polar bears. You can ascend to the top of the exhibit either via a motion-simulation helicopter "ride" or by walking. (Kids must be 42 inches tall to take the motion-simulation ride.) Lines at Wild Arctic are long just after the nearby Shamu show lets out; if you visit while one of the Shamu shows is in progress, you'll get through much more quickly.

Note: A new attraction, Journey to Atlantis, is slated to open in 1998.

The Budweiser Clydesdales are also part of the Sea World family, and children thrill at the chance to meet these huge but gentle creatures. At certain times of the day, noted on the entertainment schedule, one of the horses is taken out into a paddock, where children can get close enough to have a picture taken. The nearby Anheuser-Busch Hospitality Center is a quiet, cool oasis; there are free beer samples for adults, and the deli inside is never as crowded as the other Sea World restaurants.

Sea World is a low-stress environment, much less frenetic than the other Orlando parks. It can be easily seen in six or seven hours, and is laid out so that the crowds pretty much flow from one scheduled show to the other. Following the recommended show schedule will minimize backtracking. The park is so beautifully landscaped that you often can't see one stadium from the other, and the sense of space is a welcome change after a week spent in the Magic Kingdom or MGM. But the openness also means that children up to age 5 will benefit from a stroller; fortunately, the dolphin-shaped rental strollers are so cute that most kids climb in without a fuss.

If you're feeling guilty about taking the kids out of school, Sea World offers educational tours (*Quick:* Can you tell the difference between a sea lion and a seal?). A daily 90-minute tour, Animal Lover's Adventure, is appropriate for any age; it takes visitors into the habitats of several different Sea World animals and explores what they eat, how their group dynamics work, and how they care for their young. A better tour choice for kids 10 and up is Animal Training Discoveries; it is offered several times a week and lasts for only 45 minutes. Animal Training Discoveries focuses primarily on one animal, which varies from day to day, and allows you to meet the trainer and ask questions.

The tours are reasonably priced (adults $6, children $5), and reservations are not necessary. Either buy your tour ticket when you purchase your general-admission ticket, or, if you get the urge to join a tour after a few hours in the park, return to Guest Services near the main entrance.

Note: If more than one is tour is scheduled, don't take the first one of the day. Let the kids explore the theme park for a while and see a few shows during the empty morning hours, then return for the tour in the afternoon as the park becomes more crowded.

Small children welcome the numerous chances to get close to the beasties at Sea World. My 4-year-old son loved feeding the harmless-looking but actually quite vicious seals and the vicious-looking but actually quite harmless stingrays. For $3 you can get three small fish and toss them to the seals, sea lions, or dolphins. The dolphins and stingrays are in shallow tanks so that children can reach over and touch them as they glide by. Running a hand along the flank of a dolphin or flinging a fish into the whiskered mouth of a furiously barking sea lion is a real thrill for a child, and the experience will probably stay with her long after the shows and tours have faded from memory.

Another kick for kids is Shamu's Happy Harbor, a play area that puts those at MGM and Universal to shame. Shamu's Harbor is not only happy, it's huge—with an elaborate web of climbing nets, a ship heavy-laden with water-firing muskets, a splashy climb-through area, a variety of ball pits to sink into, and padded pyramids to climb. After a few hours spent in shows and exhibits, stop by and let the kids play for a while. There's a shaded seating area below the climbing pits so that parents can relax. A separate play area for toddlers ensures that they don't get tangled up in the webs, whacked by an older kid on a tire swing, or, worst of all, become confused in the mazes and exit far from where Mom and Dad are waiting. Because several of the play areas involve water, some parents let kids wear their bathing suits under their shorts. Shamu's Happy Harbor provides a nice in-park break on a summer day full of touring. There's a midway and arcade next door, so older kids can hang out while the younger ones play.

Sea World admission is $38 for adults, $32 for kids 3 to 11, but numerous discount coupons can be found floating around Orlando. The park opens at 9 A.M., is virtually empty until 11 A.M., and can be comfortably toured in a single day. (In fact, Sea World is a good park to visit on a day when you're planning something else, like a trip to Wet 'n Wild.) Have your hand stamped as you leave, spend the afternoon relaxing at your hotel or at one of the water parks, and return for the evening show, the fireworks, or—if you purchased tickets earlier in the day—the nightly Polynesian luau. Call (407) 351-3600 for more information.

Sea World Educational Programs

If you think your kids would benefit from a more extensive program, Camp Sea World offers many one-day classes geared for kids as young as 3. "Colorful Critters" is aimed at toddlers and preschoolers; school-age kids up to eighth grade can take "Whose Genes Are These?" There are also five-day classes that allow a more in-depth study of marine animals. The one-day classes are $45; the five-day are $100 for half-day classes, $200 for full-day. The vast majority of the offerings are in the summer. Call for the Camp Sea World brochure at least two months before your trip: 1-800-406-2244 or (407) 363-2380.

Even more fun are the sleepovers, which allow kids in grades 2 to 6 to spend the night in the Sea World park. Depending on which animal is the focus, kids will sleep in Dolphin Cove, with the manatees, or even bed down (yikes!) with the sharks in Terrors of the Deep. The sleepovers are a very reasonable $60, with supper and breakfast included. Kindergartners through third-graders can bring a parent and participate in the family sleepovers. There's an "Egg-cellent Adventure" with the penguins at Easter, "Mother's Day Memories" with baby animals and their moms in May, a "Father's Day Fishin' Trip" in June, and a Terrors of the Deep sleepover at Halloween. Cost for the family sleepovers is $40 per person.

All Camp Sea World activities are popular, so advance reservations are a must. The wonderful brochure not only outlines the available classes for every age group, but also gets you so fired up that you want to register for everything.

GATORLAND

The—*ahem*—unique ambience of Gatorland is established by the fact that you enter through a giant blue concrete gator mouth. Although most of the alligators within are rendered passive by the Florida sun, things do perk up four times a day at the Gator Jumparoo. The gators leap as high as five feet out of the water to retrieve whole chickens from the hands of the trainers. One young cynic surveyed pointed out that the animals jump highest at the first show of the day, aka "breakfast." The Gator Wrestlin' Show and Snakes of Florida are also big hits with kids.

This campy little place, which also has a small zoo and a train ride, can be easily toured in two or three hours. Children might like a souvenir shot taken of them holding either an alligator or a boa constrictor. And while Sea World certainly doesn't serve dolphin, Gatorland suffers no qualms about biting the hand that feeds it. You can pick up a few cans of Gator Chowder at the gift shop, surely a unique thank-you for those neighbors back home who are watering the plants while you're away. Gatorland admission is $12 for adults, $9 for kids 3 to 11. Call 1-800-393-JAWS or (407) 855-5496.

WET 'N WILD

The atmosphere here doesn't stack up to the Huck Finn feel of River Country or the tropical splendor of Typhoon Lagoon, but for families staying off-site, Wet 'n Wild is a great place to cool off without getting back into the mouse race.

This was the original water theme park in Orlando and in terms of sheer thrills, the preteen crowd surveyed claim it's still the best. The six-story plunge of the Der Stuka, the twisting tubes of the Mach 5, or a spiraling descent through The Black Hole are not for the faint of heart. Wet 'n Wild's wildest attraction, the Bomb Bay, sends riders on a six-second free-fall down a 76-foot slide and is, like the other big-deal attractions, strictly off-limits to children under 48 inches tall. The newest addition is the Fuji Flyer, a four-person, toboggan-like slide. These rides are enough to knock the breath out of even a strong swimmer; some kids who make the height requirements still aren't up to the intensity of the attractions, so if you have doubts, steer your 8-year-old toward the smaller slides and flumes.

Small children and others who are chicken of the sea can slide along in a Bubba Tub or float down the Lazy River in a big rubber tube. Wet 'n Wild also offers a $1.5 million children's water playground, billed as a "safe, fun environment for kids 1 to 10." Preschoolers and unsteady swimmers have their own wave pool, a miniature raging rapids, and fiberglass flumes designed for riders under 48 inches tall. It's the perfect addition for families whose children range in ages and who need a place that can be both Wet 'n Wild and Wet 'n Mild.

Tickets are $25 for adults, $20 for kids 3 to 9, but your best bet is to arrive in late afternoon or early evening, when admission is half price. Discounts take effect at 3 P.M. during the off-season and at 5 P.M. in summer, when the park stays open until 11 P.M. Crowds become far more manageable as the sun goes down, and summer evenings offer live entertainment, poolside karaoke, and the laid-back party atmosphere of a beach club. Consider one of the combo passes that let you take in Wet 'n Wild, Universal Studios, and Sea World. Wet 'n Wild is located on International Drive, which is exit 30A off I-4. Call (407) 351-1800 for details.

THE MYSTERY FUN HOUSE

A good place for rainy days, the Mystery Fun House is full of mazes, sloping floors, and optical illusions and includes a *Jurassic Park*–themed miniature golf course and arcade. Admission for all ages is $8. The Starbase Omega laser tag game next door charges $7 a head regardless of age.

Numerous discount coupons are available (some lowering the price as much as 50%) as well as a $13.85 combination ticket allowing holders access to the fun house, golf, and Starbase Omega. Call (407) 351-3355 for details.

For an even wilder thrill, check out Rickey's Rockets in the parking lot, which offers a type of bungee jumping in reverse for $20. Riders are shot up into the air slingshot-style on a bungee cord. It's worth watching, even if you're not up to the ride.

OFF-SITE DINNER SHOWS
FOR THE WHOLE FAMILY

Disney isn't the only company in Orlando that produces family dinner theaters. The dinner theaters that follow differ greatly in theme, with some more suitable for children than others, but each offers a four- or five-course meal, unlimited beer and wine, and a live show. Prices run about $34 for adults, $21 for kids 3 to 11, but discount coupons (some cutting the price of an adult dinner as much as $10) can be found all around Orlando at Guest Services booths, family-style restaurants, and those freebie magazines aimed toward vacationers. There is generally one seating nightly in the off-season, two during the on-season, so you'll need to call for exact showtimes and to make reservations. The halls hold between 400 and 1,000 people; come prepared to buddy up to that couple from Michigan.

Of the dinner-theater options listed here, Wild Bill's and Medieval Times are the best for young children, who can join the raucous action with no fear of disturbing anyone. Older kids will be able to better appreciate the music and humor of Capone's or the challenge of the Sleuth's Mystery Dinner Show.

Arabian Nights

Arabian Nights features more than 60 horses, including White Lipizzans and a "mystical unicorn." The highlight of the evening is a high-speed chariot race re-created from the movie *Ben Hur*. The main course is prime rib. Call 1-800-553-6116 or (407) 396-1787.

Wild Bill's Fort Liberty

A favorite of younger kids, this Wild West show offers knife throwers, rain dancers, lasso twirlers, and the comical soldiers from E Troop. (If you remember the old "F Troop" TV show, you get the general picture.) Barbecue, fried chicken, and corn on the cob are served up chuck-wagon style. Call 1-800-883-8181 or (407) 351-5151.

Medieval Times

Dueling swordsmen and jousting knights on horseback perform in a huge pit while guests dine on roast chicken and ribs. Several of the gentlemen surveyed gave a must-see rating to the serving wenches' costumes. Medieval Times was the favorite dinner theater of kids in the 7-to-11 age range, largely because the arena is divided into competing teams bearing different colors and the performers do a wonderful job of urging spectators to cheer for "their" knight. Call 1-800-229-8300 or (407) 239-0214.

King Henry's Feast

The portly monarch is searching for his seventh wife—portraits of her six unlucky predecessors hang in the entry hall—as magicians, jugglers, and minstrels offer a kinder, gentler version of Medieval Times. Chicken and ribs are on hand for the revelers. Call 1-800-883-8181 or (407) 351-5151.

Capone's

Expect Italian food and mobsters aplenty in this cheerful version of a Chicago prohibition-era speakeasy. Capone's offers massive portions of pasta and musical comedy in the best *Guys and Dolls* tradition. Call (407) 397-2378.

Sleuth's Mystery Dinner Show

As you munch hors d'oeuvres and mingle with suspicious characters in an English drawing room, be sure to keep your wits about you. A crime is about to unfold, and it is up to you to collect the clues, interrogate the suspects, and formulate a theory. The family who comes up with the most accurate solution wins a prize. The meal is very civilized as well—prime rib or Cornish game hen with herb dressing. Call (407) 363-1985.

Index

Branson with Kids

The Definitive Family Guide to the
Live Country Music Capital of the World

Toni Eugene

ISBN 0-7615-0248-3 / paperback / 272 pages
U.S. $14.95 / Can. $19.95

Country music lovers from around the world are flocking to the tiny town of Branson, Missouri, in huge numbers, and many of those fans are taking their kids. But how can a parent decide which of the many music shows are best for children, choose a restaurant with a menu designed for kids' tastes, or find a hotel where kids stay free? Toni Eugene has the answers to all of these questions and more. With the help of *Branson with Kids,* parents can design a headache-free family vacation in and around the Branson area.

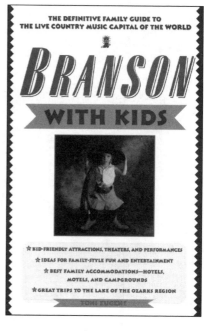

THE DEFINITIVE FAMILY GUIDE TO
THE LIVE COUNTRY MUSIC CAPITAL OF THE WORLD

BRANSON
WITH KIDS

☆ KID-FRIENDLY ATTRACTIONS, THEATERS, AND PERFORMANCES
☆ IDEAS FOR FAMILY-STYLE FUN AND ENTERTAINMENT
☆ BEST FAMILY ACCOMMODATIONS—HOTELS,
MOTELS, AND CAMPGROUNDS
☆ GREAT TRIPS TO THE LAKE OF THE OZARKS REGION

TONI EUGENE

Visit us online at www.primapublishing.com

Camping with Kids in California

The Complete Guide—Where to Go and What to Do for a Fun-Filled, Stress-Free Camping Vacation

Bill McMillon

ISBN 0-7615-0003-0 / paperback / 304 pages
U.S. $15.00 / Can. $19.95

Whether you want a true wilderness experience or the comforts of home in the great outdoors, this book will help you plan excursions sure to please every family member. You'll find details on hundreds of spectacular, family-friendly destinations, from Yosemite to Tahoe and beyond, complete with information on showers, rest rooms, and:

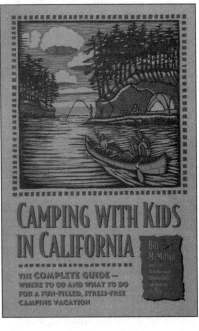

- Tips on the best time to go
- Ranger-led activities and fun educational programs
- Great hikes for campers of any age
- Health and safety tips
- The best campgrounds and rustic accommodations
- Swimming, horseback riding, bicycling, beach-combing, and much more

Visit us online at www.primapublishing.com

Ski Vacations with Kids in the U.S. & Canada

Candyce H. Stapen

ISBN 0-7615-0319-6 / paperback / 432 pages
U.S. $16.00 / Can. $21.95

All the information you need to plan an exciting and economical family ski vacation is here. With separate sections on New England, the Mid-Atlantic states, Minnesota, the American West, and Canada, this book specializes in family-friendly ski resort information, including:

FUN FOR KIDS, RELAXING FOR PARENTS

SKI VACATIONS WITH KIDS IN THE U.S. & CANADA

INCLUDES SNOWBOARDING!

INSIDE TIPS, INCLUDING:

* CHOOSING THE RIGHT SKI VACATION FOR YOUR FAMILY
* GETTING THE MOST FOR YOUR MONEY
* FINDING FAMILY-FRIENDLY DOWNHILL AND CROSS-COUNTRY SKI RESORTS AND LODGES
* DISCOVERING THE BEST CHILDREN'S SKI SCHOOLS AND PROGRAMS
* ENJOYING OFF-THE-SLOPES FAMILY FUN

CANDYCE H. STAPEN

* Great family bargains
* Downhill and cross-country skiing
* Snowboarding, with a special section on snowboard equipment and etiquette
* Kid-friendly lodgings and restaurants
* Ski schools custom-tailored for kids
* Helpful phone numbers and Web sites
* And more!

You'll even find suggestions for nonskiing activities the whole family will love, such as dogsledding, snowshoeing, and sleighriding.

Visit us online at www.primapublishing.com

Disneyland® and Southern California with Kids, 1996–1997

Kim Wright Wiley

ISBN 0-7615-0122-3 / paperback / 240 pages
U.S. $9.95 / Can. $13.95

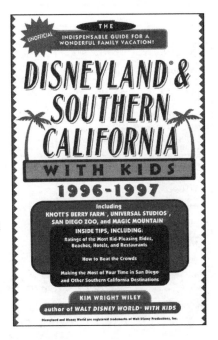

If you liked *Walt Disney World with Kids,* you'll love this book! Once again Kim Wright Wiley shows parents the secrets of the most enjoyable, hassle-free, biggest-bang-for-the-buck experience of a premiere family destination resort. This is an indispensable guide to the original Disneyland and to Southern California's other family-style attractions, including Knott's Berry Farm, Universal Studios, Magic Mountain, the San Diego Zoo, Hollywood, and Beverly Hills. Kim showcases restaurants and lodgings with surefire kid appeal, points out attractions that first-timers frequently miss, and offers invaluable tips for family travel and fun.

Visit us online at www.primapublishing.com

To Order Books

Please send me the following items:

Quantity	Title	Unit Price	Total
_____	Branson with Kids	$ 14.95	$ _____
_____	Camping with Kids in California	$ 15.00	$ _____
_____	Ski Vacations with Kids in the U.S. and Canada	$ 16.00	$ _____
_____	Disneyland and Southern California with Kids, 1996–1997	$ 9.95	$ _____
_____	_____	$ _____	$ _____

*Shipping and Handling depend on Subtotal.

Subtotal	Shipping/Handling
$0.00–$14.99	$3.00
$15.00–$29.99	$4.00
$30.00–$49.99	$6.00
$50.00–$99.99	$10.00
$100.00–$199.99	$13.50
$200.00+	Call for Quote

Foreign and all Priority Request orders:
Call Order Entry department
for price quote at 916/632-4400

This chart represents the total retail price of books only (before applicable discounts are taken).

Subtotal	$ _____
Deduct 10% when ordering 3-5 books	$ _____
7.25% Sales Tax (CA only)	$ _____
8.25% Sales Tax (TN only)	$ _____
5.0% Sales Tax (MD and IN only)	$ _____
Shipping and Handling*	$ _____
Total Order	$ _____

By Telephone: With MC or Visa, call 800-632-8676 or 916-632-4400. Mon–Fri, 8:30-4:30.

WWW: http://www.primapublishing.com

By Internet E-mail: sales@primapub.com

By Mail: Just fill out the information below and send with your remittance to:

**Prima Publishing
P.O. Box 1260BK
Rocklin, CA 95677**

My name is _____

I live at _____

City _____ State _____ ZIP _____

MC/Visa#_____ Exp. _____

Check/money order enclosed for $_____ Payable to Prima Publishing

Daytime telephone _____

Signature _____